A BOOK OF
Gardening

IDEAS · METHODS · DESIGNS

Published in association with
THE NATIONAL TRUST

A B O O K O F
Gardening

IDEAS · METHODS · DESIGNS

A PRACTICAL GUIDE BY

Penelope Hobhouse

For John, who worked with me at Tintinhull

Published in association with
THE NATIONAL TRUST (ENTERPRISES) LTD
36 Queen Anne's Gate
London SW1H 9AS

First published in Great Britain in 1986 by
PAVILION BOOKS LIMITED
26 Upper Ground, London SE1 9PD
Revised and updated 1987, 1995
This new edition published 1995

Designed by Andrew Barron & Collis Clements Associates

A CIP catalogue record for this book is available from the
British Library

ISBN 1 85793 423 7

Typeset in Horley Old Style Roman, 9^1/$_2$/11pt

Printed and bound in Hong Kong
Produced by Mandarin Offset Ltd

2 4 6 8 10 9 7 5 3 1

This book may be ordered by post direct from the publisher.
Please contact the Marketing Department.
But try your bookshop first.

*(Frontispiece) A door leading into the enclosed gardens at
Barrington Court, where planting is in the style of Gertrude Jekyll.*

Contents

PREFACE

This book is a practical guide to gardening in National Trust properties. It is not intended to be descriptive of the gardens themselves: the Trust's own guidebooks fulfil this function, as does Mr Graham Stuart Thomas's *Gardens of the National Trust*. Instead it explains how the actual gardening is done, with reference to a particular planting theme or garden feature which is only a part of a larger garden. This book, by drawing on the individual gardener's experience, is intended to bridge a gap between the theory of garden design and its appropriate and practical use.

The arrangement of the book is intended to help readers draw on National Trust gardening policy and adapt its practices to areas in their own gardens. As in all gardening practice there are guidelines rather than hard and fast rules; textbook instructions are interpreted by individual gardeners in the most practical way for the particular garden, bearing in mind the amount of labour available for maintenance through the year, and many other factors. The first chapter relates to the structural framework of gardens and includes features such as hedges, topiary and formal planting, all readily adaptable for use in any garden. Further chapters discuss garden features such as the border, the rose garden, the herb garden, the use of water, ferneries and rockeries, which may be situated inside this frame. Less structured garden styles such as the informal woodland, meadow gardening and low-maintenance techniques precede a final chapter on practical aspects of grass care, machinery and specific soil treatments.

In many places in the book a Head Gardener has contributed the details of complete planting and maintenance programmes for a garden area. During my visits I have spent many hours learning from the 'man on the spot'. My own practical gardening knowledge has been extended – and I hope that the reader will benefit from that aspect of my writing as well as from the gardeners' own contributions. (Quotations from the gardeners themselves are indicated in the text by a pair of National Trust symbols.) I could not have written this book without the help and stimulation of these dedicated gardeners. This is a chance

At Hidcote hedges and clipped topiary establish a firm garden structure, inside which hardy plants grow in box-edged beds.

not only to thank them for giving me this help, but, on behalf of the whole visiting public, to express our appreciation of the beauty of the Trust gardens and of the high standards with which they are maintained. As a former Gardening Tenant of the National Trust myself, I feel I was inspired to garden better as a result of the experience I gained while writing this book.

I also wish to thank the four Gardens Advisers who look after all the National Trust properties – Mr John Sales, Mr James Marshall, Mr Michael Calnan and Miss Sallyan Morris – for their help and encouragement. Each of them has provided an essential element of the book, contributing specialist skills and knowledge that I lack. I am particularly grateful to former Gardens Adviser Mr Anthony Lord for checking plant names.

The book would be nothing without the beautiful photographs, many of them specially commissioned. Gardening photography not only demands technical skills but, especially in a wet summer, requires perseverance and patience to achieve such perfection.

I am most grateful to Colin Webb at Pavilion Books for allowing me to plan and execute this book. Russell Ash and Penny David supervised the original manuscript; without the former I would have lacked essential encouragement at early stages of planning and writing, without the latter I could not have achieved the organization of so much detailed information. An author becomes dependent on skilled editors and I have been fortunate.

Many others helped me during the course of writing the book. Besides contributing to the book, gardeners and Gardens Advisers were frequently consulted on a personal level.

The National Trust sets a standard in garden design and maintenance which we sometimes take for granted. I hope this book shows my appreciation of all who have contributed or do contribute to this achievement.

PENELOPE HOBHOUSE

FOREWORD

Garden visiting is one of the most popular summer pastimes in Britain and reflects both our abiding love of gardens and our almost obsessive interest in gardening, which has been gathering strength for at least three hundred years. In variety, quality and quantity Britain's gardens are unrivalled in the world and the many visitors from abroad testify to their unique attraction. This practice of visiting gardens is a great stimulus to creativity and improvement. Rarely does a keen gardener return without an idea, or even a plant purchased, with which to improve his or her own garden. The unique purpose of this book is to facilitate this process by interpreting features and techniques found in the many gardens owned by the National Trust.

Never before has one organization owned so many gardens of such historic and horticultural significance, and which exhibit such enormous diversity. The Trust's gardens advisory staff visit about 160 gardens regularly, as well as another 60 or so landscape parks. These properties vary from tiny town gardens like Carlyle's House in Chelsea to large and complex historic gardens like the 31.5 hectares (78 acres) at Mount Stewart in Co. Down or the 72.8 hectares (180 acres) at Cliveden, Buckinghamshire. They cover the whole range of soil, site, climate and habitat found in these islands and contain, taken together, the world's greatest collection of cultivated plants, trees and shrubs. It is axiomatic that almost every garden style developed over the past 300 years or more can be discovered somewhere in the Trust, but much more significant is the impact of the individuals and the families that were the gardens' former owners. Like any other work of art, a great garden may be the distinctive product of a genius – or more often two individuals working together, as at Hidcote and Sissinghurst; or it may have been created like Powis and Blickling from the 'bones' of an original layout by successive generations of owners over two or three hundred years. Each successive owner adds their own contribution, in response to the fashion of the day, their interests and their means. Because of the unique stability that has existed in Britain for three centuries, this latter quality of continuity – continuous cultivation and evolution of style and planting – is rare in the world and is particularly precious.

In these respects historic gardens have much in common with

historic houses; they can be pure examples of a style or a palimpsest, reflecting the history of the house and the fortunes and tastes of its owners through the years. But gardens have another dimension – they are constantly changing. Only the artefacts in them remain comparatively unchanged unless deliberately altered or allowed to fall into disrepair. Plants, whether small and herbaceous or large and woody, are constantly growing, developing and decaying and this is what gardeners enjoy: pitting their wits against the uncertainties of plant growth and climate and exploiting to the fullest extent the limitations imposed by soil and site. A garden is more of a process than an object and for its long-term conservation a distinct and consistent policy is needed to direct inevitable change in a way that preserves the unique character of the garden. A valid policy can only be arrived at through a thorough knowledge of the garden, its history and its former owners, its circumstances and its plants.

It is one thing to make a garden to be enjoyed in one's own lifetime and quite another to anticipate change and to provide for its continuous conservation, which is the purpose of the National Trust. Not only does it demand a policy, both for the general approach to its style and character and for the details of its planting or upkeep, but it also requires a consistency of purpose that goes beyond individual Head Gardeners and tenants. Of course the effect of the person directly in charge always shows through and a positive approach is vital if a garden is to remain fresh and interesting. The Trust does not aim to stifle this stimulating influence provided that it can be accommodated within the policy, the tradition and, not least, the budget for that particular garden. Even the great artist-plantsmen and -women of this century such as Lawrence Johnston and Vita Sackville-West were always experimenting and making changes, and it is necessary for the well-being of their gardens that each part should be reworked within the character and the colour scheme originally intended.

Rarely is it possible or even advisable to revert totally and exactly to an original scheme, even if the details are precisely known, which is rarely the case. Historic gardens need constantly to be reinterpreted in response to changed circumstances, physical and financial. Gardens continue to exist only if the quantity and the quality of the upkeep is sufficient. Many Trust gardens are being run with as few as ten per cent of their original labour force, a discrepancy that requires considerable ingenuity to overcome. Without eliminating all inessentials and using every modern aid and technique to the maximum it would be impossible. But if the Trust's objects are to be met such methods have to be directed constantly towards the retention or the restoration of the special character of the garden; the temptation to make changes merely for convenience and economy must be resisted.

The advent of visitors in large numbers is a fundamental change. Paradoxically, the problem of minimizing their impact, while protecting the garden's design and as far as possible its character as a private garden, often makes it necessary to make changes. These may be aimed for example at improving circulation and spreading people out so as to avoid the appearance of overcrowding.

Clearly, then, Penelope Hobhouse has had plenty of scope from which to draw examples of designs and techniques capable of being adapted for private gardens of a different scale. While obviously avoiding the grandest schemes, she has chosen widely and wisely, covering most aspects of gardening out of doors and 'within the ha-ha'. In anything to do with the Trust it is difficult to generalize; colour schemes that might be considered vulgar in a garden influenced by Gertrude Jekyll could be just right in a Victorian scheme; techniques and planting for the rock garden at Rowallane are unlikely to suit the gigantic layout at Cragside. Penelope Hobhouse has avoided this trap very sensibly by using specific cases and inviting Head Gardeners to comment on them. By quoting some of the Trust's most skilled gardeners she has brought forth a wealth of valuable practical experience for others to share. These contributions are invariably authoritative, searching and direct, and particularly valuable when dealing with aspects of management, which is of course the key to successful garden conservation. A well-researched policy, consistently and sensitively applied, is essential. But in the absence of a resident expert tenant, it falls largely on the Head Gardener and his or her staff to provide the thoughtful, observant and energetic upkeep that distinguishes a true garden from an institutional open space.

Guided above all by its elected and voluntary national and regional committees and more directly by its expert Gardens

Panel, the Trust's gardens are managed regionally and advised nationally. In some cases the Trust is able to benefit from the presence of a resident expert donor or tenant, but in three-quarters of its gardens it relies mainly on its permanent staff. The Head Gardener or Gardener-in-Charge is accountable for the day-to-day management of the garden. Detailed advice on all aspects of conservation and upkeep is given by one of four national Gardens Advisers who visits regularly. These three – gardener, manager and adviser – discuss priorities and agree a programme of work, which is set out in some detail in the Gardens Adviser's subsequent report. With consistent aims, this continuity can achieve a great deal, little by little over the years, despite limited resources. Where there is no donor or tenant the Regional Historic Buildings Representative provides historic research and aesthetic sensitivity. From time to time help from a variety of experts inside and outside the Trust is sought, but no garden has ever been run successfully by a committee. Courageous and decisive management is essential for the long-term conservation of gardens and for their restoration.

As a former tenant Penelope Hobhouse has been part of this process at Tintinhull, where she has used her skill and artistry to great effect in the conservation of Mrs Reiss' little masterpiece. In looking beyond Tintinhull she has cast her discerning eye on some of the greatest gardens ever made. Her commentary reveals a vast range of design ideas and a wealth of practical tips from which any garden owner can select and adapt.

JOHN SALES
National Trust Chief Gardens Adviser

I

THE GARDEN

FRAMEWORK

STRUCTURAL PLANTING

Using plants or objects to suggest to the eye a division, as well as using an actual physical barrier such as a wall, fence or the continuous planting of a hedge, is an effective way of establishing the architectural structure of a garden design. Upright shapes in lines or geometrical arrangements will emphasize a ground pattern and give a third dimension to the two-dimensional garden plan. As well as being architectural features, these divisions provide seclusion, shade and an opportunity to display plants in various different ways.

The diverse subjects that constitute a garden's structure will overlap and interrelate as topics of discussion, just as the physical elements overlap and work together in the garden. Here, for convenience, they are grouped as a series of broad themes. Perhaps the most functional barriers and divisions, walls and walled enclosures, are one special case, to be considered separately later on; and hedges – barriers of living plants – are another. The training or pleaching of rows of trees to make avenues, alleys and so on, and constructions such as pergolas, form a different sort of three-dimensional element in the garden. When the effect of some of these techniques is not so much to form physical garden divisions as to become pattern and ornament for its own sake, it becomes the subject of the discussion 'Planting in patterns'.

Among the growing structural elements in the garden framework are hedges. Like walls and fences, they can mark a continuous boundary around the garden perimeter, or can divide up the space within the garden into a series of compartments. An inner hedge that appears to be a division might act as a screen, either hiding some unsightly object or area, or by first concealing a landscape view or garden feature from the visitor, introducing it as a surprise later.

An avenue is not necessarily the great landscape feature that the word is inclined to evoke. In design terms it is a series of ornamental objects – not always trees or even plants – placed at regular intervals on either side of a directional path. Size and actual spacing distances will determine the effect of linear perspective: occasionally, to increase or diminish the apparent distance, the elements are deliberately set nearer or farther apart. The scale can be proportionate to the situation. The dictionary defines an avenue as a passage or path of entrance or exit,

*Immaculate box hedging contains the beds of old shrub roses in the walled
garden at Mottisfont Abbey in Hampshire*

particularly the chief approach to a country house, usually bordered by trees – hence any broad roadway marked by objects at regular intervals. It is a dramatic device using rhythmic repetition in perspective to enhance the grandeur of the approach, or to pace the view towards a focal point.

Pleached trees suggest a continuous row and garden division but usually allow a clear view below boskage. In the Middle Ages pleaching was used as a device to create shady and secluded garden walks before it became a useful feature of garden design. By regularly cutting back new growth of specially trained trees, dense young foliage makes a solid impenetrable shape, at a deliberately chosen height. An alley is usually of pleached trees trained to meet overhead and quite distinct from the French *allée* which is a ride or walk cut through massed trees where the sides are clipped up to a considerable height. An alley (or tunnel) is very similar to a pergola, where a double row of strong supports with crossbars provides a frame for climbing plants which are bent or carefully trained and tied to it.

Treillage or trellis work, where a patterned open frame of light wood gives the appearance of a substantial division, is another structural device, and provides a frame on which to grow ornamental plants as well as being highly decorative in itself.

Many National Trust gardens contain some or all of these architectural features. Some of them will have been introduced by previous owners for comfort and use and to display plants as well as because they were fashionable at the time the garden was being made; others will have been devised as design techniques to emphasize dimension and define space. In some properties where the Trust has developed or restored a garden style appropriate to the date or historical connections of the house, new features have been introduced much more recently.

HEDGES

Hedges, which are a continuous line of planting, can make solid boundaries to protect the garden area from outsiders, and give a feeling of security to the garden owner who wishes to stress his separateness from the outside world. Equally, hedges of different heights partition the garden into inner compartments which can contain separate seasonal or planting themes.

The very first paradise gardens created by the Persians in the Middle East needed barriers to keep out wild animals (and even human enemies), and the earliest English gardens were safely within the confines of a castle keep or monastery walls. By Tudor times brightly painted palisades defined garden areas, but dwarf hedging plants – already used for making intricate knot patterns – were increasingly employed to divide gardens into separate areas. All through the seventeenth century and in the early years of the eighteenth, fashionable garden designs were based on the ideal of the Italian Renaissance gardens, where a series of outside 'rooms' were linked together and to the house by pathways and terraces, and by steps between different levels. Hedging plants and walls built of local brick and stone were used to make these barriers, materials for building varying greatly in different regions.

The history of gardening shows how the development of design depends as much on the availability of plants and a knowledge of how to grow them as on the quirks of fashionable thought or philosophy. It is worth remembering that in these early gardens the cost of labour was negligible, local stone and brick was cheap, but nurseries to supply suitable hedging plants, in sufficient quantity, were few and far between. Today, on the other hand, the cost of good masonry barriers is almost totally prohibitive, and even the National Trust, intent on an accurate historical reconstruction, can seldom do more than mend existing walls. Fortunately they can make the best use of local skilled craftsmen and masons, and do even, as at KINGSTON LACY, reopen stone quarries long deemed uneconomical to work.

Many Trust properties have houses and gardens which date from Tudor or Restoration times, when garden areas were separated from the countryside and divided up by walls and hedges; the latter of plants such as yew (*Taxus baccata*), holly (*Ilex aquifolium*), hornbeam (*Carpinus betulus*) and beech (*Fagus sylvatica*). For more rustic barriers the common 'quick' (*Crataegus monogyna*) was often planted, although native common privet (*Ligustrum vulgare*), box (*Buxus sempervirens*) from chalky uplands, hornbeam, sweet briar and common holly proved effective when locally available. Genera were frequently mixed, as in the replanted hedges at IGHTHAM MOTE and LITTLE MORETON HALL. Beech has become more popular in the last hunded years, its pleasant habit of retaining buff-coloured leaves all through the winter making it an attractive alternative to other deciduous hedge plants. The purple-leaved beech, today usually *Fagus sylvatica* 'Riversii' (introduced in the late nineteenth century) or one of its variants, is sometimes used for hedging, often mixed with the ordinary green-leaved species to produce a tapestry effect. Incidentally, Lady Stamford's rose garden at DUNHAM MASSEY was originally surrounded by a hedge of purple beech kept clipped to 1.5–1.8 m (5–6 ft), admitting plenty of sun and air. Today the neglected beech plants have grown to trees 9 m (30 ft) tall, completely altering the character of the site by turning it into shady woodland where mosses thrive, instead of airy, open sunlit garden.

In his discourse *Sylva* (1664), John Evelyn did much to popularize the ordinary English yew as a plant for inner hedges (where its poisonous qualities would be harmless to stock): 'I do name them for hedges, preferable for beauty and a stiff defence, to any plant I have ever seen and may . . . without vanity be said to have been the first who brought it in to fashion.' Many of the places where Evelyn's advice was taken were typical of the seventeenth-century gardens which are now in the care of the Trust, for example WESTBURY COURT and POWIS CASTLE.

Often all barriers and divisions made by walls or plants were swept away in the second half of the eighteenth century, when landscape parks came up to the windows of the great house, and the only dividing line allowed was the 'invisible' ha-ha. The Trust has 'restored' landscape gardens, allowing the eye once again to travel uninterruptedly across parkland and to distant views. At KILLERTON in the 1960s the Trust removed hedges which obscured the view, and built ha-has here and at SALTRAM, but by far the longest and finest, complete with stone facing, has been built at FLORENCE COURT between the Pleasure Ground and the Park. With modern earth-moving machinery the cost of excavation is relatively low, although building the retaining wall is expensive in materials and labour. To most of us increasingly used to a mainly urban landscape this extension of outlook seems even more important today than it must have been to the casual visitor in the eighteenth century. The initial expense is fully compensated for by the relative cheapness of subsequent upkeep, and the advantages of a ha-ha are not to be disregarded even by the private owner, for a site in unspoilt countryside.

By the twentieth century, when the National Trust started to acquire or receive properties, many of the landscape parks attached to classical eighteenth-century houses had already had some form of more intimate gardening style incorporated into their designs. Earlier Elizabethan or Jacobean houses retained the vestiges of their contemporary layout, or in Edwardian times had had their gardens reconstructed into a series of compartments, sometimes closely related to the seventeenth-century style. Even Victorian gardens, although not always strictly compartmental, often had areas of the so-called Italianate or 'Dutch' style: for example, ICKWORTH and ASCOTT respectively, where evergreen hedges and topiary helped frame elaborate parterres. The Trust has been able to restore gardens to the original plan when it is considered appropriate.

Edwardian gardens, despite William Robinson's influence on planting, remained firmly structured. (The more naturalistic woodland and 'wild' garden of the period is discussed in Part IV). In the main, garden architecture led by Blomfield, Lutyens (inspired by Gertrude Jekyll and often with her practical help), Sedding and Peto stressed the importance of strong directional lines and vertical and horizontal surfaces. Lutyens was responsible for the fortress-like hedges at CASTLE DROGO, Sedding worked at ASCOTT and Peto designed the hedge-lined water garden that drops down to the lake at BUSCOT PARK. Hedges or walled enclosures were arranged in geometric patterns around a house, and this rigid framework provided the perfect foil for the more flowing plant shapes which furnished the area. Stone, patterned brick or just grass linked the separate areas so that the garden was united as an integral whole, and was not just a collection of disparate parts and themes. Essentially this seems a garden 'fashion' eminently suitable for large or small gardens, a firm architectural structure providing the setting and frame for more free-flowing and informal planting. It is as adaptable for a large country garden as it is for subdividing the elongated town plot.

Two of the most important National Trust gardens, HIDCOTE and SISSINGHURST CASTLE, depend for their effects on hedges which partition the garden areas. Both gardens were made in this century and represent the epitome of this style. A strong rigid framework provides the perfect foil and background for the massed colours and fluid shapes of cottage-type planting. Inside each garden division plants are tightly packed to perform at their best in a particular season, or arranged in definite colour schemes or planting themes. Hedges are in yew, hornbeam, box and holly, all giving different 'green' effects as their individual leaves and habits of growth reflect light in different ways. Further interest is given by the shapes and angles at which the hedge sides and tops are cut. TINTINHULL HOUSE, a much smaller garden owned by the Trust, has a similar design, the system of axial paths and hedged and walled enclosures making the two-acre garden seem much larger than it is.

Hedges in design terms provide not only straight lines to contrast with the more billowing shapes of other plants, as at ICKWORTH. Sometimes hedges of different plant materials are seen by the observer as horizontal bands of contrasting foliage and texture. A tall hedge in the distance will tower above a nearer lower planting. At LYTES CARY a row of pleached lime outside the garden backs the long inner boundary hedge of privet, revealing interesting variation in leaf 'greens' as well as varying density and habit of growth. At TINTINHULL the low hedge of *Lonicera nitida* makes a line of dense twiggy growth in quite a different green to the dark yew hedge silhouetted against the light behind it. Elsewhere, glossy bright green box contrasts with the dull heavy yew foliage in a similar way.

When hedges divide up the available space in a garden into a series of inner compartments, they make the whole area seem larger than the sum of its parts. Furthermore, each line of hedging provides shelter and an attractive background for other planting. Straight horizontal lines, trimmed to a regular height, and vertical or sloping 'battered' sides all provide the contrast with curving and billowing plant shapes which makes a garden stimulating. As Ruskin said, 'Straight lines are the best foil to the grace of natural curves in plant and flower'. Among the taller-growing evergreens which make satisfactory hedging plants are the traditional English yew (*Taxus baccata*), holly (usually common for cheapness, but sometimes cultivars of *Ilex* × *altaclerensis* or *I. aquifolium*) and narrow-leaved conifers. The evergreen oak (*Quercus ilex*) is suitable only for mild or sheltered areas.

Lower-growing plants such as the dwarf form of box (*Buxus sempervirens* 'Suffruticosa'), santolina, rosemary and lavender can be clipped into neat little hedges. These will divide areas visually into further subcompartments and can be used for making patterns such as knots. Other plants with a more casual form of growth including shrub roses, potentillas and non-woody perennials such as catmint make a less strictly geometrical delineation.

Whether for boundary or inner division, the plant chosen must be 'right' for the type and period of house and garden. Its ultimate height and shape, how its top and sides are contoured, and its leaf colour and texture, will determine the character of the space enclosed. Darker leaves make a space seem smaller and the walls of hedges close in, while pale foliage increases dimensions and gives a feeling of freedom. A hedge of dark yew is sombre all the year, although young growth in early summer contributes interwoven leaves of a paler colour, and provides perhaps the best of all backgrounds to flowering plants through the seasons. Hornbeam and beech leaves change from fresh light airy green to a heavier mature texture in late summer and the dead leaves in winter have a warm rusty-buff colouring.

In a modern garden creating barriers with green and living plants is usually a much cheaper option than introducing any form of masonry, although they are more expensive to maintain. When making a choice of available plants it is worth considering various factors. First, which plants will make the most beautiful feature in the particular garden, and which will thrive on the site? Which plants will need the most care in planting and later maintenance? Which will grow most rapidly and therefore will most quickly establish the 'pattern' of the garden, providing the vital framework in which all other planting is best displayed? There are pitfalls here for the unwary. Hedges which grow quickest have to be clipped most often. *Lonicera nitida*, introduced from western China only at the beginning of this century (1908), has a dense twiggy habit and small evergreen leaves, and responds well to cutting back. Popular after its introduction for speed and density of growth, easily reproduced by the nursery trade, hardy, vigorous, and pleasant to look at, yet it has disadvantages. It is rather greedy and takes much goodness out of the soil, to the disadvantage of neighbouring plants. It needs cutting back at least four or five times annually. Its density makes it particularly vulnerable to collapse from heavy snowfalls.

Successfully creating a new hedge requires good preparation and the correct choice of young plants. Hedges consist of a row of identical plants. Where uniformity is the aim, as with avenues and topiary, take cuttings from one clone, since seedlings have a considerable variation in colour and form. Because they are planted unnaturally close, these living plants need special care. The soil should be well dug to a depth of at least two spits. If the subsoil is of poor quality, break it up with a pickaxe. Preparing the soil to a considerable depth encourages roots to delve deep rather than to straggle laterally searching for moisture or food. A layer of organic manure is then placed in the trench and covered with soil. Today most evergreens such as yew, holly and *Quercus ilex* are container-grown and can be planted in March or April; deciduous hedging plants of beech and hornbeam usually come bare-rooted and should be planted in autumn, to get well established before the following growing season. In Trust gardens hedges are planted to last for the foreseeable future and it is more important to choose the best subject for the long term than to aim simply for quick effects. It seems generally accepted now that single-line planting at an appropriate distance for the type of plant is better than 'staggered' rows, previously favoured for making thick and solid hedge bottoms. Frequent trimming of the sides during the first few years ensures bushy uniform growth. And cutting fiercely where growth is thinnest (against natural instinct) immediately stimulates growing points.

In Trust properties only recently acquired it is found that many of the old hedges have grown both too high and too wide through years of comparative neglect. This was especially true when labour was scarce during the 1939–45 war. In fact hedges fifty years old or so, even if well maintained, will also tend to grow beyond the proportions which are convenient. The private owner acquiring an old property may find himself faced with similar problems, even if on a smaller scale.

At MOUNT STEWART Lady Londonderry used the Monterey cypress (*Cupressus macrocarpa*) to make inner garden compartments in the 1920s. High hedges and a pergola surrounded a sunken garden, and to the west of the house a Spanish-style garden was lined with the macrocarpa, in which arcaded windows were cut, very similar to the arcades of Italian cypress (*Cupressus sempervirens*) which frame the view of the city of Florence from the terraces of Villa Gamberaia. By the late 1960s the macrocarpa, attractive with its fine textured foliage of bright green, had become bare and woody at the base and a series of bad winters had cut it back, even in this very sheltered Irish garden. The Trust has now replaced it with the darker green Leyland cypress (× *Cupressocyparis leylandii*), which is reliably hardy and quick-growing. In other parts of the garden the macrocarpa has been replaced with yew. Low hedging of coloured foliage – berberis, thuja and rue – is used at Mount Stewart to enclose flower beds in patterned colours. Their coordinated colour schemes and maintenance are described more fully by Mr Nigel Marshall in Part II.

At POWIS CASTLE, SISSINGHURST CASTLE, LYTES CARY and more recently at CHARTWELL, KNIGHTSHAYES and MONTACUTE, overgrown yew has been treated severely. At first the top and one side is pruned right back to the main stem; within a season or two, as these make new healthy young shoots, the second side is trimmed back. Liberal mulching with organic manure or compost plus feeding with slow-acting artificial fertilizers promotes and maintains growth. At HARDWICK HALL both the yew and hornbeam alleys which meet at a *rond-point* have had similar and successful treatment. Beech responds more slowly but has been successfully reduced at ANGLESEY ABBEY, where the hedges are a special feature.

Often the problem with an old yew hedge is an outward-curving bow from the base upwards, instead of sides sloping slightly inwards on a 'batter' from a wider base, which allows maximum light to reach the lower part. A good shapely 2.4 m (8 ft) hedge

Half a mile of boxwood hedging is used to edge the borders in the walled garden at Felbrigg Hall in Norfolk.

may have a 1.5 m (5 ft) spread at the base (preferably less) and slope gradually inwards towards the top so that all the surfaces get plenty of light. With very old and misshapen yew it is not possible to use half measures. All branches have to be 'stumped' right back, ideally back to the main stem: simply cutting back into bare wood will not induce rejuvenation. The ideal time to do this is late winter or early spring, but in many gardens it is done in late autumn when there is relatively less pressure of work. Trees and bushes are mulched with well-rotted organic matter (compost or manure) or fed with a balanced general fertilizer with trace elements, such as Vitax Q4, as growth begins in the spring. If the sun is very strong in April and May the new fuzzy growth may even be scorched when it is at its most vulnerable.

Apart from the famous topiary yews planted at the end of the seventeenth century, all of the yew hedges in the lower garden at POWIS CASTLE were first planted by the wife of the Fourth Earl in the years just before the outbreak of the First World War. Now over 80 years old, the planting suffered from two wartime periods of neglect and by the time the Trust acquired the property in 1952 it found many of the formal hedges, so important in outlining the structure of the garden, had grown to widths of over 2.4 m (8 ft), and had lost their 'batter'. The Head Gardener, Mr Jimmy Hancock, described the process of improving the overgrown hedges as well as the routine maintenance. One side of yew is cut back right to the main trunk, and the tops are cut down to the required height. Yew starts to sprout and make fuzzy growth in the following spring and summer. After three years of regeneration the other side is cut, the whole operation taking almost eight years before hedges are neat and trim again. Feeding of any high-nitrogen fertilizer is maintained over this period. In one place at Powis where the hedge had been cut down to 1.2 m (4 ft) some years ago to save work, each plant was cut back to ground level, and is now growing on to the required height to match another hedge with which it forms a yew walk.

This sort of treatment seems drastic but results are worth while. Now at Powis, using machines with reciprocating double-action blades, annual clipping begins for both the yew hedges and the topiary shapes in early September and continues until the third week in October. Gardening staff working an eight-hour day at this gruelling work need the lightest practical machine. For clipping the very high yew a petrol-driven engine would be too heavy to use each day for several weeks at a time.

The great informal yews where the contoured shapes which have evolved over almost three hundred years are carefully and smoothly followed, are started in September and take six weeks to complete. Now very tall, in places to 9 m (30 ft) but on steep terraces needing a ladder to 16 m (52 ft), the work has to be carefully planned and safety systems coordinated. For ordinary hedging scaffolding is used, but when doing these strange-shaped giants the ladders are tied to the yew. As branches of yew die back (often due to 'ringing' of bark by mice or squirrels, or by some taut wire overlooked during the years) new moulded shapes emerge.

The box hedges at Powis, *Buxus sempervirens*, are cut earlier, in June or July, when young growth is still soft. This prevents box suckers (*Psylla buxi*) from doing damage, although some occurs on the taller hedges during warm springs, and allows clipping time to be staggered throughout the summer months. The lower box plants which edge the terrace borders and the flower beds in the old orchards below are cut in June, the taller hedges in early July. The latter suffer in places from being shaded by overhanging trees, which leads to die-back and bare woody growth. In the winding path lined with tall box which descends to the formal garden below the terraces, growth is weak and bare at the base, where there is less light.

Box is slow-growing, especially in such shady situations, and its tailored shapes are very vulnerable to damage. Heavy snow or any sort of abuse can make unsightly holes which takes years to recover. At PACKWOOD HOUSE the boxwood on the spiral path was completely replanted in 1975. Butcher's broom (*Ruscus aculeatus*) was placed at the base of the inner edge of the well-trodden path, creating a protective barrier prickly enough to discourage children from falling against the hedge in play and causing damage. It is possible in favoured situations to restore straggly and woody dwarf box by the drastic method of cutting it back to ground level, but certainly there is a greater risk with box than with yew. It is a technique which **Mr Ted Bullock**, the Head Gardener, has used with success at FELBRIGG HALL. There, half a mile of low box hedging has to be cut with a sloping batter. By cutting in this way not only do the plants do well, remaining thick and bushy right to the ground, but the sloping sides reveal colour and texture as light is reflected at different angles. Mr Bullock writes:

❧ At Felbrigg the boxwood hedging in the walled garden is over half a mile in length. It is 38 cm (15 in) high and 20 cm (8 in) across the top with sloping sides making a wide base. Cut in August, the top is trimmed with a petrol-driven hedge cutter (a Japanese Tondu) and the sloping sides are cut with hand shears. On straight sections strings and rods are used to obtain a good level; curved sections are done by eye. We usually trim our box hedging once a year only. Box does benefit from an application of Vitax Q4 fertilizer applied in the spring.

We have successfully renovated old leggy box by cutting back to 10 cm (4 in) in March, and giving a feed of fertilizer when there are signs of regrowth. ❧

Incidentally, Ted Bullock finds that box hedging is easier to cut when wet, and even uses a watering can to moisten the leaves and stems in the section ahead of him as he works.

AVENUES

Avenues are usually of live growing trees, shrubs or plants, and this is the sense in which Evelyn used the term in the seventeenth century. In garden design an avenue can equally be composed of a row of stakes or a series of ornamental statues or, on a smaller scale, of flowerpots. In the past, the grand avenues of country houses linked the house, garden and landscape. Trees lining the approach road, rather than striding through the countryside, framed the house itself at the end of a vista, the narrowing perspective making it appear far away.

Such grand design features may seem to have little relevance to the more modest gardener today, but in any layout the same principles are involved: the eye needs direction; diminishing height in perspective adjusts scale, and space is divided to create compartments and define perimeters. The eye picks up rhythms established by anything in a simple repeating pattern, just as even a single pair of similar plants or architectural features will make the eye concentrate on what they frame.

The essence of an avenue is its even and regular appearance. It is important for its ultimate success to ensure that plants grow at a similar rate. The trees or plants placed at regular intervals must have enough light and space to thrive. Obviously the distance apart will vary with each tree type, and depends greatly on whether the trees are of fastigiate habit or have broad spreading heads. A double row of trees, too, must be adequately spaced out. The choice of young plants is important. Seedlings vary enormously in characteristics and while this can create an attractive and even desirable tapestry effect in hedging, it can spoil the symmetry which is so important in a classic avenue. For the best results, choose young plants propagated vegetatively from one clone, or grafted on to a stock plant characterized by uniform habit and growth, to ensure complete regularity in the future. A subtle exception to this rule is at WIMPOLE, where six clones of hybrid lime from the park have been mixed along the 6.4-km (4-mile) double avenue to give a degree of diversity and to simulate the variation that exists in many ancient avenues.

In many great Trust parks variations in conditions such as aspect, shelter, sun or shade, and soil moisture will lead to some difference in performance and growth rate between trees at one end of an avenue and those at the other. At BUSCOT PARK willow, poplar and lime avenues radiate from the plateau on which the house itself stands, diving down into the depths of damp frost-filled valleys and rising steeply again to the heights of windswept hills. It is impossible to ensure uniform growth in such circumstances: the undulating nature of the English countryside has always made it difficult to copy the French style of the seventeenth century. Whereas avenues in France were often cut through blocks of natural forest and were planned to give a feeling of distance as well as being aligned on some focal point (an effect that the Trust has consciously aimed at north of the house at DUNHAM MASSEY), trees in England had to be planted in open countryside and were exposed to variations of weather and conditions. For this as well as other reasons, many avenues planted in the second half of the seventeenth and beginning of the eighteenth centuries were swept away in the landscape movement. In fact, although avenues are traditionally reputed to be of great age, there are few complete avenues in existence which date from more than two hundred years ago. Among the exceptions are the oldest, that of sweet chestnuts (*Castanea sativa*) at CROFT CASTLE, the common limes (*Tilia × europaea*) at CHARLECOTE PARK and the sycamore (*Acer pseudoplatanus*) and beech (*Fagus sylvatica*) at LANHYDROCK. Among others which escaped the change in style of the eighteenth century are the lime avenues of CLIVEDEN, DUNHAM MASSEY and KINGSTON LACY, and the original approach avenue of beech at TATTON PARK.

Just as plants chosen for any part of a garden will depend on their ready availability through the nursery trade, so the actual trees used for avenue planting were apt to change as new types were introduced from abroad or as nurseries such as those in Holland in the seventeenth century discovered how uniform was the growth of the common lime, itself a sterile hybrid, but very easily propagated from basal shoots. Today this characteristic makes it less desirable. When in 1963 at SIZERGH CASTLE it was decided to plant a lime avenue leading to a memorial seat, the small-growing *Tilia × euchlora*, with an elegant arching habit and shining dark green leaves, was chosen rather than either *Tilia × europaea* or *T. platyphyllos*, both of which are susceptible to attacks from aphids causing honeydew, which is a nuisance as it is dropped in the summer. Sadly, however, after twenty years the young *T. × euchlora* specimens at Sizergh have become diseased with lime-flux bacteria. The entire avenue is to be replaced by *Sorbus aucuparia* 'Beissneri', an unusual mountain ash with a decorative orange-brown stem and autumn colouring. Its fruits are very freely carried.

Native beech, oaks and chestnut grow easily from seed, but produce variable plants. At CHARLECOTE the west avenue of elms, killed by Dutch elm disease since 1970, has been replaced by Turkey oaks (*Quercus cerris*), which thrive on the poor dry Warwickshire soil. The Church avenue, which runs at an oblique angle to the avenue of oaks, is of the disease-resistant clone of the Huntingdon elm (*Ulmus* × *hollandica* 'Commelin', syn. *U.* × *vegeta* 'Commelin') with slightly narrower habit and narrower leaves than the type. At HIDCOTE the approach avenue of Huntingdon elm, also dead from the disease, has been replaced with alternating hornbeam (*Carpinus betulus*) and Turkey oak. In the long term either the hornbeam or the oak will be removed.

Among the most spectacular avenues planted in this century was that of the quadruple rows of alternating horse chestnut (*Aesculus hippocastanum*) and London plane (*Platanus* × *acerifolia*) at ANGLESEY ABBEY planted by Lord Fairhaven in limy Cambridgeshire soil in the thirties. In this case the young London planes unexpectedly began to break up in the wind and were renewed, but have now been taken out and the chestnuts are being thinned. Very much in the French grand style of the seventeenth century, the avenues at Anglesey run along almost level ground, and visual effects are increased by cutting grass at different heights, allowing the horizontal surfaces to further emphasize the direction and scope of the broad-headed tree shapes.

New narrow avenues of *Tilia cordata*, the small-leaved lime, were planted in triple rows at DUNHAM MASSEY in 1983, each tree closely spaced at 3 m (10 ft). Limes often grow upwards too fast for stability; complete and immediate trimming back of side shoots encourages a young plant to grow tall and thin, lacking wind resistance. Instead, 'feathering' promotes a gradual thickening and swelling of the trunk. On one-year-old trees which have been newly planted, side shoots or 'feathers' are allowed to develop to encourage the sap to spread horizontally; these side shoots are later trimmed back flush with the main stem. This process is repeated until the young trees have established a sturdy trunk.

Where avenues are in pasture or deer park, elaborate tree

guards have to be built and maintained, and the National Trust has developed its own designs, which are functional as well as elegant. One guard is composed of pressure-treated softwood rails and 2.4 m (8 ft) strong posts. The Trust, with plenty of commercial woodland, can make such guards very cheaply. Lines of barbed wire, or even sheep netting to 90 cm (3 ft) from ground level, can reinforce effectiveness. Where the newly planted trees do not have to be stock-proof, spiral-shaped plastic guards are usually effective against rabbits and partially effective against squirrels. Although 'maidens' (young trees the first year after budding or grafting, where no attempt has yet been made to clean the stem) are much cheaper to buy, to stake and maintain, most private owners will plant trees, even in avenue quantities, as standards (having a clean stem to 1.65 m or 5 ft 6 in) or half-standard (stem 1.35 m or 4 ft 6 in) and will prepare the site and soil as in planting any garden tree. In windy sites avenue trees may need careful staking, but the Trust has no fixed policy about whether to use one or two stakes. If two stakes are employed, neither touches the tree stem, which is linked to them by a cross-bar support. More usually one strong stake is quite sufficient. A rigid plastic tie providing a buffer between the stake and the stem can be expanded as the girth of the tree stem increases. An important principle is that staking should be the minimum practicable (30 cm/12 in above the ground) to prevent the tree from rocking or blowing over, and ties placed as low as possible to encourage the tree to thicken naturally.

Throughout Trust properties many different trees and shrubs are used to create avenue effects, from the grand parkland features discussed above to the rather surprising avenues of palm (*Trachycarpus fortunei*) at SHEFFIELD PARK and in the almost tropical garden at OVERBECKS. In the walled garden at ACORN BANK, orchard planting is divided by a grass path lined with a yew hedge cut to a level of 1.2–1.5 m (4–5 ft), on the outside of which young trees of *Prunus cerasus* 'Rhexii' make an evenly spaced avenue, stressing the line and direction of the yew. This cherry with attractive double white flowers has been grown in England since the sixteenth century, and is an appropriate choice where a more recent exotic would be out of place, linking the two parts of this domestic orchard of mixed pears, apples, medlars and mulberries. On the grand scale at MONTACUTE HOUSE, the west front of the Elizabethan house looks down a wide

Guards to protect young trees against livestock are decorative in themselves in the park at Felbrigg.

sweep of grass edged by an avenue of sentinel Irish yews (*Taxus baccata* 'Fastigiata') backed with mixed planting of limes and beeches and a recently planted outer avenue of wellingtonias (*Sequoiadendron giganteum*) behind.

On a much more intimate scale at nearby TINTINHULL HOUSE, a double line of box (*Buxus sempervirens*) edges the axial path which takes the eye to the bottom of the garden. The formal symmetry requires that each dome should have just the same curved pudding shape, and those near to the greedy roots of an overhanging holm oak (*Quercus ilex*) need extra watering and feeding in dry spells. Box, like yew, needs clipping only once a year when it is mature or has reached the desired height and width, but can be made to grow more quickly when young by more frequent cuts, which are combined with extra feeding. The Tintinhull domes are fed with Vitax Q4 in March. Feature plants such as this can seldom be fed with heavy mulches of organic manure, as birds scratch and scatter the loose substance over edge and lawn. At WIGHTWICK MANOR clipped yew 'thimbles' have flat heads and line a central pathway from the house, framing the view of a paddock beyond. Planted in the early years

Avenues are not always grand. At Tintinhull House in Somerset, spaced domes of clipped box lead the eye down the long axial path.

of this century, they mark the period when Thomas Mawson gave advice here, although much of the earlier yew hedging and topiary were planned by Alfred Parsons some years before. Round the base of the yew shapes the grass is tightly mown, while panels of longer-textured turf fill in at the sides of the lawn.

At HIDCOTE, in the Pillar Garden, where twenty-two tall yews dominate a mixed border of peonies, fuchsias and roses, an avenue effect is created by the regular spacing between the meticulously sculptured yews. Here an annual cut keeps the yews in shape and feeding is part of the maintenance programme for the whole double border area. In the Stilt Garden is another sort of avenue. A double line of hornbeam (*Carpinus betulus*), fourteen trees on each side, in two rows of seven, are grown with trunks bare to 1.8 m (6 ft). The sides and tops are clipped to make growth which is not only rectangular in form, but dense and very green in summer, and matted and twiggy in winter. To step inside the ranks of trees is like being in a tree room, with walls and ceiling.

Many other Trust gardens have avenues as features inside quite small garden enclosures. At PENRHYN CASTLE, where the soil is acid, an avenue of elegant pinnate-leaved *Eucryphia gluti-nosa* lines the central path below the top terrace in the walled garden. The irregular, spreading crown of these deciduous eucryphias makes them an excellent choice to define a pathway, and the creamy-white flowers which are carried so freely on the upright branches in July and August are an extra bonus. The leaves colour rich orange, brown and russet before falling in autumn. At ERDDIG Portugal laurel (*Prunus lusitanica*) bushes appear to be planted in ornamental Versailles wooden contain-ers, and line a gravel pathway stretching out to the south of the house, between rows of pleached lime. In fact the laurel is planted directly in the ground to save watering, and the wooden surrounds are 'dummies' and give protection in winter.

PLEACHING
ARBOURS AND TREE TUNNELS

The pleaching of living trees and bushes into what is now often called an aerial hedge is a device usually used to delineate inner garden compartments, but may also be used to provide addi-tional height at the boundaries of town gardens. The technique makes a valuable architectural feature which becomes an impor-tant part of the whole garden design. Because pleaching, or 'plashing' as it is sometimes called, is a very old gardening prac-tice, the National Trust finds, where precedent dictates it, that its function in defining separate garden areas, as at ERDDIG, is appropriate when recreating gardens around houses which date back to the sixteenth and seventeenth centuries, as well as in those Edwardian-style gardens which based their design on this earlier fashion. The technique can equally be used to make shady tunnel walks where living plants arch overhead, or to form the corner or central arbour or bower (there is one covered with elm at SHUGBOROUGH) which protects and shades a sitting place. Sometimes the Trust has taken over properties where pleached trees are already a feature. The famous hornbeams at HIDCOTE, perhaps the first to be known as 'houses on stilts', and the pleached lime walk at MOTTISFONT ABBEY, are examples. Such features have to be maintained and often in due course completely renewed and replanted.

Pleaching, from the French *plessier* meaning to plait or inter-twine, seems to have been a known garden practice all through the Middle Ages, and was probably less common in England than in Europe, where the hot summers made shady walks even more desirable. However, pleaching is first recorded in England as early as 1324, when workmen were paid a penny for every two perches completed – a perch being the equivalent of about five and a half yards. There has occasionally been some confusion between the terms 'plashing' and 'pleaching', the former possibly applying to the process of cutting and laying a farm hedge (which will often have been of quickthorn). The use of plashing to make a perimeter hedge dense and stock-proof is described in the Oxford dictionary with a reference to 1563: 'Cutting young trees half a sunder and bowying downe theyr toppes to the grounde, and *plasshying* the boughes that growe thicke oute of the sydes wyth bushes and thornes betwene them, they brought to passe that their hedges were as good a defence to them as a wal.' Pleaching, on the other hand, has over the years come to mean *overhead* work.

Young flat-headed trees are planted at regular intervals, in a line, each one tied to a post at least 3 m (10 ft) high. Horizontal wires about 30 cm (12 in) apart are stretched tight between the posts; the young side branches are trained on them and pruned hard annually. All growth that points in the wrong direction is removed. Usually the sides of leafy growth, above the stems or trunks – which are bare to 60–90 cm (2–3 ft) or more – are kept formally clipped. On a grand scale such as at ERDDIG, once the trees have grown tall, special equipment is necessary for the annual pruning. Platforms on high trestles, on wheeled trolleys as in France, or on hydraulic platforms lighten the work.

When plant material such as hornbeam (*Carpinus betulus*) is treated in this way, its thick twiggy growth makes it possible to produce the dense effect of solid rectangular shapes sitting atop the bare trunks, as in the Stilt Garden at HIDCOTE. Lime trees, too, and in particular *Tilia platyphyllos*, are frequently used for pleaching. Their fresh pale green leaves flutter slightly in the breeze, giving a sense of movement and freedom in the garden that is not present when dense small-leaved plants are used for barriers. Pleaching has the practical advantage of acting as a wind-filter where a solid hedge can cause turbulence as great as that around masonry walls. *Tilia* × *euchlora*, planted in 1975 when the formal early-eighteenth-century garden at ERDDIG was carefully restored by the Trust, will eventually grow to give the effect of aerial hedges. Facing each other across the central walk

The pleached hornbeams at Hidcote Manor in Gloucestershire are like clipped hedges on stilts.

south of the house, two double rows of pleached limes will partly conceal the pyramid-shaped fruit trees.

Pleached trees and shrubs that lose their foliage make ideal frames for spring gardens as well as becoming comfortable shady places in the hot summer months. At LYTES CARY the fresh green leaves of the short avenue of pleached limes that borders the approach to the house offers an attractive tonal and textural contrast with the dark solid shapes of clipped yew near by.

Pehaps the best-known pleached lime walk is at SISSINGHURST CASTLE. Its history carries a relevant warning to gardeners keen to reproduce similar features elsewhere. Vita Sackville-West (Mrs Harold Nicolson) originally planted the common lime (*Tilia × europaea*). This produced its vigorous suckering basal shoots, spoiling the purity of design and disguising the clean straight trunks, so carefully underplanted with a riot of many-coloured spring bulbs. It was also prone to aphids, which deposit a soot-like film of honeydew on plant leaves underneath the trees. In 1976, ten years after the property was given to the Trust, it was decided to replace these unsatisfactory trees with the non-suckering lime, *Tilia × platyphyllos*. (This 'clean' hybrid

*Kipling's alley of pears is an architectural feature in the garden at Bateman's.
Small plants thrive under the light shade of the pear foliage and
later-flowering clematis twine through the framework.*

lime, incidentally, has flowers narcotic to bees: do not plant it
near a swimming pool or even a children's playground.) At the
same time the central pathway was repaved. Now each spring,
sheets of blue *Anemone apennina*, forget-me-nots, scillas, grape
hyacinths, small daffodils, fritillaries and erythroniums carpet
the ground while the lime branches are still bare.

Pollarding is just another form of pleaching, where rounded
heads are produced on tall trunks. It was originally adopted as a
method of protecting young growth on trees which would be
coppiced annually, to keep the heads just out of reach of livestock, but is now used ornamentally and, in hot countries, to create shade. A row of pollarded willows or, on a larger scale, plane
trees can be an attractive garden feature with their mop growth.
At BLICKLING HALL high limes on either side of the south
approach to the house are pollarded every three years. At ICK-
WORTH the holm oaks in the formal garden are occasionally pollarded to keep them in scale.

Extended pollarding can play a number of roles in garden
design. The walk of pollarded limes designed by Geoffrey Jellicoe at MOTTISFONT in 1936 has more the effect of an avenue

than of a barrier. The lime walk is effective in spring with its underplanting of glory of the snow (*Chionodoxa luciliae*) happily established in the short turf.

A further form of pleaching is that used for making tree arbours or tunnels, sometimes called 'alleys' (not to be confused with the French term *allée*). Strictly speaking, alleys are pathways lined with enclosing hedges as in the wilderness at HAM HOUSE or as defined in yew at LYTES CARY. Arbours, on the other hand, are made by training supple young shoots from two rows of trees planted perhaps 2.4 m (8 ft) apart. These are bent over metal or plastic-coated hoops to form a covered walk, at least 2.1 m (7 ft) high in the centre. Originally a rough framework of laths would have been used, and this framework developed into the more elegant trellis work seen in French Renaissance gardens. Sometimes the shoots overhead are grafted together where they meet: 'Overhead the branches joined one another and their foliage intermingled; nature itself seemed a work of art.'

At BATEMAN'S Rudyard Kipling designed a spacious pear alley shortly after his move there in 1902. Spring flowers grow at the base of the pear trees, which themselves make a froth of white blossom in May. Clematis planted outside the pears twine among the branches to give a summer display. At the end of the alley a wide seat is welcoming. **Mr Alan Champion**, the former Gardener-in-Charge at Bateman's, wrote about the maintenance of the alley (updated by the current Gardener-in-Charge, **Mr Derek Bobin**):

❧ The pear trees, which are a mixture of 'Conference', 'Doyenné du Comice' and 'Winter Nelis', are pruned in winter. All unwanted lateral growth is cut back to three or four buds: some are needed to train to replace dead branches. All dead wood is removed. It is usual with pears to summer-prune as well, but this is impractical here because of the clematis and honeysuckle which help clothe the arch in summer. To prevent excessive growth the tree trunks have been given two opposing cuts like two horseshoes one above the other about 5–7 cm (2–3 in) apart. This slows down the whole growth of the tree, but the trees here are for decoration rather than fruit. This is a task which should only be undertaken by an experienced person; if incorrectly carried out the tree will die. The cuts slowly heal themselves and need to be cleaned out ever two or three years. After cutting the wounds are painted with Arbrex as a cosmetic.

After the pear trees are pruned, the honeysuckle (*Lonicera etrusca*) which is trained over the seat at one end of the arch is cut back to a framework. Then the clematis are pruned back to ground level, leaving some stems to lengthen the flowering season the following year. These will be removed completely in the next pruning season and others left in their place.

The beds beneath the pear arch are weeded, edged and mulched. The clematis are given fertilizer and a sprinkling of lime. Most of the plants are shade-loving ground-cover plants which need little maintenance. The main clumps of plants are kept together, but any odd plants which come up unexpectedly are normally left to help cover the beds and give a natural look. As things die back in the autumn the foliage is tidied, ending with the vincas which are cut back at Christmas. ❧

PLANTS UNDER THE PEAR ARCH AT BATEMAN'S

Ajuga pyramidalis	*Geranium endressii*	*Pachyphragma*
A. reptans 'Multicolor'	*G. macrorrhizum*	*macrophyllum*
Allium moly	*Helleborus corsicus*	*Pachysandra terminalis*
Anemone coronaria	*H. foetidus*	*Polygonatum* × *hybridum*
Bergenias	Hostas	Primroses
Bluebells	Hyacinths	*Pulmonaria officinalis*
Brunnera macrophylla	*Lamium maculatum*	*Saxifraga fortunei*
Camassia leichtlinii	*L.m.* 'Aureum'	*Symphytum grandiflorum*
Colchicums	*L.* 'Beacon Silver'	*Tiarella cordifolia*
Convallaria majalis	*Leucojum aestivum*	*Vinca minor*
'Fortin's Giant'	'Gravetye'	*Viola cornuta* Alba Group
Epimedium × *versicolor*	*Lilium candidum*	*V. riviniana* Purpurea Group
Ferns	*Liriope muscari*	*V. odorata* 'Sulphurea'
Galanthus nivalis	Narcissus	

CLEMATIS ALTERNATING WITH PEAR TREES

C. 'Alice Fisk'	*C.* 'Jackmanii Rubra'	*C.* 'Madame Baron
C. 'Barbara Jackman'	*C.* 'Jackmanii Superba'	Veillard'
C. 'Gipsy Queen'	*C.* 'Lady Betty Balfour'	*C.* 'Miss Bateman'
C. 'Huldine'		*C. viticella*

At BENINGBROUGH HALL old pear espalier trees have been adapted to make attractive arches in the walled garden which has now been grassed over. Originally lining the central path, in traditional kitchen-garden fashion, the espalier trees seemed to have no function once paths and beds had disappeared. Long new shoots, instead of being cut off, have been trained across hoops to meet the shoots of espaliers on the opposite side. These archways make a feature down the middle of the garden.

Apple trees can also be trained to arch overhead, but the harder wood curves less elegantly, and the visual effect is harsher and stiffer. To plant up a new pear arch use two-year-old bushes already trained as cordons and give plenty of support, tying in loose shoots tightly and continually. For good crops of fruit as well as the ornamental effect, careful systematic pruning is necessary, cutting the previous year's growth back to a hand's breadth, to leave six or eight buds at the most as the fruiting spurs of the future.

The *berceau*, a form of trellis work covering a walk, makes a support for greenery and was a feature of early French and Dutch gardens, the forerunner of the more substantial pergola. Trellis work or *treillage* gives the appearance of a more solid architectural feature, yet is made in light, relatively flimsy batons in either square or diamond patterns. Its versatility makes it useful as a tool in garden design, where tricks with false perspective can control garden dimensions and narrowing bars of trellis work give the effects of distance or frame a fictitious distant path. In mediaeval gardens even the great bindweed (*Calystegia sepium*), known as poor man's rope, and with handsome bell-shaped flowers, was sometimes used for ornamental display on trellis. Today this most invasive deep-rooting weed is seldom allowed a place of importance; indeed, no well-maintained Trust garden allows it to flourish. More usually, fruiting vines combined use with beauty, just as today at FELBRIGG HALL grapevines are trained on timber pyramids, giving a strong architectural flavour to the garden and reminiscent of a French potager.

Bowers and arbours are places for sitting in for rest or contemplation. They can be angular, like sentry boxes of woodwork or trellis, or smoothly curved frames on which plants can twine. At WESTBURY COURT in the walled garden where shrub roses mingle with seventeenth-century herbs (or at least plants known in

At Moseley Old Hall in Staffordshire, where planting is seventeenth-century in style, the design of the wooden arbour is taken from Thomas Hill's A Gardener's Labyrinth *(1577).*

English gardens by 1700), corner hooped arbours very much like those at the Château de Villandry on the Loire, but on an appropriately smaller scale, provide the structure on which climbing roses flourish. Other shady arbours can be of one tree or climbing plant only. The oriental plane tree (*Platanus orientalis*) can be trained or Boston ivy (*Parthenocissus tricuspidata* 'Veitchii'), often wrongly known as Virginia creeper (actually P. *quinquefolia*), will provide cool shade through the hottest months, and the red grape (*Vitis vinefera* 'Purpurea') makes a crimson umbrella in late summer.

At MOSELEY OLD HALL a wooden arbour leads to a shady hornbeam tunnel across a corner. The decorative arbour, its pattern taken from Thomas Hill's *A Gardener's Labyrinth* (1577) is the frame on which climbers known at the period have been encouraged to twine. The dark-leaved claret vine, V. *vinifera* 'Purpurea' is interlaced with the fragrant virgin's bower (*Clematis flammula*) and purple virgin's bower (*C. viticella*), both European natives. Under the arbour and edging the walk are hedges of old English lavender (*Lavandula × intermedia*) with grey-blue leaves and dense spikes of blue. The visitor then emerges to a pathway lined with nut trees which leads on to a simple apple orchard.

A tree tunnel or shady arbour at LYTES CARY conceals a pathway linking separate garden areas and the leafy greenness prepares the eye for appreciating more colourful garden flowers beyond. Although the garden at Lytes Cary is Edwardian, it is laid out as a series of formal garden rooms and yew alleys which might well have been its pattern in the sixteenth century, when it was lived in by Sir Henry Lyte (1529–1607). He was the author of *A niewe Herball or Historie of Plants* (first published in 1578 and basically a translation of De l'Ecluse's French edition of Dodoens' *Cruydeboeck*). Appearing before Gerard's *Herball* of 1597, and well before Parkinson's *Paradisi in Sole Paradisus Terrestris* (1629), his book described plants only for their medicinal qualities.

At a focal point where a south vista from the house meets a terraced yew alley at a central stone-edged pool, the hornbeam tunnel leads on to a secret garden in the shape of an ellipse. The tunnel is 21 m (70 ft) long and 2 m (6 ft) across, with the hornbeams (*Carpinus betulus*) planted at a spacing of about a yard. The hornbeam is trained to meet overhead and needs careful pruning and tying once a year. Beyond the tunnel a lawn and statues of Flora and Diana are surrounded by a ring of *Weigela* 'Florida Variegata', underplanted with the spreading *Euphorbia amygdaloides robbiae,* an almost evergreen spurge from Asia Minor with lime-green flowers, which rapidly colonizes the ground in sun or shade.

It is perhaps hard to draw a clear distinction between tunnels and pergolas, which have a formal framework of brick, stone or wooden uprights, with crossbars in lighter wood. Once clothed in climbing plants a pergola performs many of the same functions as a tunnel, linking areas of the garden and creating shady and secret retreats, as well as providing a frame for a wide range of plants. The framework creates a three-dimensional garden feature and the straight lines contrast firmly with flowing plant shapes. It is possible to intertwine many natural climbers, extending the season for both flower and foliage interest, and at the feet of the upright supports more flower-bed space allows low-growing shrubs and herbaceous plants to line a central pathway.

One of the most spectacular and showy pergolas is that at MOUNT STEWART in Co. Down, where the winter climate compares favourably with gardens in Cornwall although it is on the same latitude as Glasgow. A very humid atmosphere and comparatively little frost permit plants such as mutisias and the scented almost evergreen Himalayan rose, *Rosa gigantea,* with wide yellowish-white single flowers followed by red autumn fruits, and a very vigorous habit, to flourish and twine overhead. Not only tender plants are grown, however, and *Lonicera etrusca* and lavender-mauve *Solanum crispum* 'Glasnevin' extend the blue and yellow theme of planting in the beds below. Although many of the plants that flourish in a favourable site like Mount Stewart are of doubtful hardiness it is, in fact, well worth while attempting to grow them in the average garden. Provided that they are well protected from harsh winds and low temperatures during their early years while they become established, many such plants can prove surprisingly tough.

At Mount Stewart the pergola on a raised terrace closes in the three sides of the sunken garden, west of the house. It is now sheltered by a tall hedge of the Leyland cypress (× *Cupressocyparis leylandii*). Below the frame, shrubs and perennials scramble in shade and sun, taking advantage of the well-drained soil.

The pergola pillars are made of sandstone, known locally as Scrabo, the name of the hill above Newtownards from where it comes. Each 45 cm (18 in) square pillar is placed about 6 m (20 ft) apart, and the overhead frame is of Douglas fir (*Pseudotsuga menziesii*), which proves hard-wearing and durable. It was last renewed in 1965.

In shade to the south the scarlet-flowered *Mitraria coccinea*, honeysuckle and small-flowered clematis species on the pillars are mixed with roses. On the sunnier sides the rare *Mutisia decurrens*, callistemon, *Jovellana violacea* and little violas grow beneath the pergola where the roses 'Easlea's Golden Rambler', 'Climbing Lady Hillingdon' and 'Rêve d'Or' make a lot of growth. Recent severe winters have killed the rare *Dendromecon rigida* from California, which is so difficult to propagate, with its narrow hard glaucous leaves and poppy-like buttercup-yellow flowers, but *Lardizabala biternata* from Chile, a twining evergreen with chocolate-purple flowers still survives. Mr Nigel Marshall, the Head Gardener, feels that the tender dendromecon would do better against a warm wall, and is not really suited to an open pergola.

A large plant of the Chinese gooseberry (*Actinidia deliciosa*, syn. *A. chinensis*), which bears fruit at Mount Stewart, scrambles over the pergola frame. Vines, the more delicate *Billardiera longiflora* from Tasmania with greenish-cream bell-flowers, *Clematis* 'Etoile Violette', *C* × *durandii* and the yellow rose 'Lawrence Johnston' named for the maker of the gardens at Hidcote (perhaps in its colour patterns a model for some of Lady Londonderry's schemes at Mount Stewart) all grow luxuriantly. Under the pergola flourish shade-loving *Waldsteinia ternata*, moon trefoil (*Medicago arborea*) with clusters of yellow peaflowers through the summer, and the little *Felicia amoena*, and there are large plants of *Ceanothus* 'Autumnal Blue' and *Chaenomeles speciosa* 'Falconnet Charlet' with double pink flowers which appear before the leaves in spring. Clumps of *Calceolaria integrifolia* and orange-flowered *Alstroemeria aurea* (*A. aurantiaca*) match the planting of yellow and orange in the sunken garden below.

Steps lined with *Erica lusitanica* lead down to this lower garden, where Gertrude Jekyll made designs for the planting. These beds reflect the same attention to colour detail as in the Italian garden to the south of the house, and are linked deliberately with the flower colour on the pergola above. With house and pergola

*The curving trellis-work pergola on the lower terraces at
Bodnant makes a frame for climbing roses. In the beds
below, grassy-leaved libertia flourish in half-shade.*

on three sides, the sense of enclosure is very strong. On the
house terrace formal clipped bays are interrupted by beds of the
apricot-flowered bush rose 'Mrs Oakley Fisher'. These roses are
underplanted with bronze-leaved *Crocosmia* 'Solfatare' with
apricot-yellow flowers on 60 cm (2 ft) stems and pale blue *Salvia
patens* 'Cambridge Blue', a colour-scheme which might be copied,
even if, in less favoured gardens, other plants had to be used.

At BODNANT steps descend below the lily terrace and lead to
curving walls over which light wooden pergola frames are covered with climbing roses, mauve-flowered *Solanum crispum*
'Glasenevin', the spring-flowering evergreen *Clematis armandii*,
and the Chilean coral plant, *Berberidopsis corallina*. Tied back
against the walls and given shelter by the pergola and the twining overhead plants are wall shrubs such as ceanothus, lep-
tospermum, tree heaths, *Drimys winteri*, the tender *Photinia
glomerata* with almost translucent young growth, and *Rhododendron edgeworthii*. In summer white libertia (*Libertia formosa*) and
in September dark pink Japanese anemones make a flowery
underplanting, and blue campanulas seed in the dry wall.

Perhaps most famous of all at Bodnant is the spectacular laburnum walk which flowers from mid-May to mid-June. Planted already at the end of the nineteenth century by the present Lord Aberconway's great-grandfather, the tunnel curves gently and is formed by training pleached laburnums over metal hoops held on a rigid frame. The original bushes will have been the common European laburnum (*Laburnum anagyroides*), but over the years these have been replaced with the newer 1875 hybrid cultivar *L. × watereri* 'Vossii' with longer, very free-flowering racemes. The bushes are trained and pruned in the same way as is described for pleached lime trees.

At GREYS COURT plants of the giant Japanese wisteria (*Wisteria floribunda*) cover an area between two walled gardens, and gnarled trunks, of considerable age, have to be supported by strong wooden props. Large wisterias can seldom be pruned twice a year as recommended, with a quick tidy in summer immediately after flowering followed by heavy pruning in winter before the sap rises again for a new season. Like so many plants it is in the first few years that particular care has to be taken; as wisteria matures, it continues to perform well with little attention and still flowers profusely if given only the winter cut-back. Under this wisteria in almost total shade the blue-flowered *Buglossoides purpurocaerulea* thrives and gives interest in summer, making a weed-suppressing mass.

PLANTING IN PATTERNS

The idea of pattern takes the controlling element – the shaping of trees and hedging plants – a stage further; instead of using plants structurally, as barriers, planting is for decoration and artifice. While topiary may vertically emphasize the structure of a layout, its clipped shape is pure ornament. In the horizontal plane, knots and parterres use dwarf hedging as outlines for garden conceits. When the neat clipped lines contain freer plant forms, the decorative effect is richer; when colour is also present, the patterns become luxury items – jewelled embroideries.

Such patterns are quite deliberately contrived, emphasizing rather than modifying the artifice of gardening. They become the central and dominant feature and need to be framed accordingly by cool green lawn and simple lines of hedging. These geometric designs, often elaborate and grandiose on a large scale, can be effectively modified for a small area; in fact are more suitable than 'naturalistic' curves in confined spaces.

TOPIARY

The cutting of trees and shrubs to ornament the garden has been practised since Roman times. In Pliny's garden, box was clipped into innumerable shapes, some even as letters spelling out the name of the gardener or his master. Originally the word 'topiary' came from the Latin *topiarius*, correctly translated as the person tending the garden, but it quickly assumed a more specific definition, until *ars topiaria* implied a degree of skill in shaping living plants. The art of topiary was revived in Renaissance Italy, when humanist writers and architects looked to classical sources of inspiration. First described in the Rucellai garden at Villa Quaracchi in Florence, shapes were varied and eclectic: 'spheres, porticoes, temples, vases, urns, apes, donkeys, oxen, a bear, giants, men, women, warriors, a harpy, philosophers, popes and cardinals'. The fashion for topiary spread from Italy through France and Holland to reach England by the seventeenth century.

These clipped shapes become important in garden design whether taking the place of statues, or emphasizing a focal point, or simply contrasting with freer plant growth. For topiary, plants should be slow-growing, of dense habit and amenable to regular cutting. Evergreens such as box, yew and holly (although the latter is less satisfactorily close-growing) are most often used. Forms of phillyrea also respond well, and both *Phillyrea latifolia* and *P. angustifolia* were much used in English seventeenth-century gardens, and are now coming back into fashion. At WESTBURY COURT phillyreas are used as clipped specimens in the Trust's restoration of the garden to its original appearance dating back to the end of the seventeenth century. Juniper (the common native *Juniperus communis*) is also practical for topiary; seldom used today, it did feature in English Restoration gardens. Portugal laurel (*Prunus lusitanica*) can be clipped into regular geometric shapes, but like beech or hornbeam does not grow densely enough to make elaborate topiary specimens. The more tender bay (*Laurus nobilis*) and holm oak (*Quercus ilex*) also make attractive textured shapes, but cannot be clipped into the more complicated structures.

Fashions come and go, and even in 1625, when the craze for topiary shapes had still a hundred years of popularity to run, Francis Bacon, writing *Of Gardens*, is scornful: '. . . images cut out in juniper or other garden stuff be for children'. By 1712 Joseph Addison writes in *The Spectator*, objecting to the fashion ('We see the marks of the Scissors on every bush'), while Alexander Pope in the following year in *The Guardian* invents a 'Catalogue of Greens' to be used by an aspiring gardener: '. . . A pair of Giants, stunted, to be sold cheap . . . A Queen Elizabeth in Phylyraea, a little inclining to the Green Sickness, but full of growth.' In the grander gardens, topiary ceased to be popular, and gardens became landscape parks. Even hedges enclosing separate garden areas were swept away to allow fields with grazing cattle and sheep to sweep up to the mansion windows.

By the middle of the nineteenth century, Charles Barry and W. A. Nesfield were again designing gardens in Italianate style where domes or cylinders of green or golden yew or variegated hollies defined garden patterns. At BLICKLING HALL Nesfield designed the parterre on the east terrace, and strangely shaped dense yew blocks known as the 'grand pianos' still sit on the lawn today. At the corners of the square beds, redesigned for herbaceous planting by Mrs Norah Lindsay in the 1930s, yews are sentinel acorns.

Although most of the tall tapering yews were planted only in the 1850s, the yew garden at PACKWOOD HOUSE represents the topiary style of the Restoration. To today's eyes successful topiary effects depend not only on the outline and solidity of the shape, but also on the textural contrasts and on the incidence of light falling on horizontal, vertical and curved surfaces. In the area where the tall yew shapes and yew arbour planted by John Ferguson *circa* 1660, dominate the upper garden at Packwood, the lawn is edged with old box bushes, interesting in the variability of surface colour and the shape of the box leaves. Although remaining botanically identifiable as *Buxus sempervirens*, individual box plants can vary greatly from one another and show a wide range of different colours and textures. Box shares this characteristic with yew. The side hedges and cross hedge just below the Mount with its spiralling path of box, has a tapestry pattern in different green tones. Grown thick and bulky with age, it makes great mounded waves, almost as interesting as the soaring yew shapes. The Trust are replanting a considerable

We hope you will enjoy this book: your comments are most welcome.

Title of Book: _____   How I learned of this book: _____

Comments: _____

Bought at: _____   Gift: _____   My Business or Profession: _____

Please send me, free of charge, your latest catalogue.
I am interested in books on the following subjects (tick relevant boxes)

☐ Cricket/Sport	☐ Gardening	☐ Humour
☐ Film, theatre and music	☐ Science and Nature	☐ Literature and anthologies
☐ Cookery	☐ Travel and guides	☐ Heritage
☐ Art, architecture & photography	☐ Children's books	☐ Biography and autobiography

NAME (BLOCK CAPITALS PLEASE) _____

ADDRESS _____

_____   DATE: _____

Do not affix postage stamps
if posted in Gt Britain, Channel Islands,
N Ireland or the Isle of Man

Pavilion Books Limited
FREEPOST WC 5141
LONDON
SE1 1BT

Yews are clipped into massive shapes at Blickling Hall in Norfolk. Probably planted by W. A. Nesfield in the nineteenth century, these dense masses are known as the 'grand pianos' and give architectural interest.

number of the box bushes, as with age and clipping it is almost impossible to keep the base from getting bare and woody.

Yew hedges and yew specimens for topiary cutting or for more bulky shapes may be grown from seed, and plants are then selected for their suitably dense habit of growth, but for the best results the plants should be vegetatively produced from the same sturdy clone. In fact, a batch of yew plants bought in from a nursery may be very variable; worse, plants taken as cuttings from side shoots will fail to make leaders, but will put on considerable horizontal growth. Seedling yews also vary in density of growing habit and in leaf colours. For both topiary and hedges a dense habit will permit much more tailored effects; in a hedge colour variation is often attractive, but in shaped topiary conformity of colour and texture is usually desirable.

At both PACKWOOD and NYMANS die-back to a few inches became noticeable and insightly in 1985. It was discovered that the tortrix moth (*Ditula angurosina*) was laying eggs in the yew hedges: the hatched caterpillars hibernated through the winter, and then 'barked' the ends of the young shoots in spring. The caterpillar is about 1 cm (½ in) long, greenish-greyish in colour, and affects malus, pyrus and prunus as well as yew. An insecticide containing permethrin, to which caterpillars and aphids do not build up a resistance, is effective. Bats, which have now become rare, are thought in the past to have been the natural predator of the tortrix moth. An even greater problem now exists with phytophthora die-back.

At Packwood the Multitude area contains tall yews dating back to the 1840s which were actually beginning to die by the 1970s. This was due not to old age, but to a combination of factors: the heavy, sticky clay soil caused waterlogging and surface rooting; there was competition (from grass) for water in a series of dry seasons and increased numbers of visitors caused compaction. The situation is now being relieved by an extensive drainage system, particularly surface drainage; by top dressing with sharp sand; by frequent spiking and by replanting on slight mounds. The yews were also cut back drastically to the bare stem, and are rejuvenating successfully. Watering in the growing season after cutting back is critical.

At POWIS CASTLE Mr Jimmy Hancock, the Head Gardener, finds that die-back in yew branches halfway up a hedge or in a cut topiary shape is often caused by nibbling of squirrels, voles and mice, which 'bark' a stem completely round. These stems have to be cut out, and it is several years before the surface returns to one smooth plane. The strange mounded 'waves' in very old yew such as that at Powis and MONTACUTE HOUSE may orginally derive from a cause such as this, and make it difficult to clip them evenly. The Irish yews (*Taxus baccata* 'Fastigiata') that make such satisfactory free-standing specimens, and in paired alignment make superb avenues, all derive from the yew discovered in 1780 at Florence Court in Northern Ireland. They must all be vegetatively produced from cuttings. The branches grow upwards almost vertically. Interestingly, Mr Alan Mitchell has remarked that the most fastigiate forms from Ireland grow less tall and narrow the farther east in Great Britain they are planted. At FELBRIGG HALL in Norfolk, for example, their habit is markedly dumpier and less soaring.

The best way to shape the trees is to clip or prune the outside annually, as is done at ERDDIG, MONTACUTE, ROWALLANE and SNOWSHILL. A traditional practice has been to use wires to hold the branches in place and maintain a good shape, but this is not recommended: it creates work, and causes damage to stems. Unfortunately once begun it has to be continued, and any necessary cutting out of dead wood has to be done by pulling down the outer branches, as is the practice with Italian cypresses.

Many topiary gardens disappeared in the landscape movement, and the Trust now often reintroduces some appropriate form of clipped ornament when restoring a garden attached to a seventeenth-century house. In the front entrance garden at MOSELEY OLD HALL, where the surrounding border is composed of plants known in the seventeenth century, the central grass panels flanking the path to the front door are decorated in period style with finials and corkscrew spirals of box.

Other Trust gardens have old and intricate topiary. The complete restoration of misshapen peacocks or even of more simple cones, spheres and finials is difficult, as few evergreens will 'break' from dead wood, but need the slow process of 'stumping' back to a main stem or trunk. Many Victorian gardens which have passed into Trust ownership still have evidence of topiary which can be reshaped, however overgrown. The great domes of golden yew on the terraces to the east of the house at SHUGBOR-OUGH were nursed back to shape but did not need completely 'stumping' back as has been necessary where neglect has been more severe over a long period.

Just as hedges, arbours and tunnels give architectural interest, so an element of clipped topiary adds a feeling of maturity and permanence to a garden, and does not take many years to look good. Shaping should begin when a plant is still young, although not for the first two years, and is at first usually done methodically with secateurs; later as the outline becomes defined, electric clippers can be used. The more the plant is cut the more feeding it needs as it struggles to put out new shoots, so well prepared soil and plenty of moisture in the growing season are essential. Plants need feeding with organic humus-making fertilizers, as well as artificial compound fertilizers which should be given as growth starts in the spring.

Many of the larger topiary features are produced by planting a group of three or four together. It is essential that these should all be taken from the same clone. After the first two seasons, clip hard and feed liberally to encourage dense growth, gradually tying shoots to a frame of stout galvanized wire or wickerwork

Yews can be trained into any topiary shape: at Hidcote Manor yew peacocks
have recently been renovated by 'stumping' back to the main branches.

to achieve a perfect shape. Leaders are chosen to grow on, and young shoots are tied into position or cut back to make bushy growth. The wicker or wire frame soon becomes completely concealed with boskage as the specimen matures. It is not difficult to keep the bush to the desired shape as long as cutting is done frequently; it can be a problem to reshape a very woody subject.

A frame is helpful even when training plants to make simple archways or recessed niches. At HARDWICK HALL a network of metal defines the recesses which frame statues in the *rond-point* where yew and hornbeam hedges meet. For elaborate shapes, special frames may be contrived. At MOUNT STEWART in Co. Down Lady Londonderry had shaped metal frames made by a blacksmith in Co. Fermanagh, on which she trained some of her topiary figures, including the complex Irish harp. The clipped bay bushes which frame the house terrace, on the other hand, were imported from Belgium in 1923 ready-shaped as mature specimens already fifty years old.

These topiary techniques for clipping and trimming of woody plants can be applied to making hedges more complicated, with

At Nymans yew topiary shaped as crowns marks four corners and frames an Italian fountain.

shapes cut out along the top, sometimes in scallops or battle-mented as at CASTLE DROGO. Buttresses project to make frames for statuary or flower beds. Single plant specimens (or groups of the same plant) are cut to represent cones, balls, birds or beasts. A fox hunt in yew runs along the broad top of a yew hedge at KNIGHTSHAYES, and finials and spheres in holly protrude from the hedges which line the water canals at WESTBURY COURT. Simple solid rectangles of box outside the west door at MONTA-CUTE HOUSE (planted in 1973), the 'grand pianos' in yew at BLICKING HALL, and the 'drums' at WIGHTWICK MANOR seem to anchor the garden with the house into the lanscape, and seem an essential part of the framework of the overall design.

The great yew shapes at POWIS CASTLE date from the end of the seventeenth century; the topiary yews at CHIRK CASTLE were planted only at the end of the last century, but have grown high with wide bases to resemble Welsh hats. More elaborate repre-sentational topiary such as the Hidcote or Wightwick peacocks, the elaborate 'crowns' which frame the Italian fountain at NYMANS, and the chase at KNIGHTSHAYES have been made only in this century. The Trust is also in the process of restoring the extraordinary topiary around the Shamrock Garden at MOUNT STEWART.

At WIGHTWICK MANOR the formal garden, designed by Alfred Parsons, is a series of yew enclosures, the hedges themselves with protruding buttresses and strange acute angles, emphasizing light and shadow effects. At the entrance to the rose garden, large cylinders of yew are topped with clipped peacocks.

The green alley, flanked by stone crowns, is 70 m (some 75 yd) long and 3–4 m (10–13 ft) wide and carries the eye to a wooden seat at the end. The yew had grown to 2.4 m (8 ft) in width and almost 6 m (20 ft) high. This has been reduced to a more manageable 90 cm by 2.1 m (3 × 7 ft). At cross entrances the yew arches are accentuated by being framed in a solid clipped box-like shape which projects forwards and upwards over the long line of yew. The designer Thomas Mawson also worked here later, and the drum-shaped golden yews in the rose garden are part of his contribution. Mawson liked to contrast leaf colours in topiary, budding a golden-leaved yew to the leading shoot of clipped hemisphere in plain green, and training and clipping this golden cap to complete the sphere. Similar tricks are played when variegated holly is contrasted with a plain green form, and shaped into a ball on top of a solid base. At Wightwick Mawson also planted bushes of brightly coloured variegated holly, *Ilex aquifolium* 'Golden Queen', along a walk edging the orchard. These are now clipped into domed cylinders.

Perhaps topiary is most pleasing when it seems to belong quite simply to its context. In the pillar garden at HIDCOTE each soaring yew shape springs from a solid cube which anchors it firmly to its place, a stabilizing foil in flower beds packed with extravagant plant shapes. At POWIS the 300-year-old yews, now 9 m (30 ft) high, have a monumental scale in keeping with the castle's grandeur, and additional bastion to its fortifications. At LYTES CARY where a garden path is flanked with cottage-loaf yews, large mounded cylinders of box against a stone wall quietly echo the rounded dome of a dovecote in the parkland beyond. More fanciful contrived ornamental shapes, appropriate in a period garden, seem decoration rather than permanent garden features. The quiet solidity and flowing smooth clipped lines of more architectural structures add a stabilizing quality to a garden scene and, because topiary grows slowly and take years to mature, imply a belief in the garden's continued development.

KNOTS AND MAZES

Knot designs in gardens derived from embroidery and the medieval passion for intricate patterns. The 'over and under' worked in silk or wool was imitated in the garden by using foliage plants with distinct leaf colours. Similarly, the intricate designs of Persian carpets, the strapwork in wooden panelling and plaster ceilings in Elizabethan and Jacobean great houses were copied in the garden in the forms of interlacing knots. The idea is much the same as making a framework with some low-growing plant, usually box, santolina, rue or germander, small-leaved and dense in habit, and then further subdividing the framed area into smaller flower beds. Early ecclesiastical gardens would have had a simple and quite functional pattern, dividing herbs for cooking and medicine from each other; later the patterns became more elaborate and developed into the French *parterre de broderie* where there were no inner flower beds, but elegant scrolls of box were laid out on a background of plain or coloured gravels.

In the garden a continuous interlacing line of one plant, like a weaving thread, would be called a 'closed' knot, while when the plants remained in separate distinct areas each section would be termed an 'open' knot. These patterns, usually of low clipped evergreen bushes, outlined miniature flower beds, in which flowering herbs or even coloured sands or brick dust were placed.

Essentially these patterns were most effective if they could be viewed from above; many knots were in garden areas directly outside the house window or sometimes in a sunken plot to be viewed from a terrace or steps. The Elizabethan raised walk and the mount not only allowed the country side to be glimpsed from within the security of the garden, but also gave the elevation necessary to appreciate the complicated designs laid out like a carpet within the garden perimeters.

The maze or labyrinth, as a conception, probably came first from the mythological tortuous windings of the minotaur at Knossos. Later representing the path the Christian believer must follow to reach a spiritual goal, it became a common religious symbol marked out in church floors or outside pavements, during the late Middle Ages. The journey through a maze became a substitute for a pilgrimage to the Holy Land, and as a penance the faithful might follow its meanderings on their knees. An early maze in masonry is recorded in the twelfth century at Woodstock, where Henry II chased the 'fair Rosamund'. At first mazes were cut in stone, rock or turf; later they were delineated with low hedges.

At GREYS COURT a modern turf maze was commissioned by Lady Brunner in 1980 and designed by Mr Adrian Fisher. Basically dictated by Christian symbolism, it represents the 'Chemin de Jerusalem', the pilgrim's path to the Holy Land, and his ultimate salvation. The maze is a puzzle with choices at the cruciform junctions. The entire maze can be walked once and once only, by crossing over each of the diamond-shaped thorns, and this path becomes the Path of Life or an allegory of the pilgrimage through life and death to the beginning of Eternal Life, then judgement and finally Salvation when all is reconciled. Although the maze is only 25 m (85 ft) across, the total length of path is exactly a quarter of a mile. The seven rings of paths represent the seven days of creation; the diameter of the centre is nine times the span between each part, and represents the ninth hour of agony; the two arms of the Byzantine cross from finial to finial total 10 m (33 ft), the age of Christ at his death. The overall design represents the Crown of Thorns.

The laurel maze at Glendurgan (below and right) has no logical pattern or philosophical meaning, but introduces formality into a woodland garden.

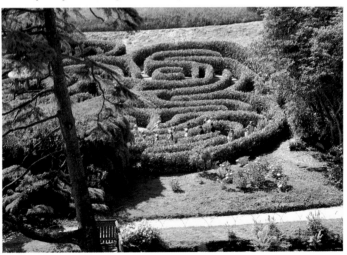

A shallow track or pathway is set in the grass turf. Three bricks on edge make the pathway 33 cm (13 in) wide; 4,500 bricks are used to complete the 320 m (350 yd) stretch. The pathway starts across a bridge in the orchard and leads a traveller into the maze of seven rings to the east, and ultimately to a central sundial. The sundial consists of a wrought-iron globe on a stone pillar. Brass strips set into the stone represent the continents of the world. A golden shaft represents the Light of the World, and protrudes out of the globe. A series of numerals runs round the globe, indicating the hour as the shadow of the golden shaft reaches them. The pillar itself has four faces, each containing an inscription carved in slate set into the pillar. The pillar stands at the intersection of two superimposed crosses; one, a plain Roman cross of native hardwood, lies within the second more elaborate Byzantine cross, which is of coloured marbles and stones.

Although grass-cutting is simple as a rotary mower slides smoothly over the 33 cm (13 in) path, edging neatly is a problem. The curve of the sunken pathway or channel is too tight for a conventional edging machine. Instead, a Wolflawn Flite edger, basically a knife on a stick with wheel blade, is used, but the process takes eight hours a week. The bricks were set in soft pointing, eight buckets of sand to half of cement, which was brushed between the bricks and then wetted. As a result weeds can get a foothold and, again because of the narrowness of the gully, maintenance is time-consuming.

Mazes in the Middle Ages derived from ritual or religious ideals, but by the fifteenth century, they lost their more philosophical significance and came to be used as ornamental features in Italian and French gardens. A book published in Venice in 1499 *Hypnerotomachia Poliphili* (The Strife of Love in a Dream) probably by the monk Francesco Colonna, influenced the development of Renaissance garden design. It included sections of fantasy on different garden themes. Ideas from Christian tradition and pagan myths were united to describe intricate knots, laybrinths in water, forests and 'flowery medes', fine wooden arbours twined with jasmine, ruins and strange sculptures, all illustrated with precise woodcuts. After its publication, no European Renaissance garden could be without a maze or some other of the features described. As in the 'Dream', the garden labyrinth and flower bed was linked with astrology. The square represented earth and all its elements; the circle became a symbol of heaven, and each herb had to have a 'correct' position in its new environment, sometimes worked out with mathematical finesse. The labyrinth with its richness of magical and Christian meaning became the basis for designs for intricate garden beds, divided into precise geometric patterns. These early mazes were cut low, with no obvious intention to confuse; like the knot, they were meant to be viewed from above. The taste for these garden features, later developing into French *broderie* and *parterres*, remained a fundamental part of garden design through the sixteenth and seventeenth centuries.

It was not until the end of the seventeenth century that the head-high maze was introduced, as at Hampton Court in 1690, with the deliberate idea of amusement through confusion. At Hampton Court the maze, made in yew, is trapezoid in shape, and measures some 66 m × 25 m (222 ft × 82 ft). A rectangular beech maze at TATTON PARK measuring 34 m × 18 m (114 ft × 60 ft) was planted in 1890. It lies almost at the centre of the pleasure gardens, and its presence is hidden by trees and shrubs. Although almost a copy of the maze at Hampton Court, the surroundings are thus quite different. The seventeenth-century original that inspired the Tatton maze would itself have been surrounded and framed by a rectangular compartment as part of a formal garden layout.

At GLENDURGAN in Cornwall the Trust maintain a maze with an unusual design. The hedges are of cherry laurel (*Prunus lauro-cerasus*) and stand at waist height. First planted in 1833 by Alfred Fox, whose descendants still live at Glendurgan, copied the design of a maze at Sydney Gardens, Bath (maze no longer in existence). In his journal for 5th October 1833 Mr Fox wrote: 'Began the preparation for a labyrinth at Glendurgan.' On 1st November: 'I rose at 5 a.m. and went on the water till breakfast. The men still busy with the labyrinth.' On 1st December: 'Nearly all the laurels planted to form our new labyrinth,' and on the 20th of the month he 'examined the apple and pear trees planted near the labyrinth'.

The maze lies on a steep slope leading down to the valley of the River Helford below. Strange in its asymmetrical shape, it seems almost as exotic as the rare magnolias, tree ferns and American agaves, much later additions, which today thrive in this almost frost-free garden. By 1979 the laurel had become weak and bare at the base and was infested with sycamore, brambles and other woody weeds. It was pruned back hard and fed liberally and the brushwood was cut out and painted with Roundup. At the same time the land-drains which had become blocked over the years were cleared.

Because they are precise, existing plans for elaborate flower beds, published in sixteenth- and seventeenth-century books, are relatively easy to follow. In some Trust gardens where a complete reconstruction is necessary, knot gardens have been made typical of the style of the period of the house. At MOSELEY OLD HALL a simple knot in box has been laid out. Taken from a 1640 garden plan found in a manuscript at Magdalen College, Oxford, the box pattern is emphasized by different coloured gravels and large pebbles, and the whole area is surrounded by a boxwood hedge. A layer of plastic under the gravel and close to the base of the box reduces maintenance to an annual clipping and periodic raking. At HAM HOUSE a reconstruction of the garden as it was *circa* 1670 has been carried out. To the east of the house a parterre of diaper-pattern, box-edged beds is filled alternatively with trimmed silvery *Santolina chamaecyparissus* and lavender. Box cones accentuate the corners. Maintenance consists of annual tight clipping.

On a more intimate scale, at MOTTISFONT ABBEY a box-edged parterre was designed by Mrs Norah Lindsay at the turn of the century. This is on a scale suitable for a small modern garden. Incidentally, at both LITTLE MORETON HALL and FENTON HOUSE, gooseberry bushes are used in reconstructions of seventeenth-century formal garden patterns, an ideal space-saving technique.

In the small west formal garden at BENINGBROUGH, a disarmingly simple modern knot pattern has been laid out by the Trust. A surrounding low box hedge makes a square which encloses another square at an angle across the corners. In the centre lilies grow through golden origanum, and the remaining triangles are planted with yellow bidens and scarlet calceolarias making solid blocks of colour.

PARTERRES

Of French origin, the *parterre de broderie* is an extension of earlier knot patterns and labyrinthine flower beds which were generally enclosed by walls and hedges. Traditionally they are an invention of the royal gardener Claude Mollet, working in the sixteenth century for the Italian Queen of France, Catherine de Medici. In the parterre, usually on a level area (often the terrace near a house), plants and possibly ornaments are arranged in a perfectly symmetrical way, more carefully balanced than in knots, on a larger scale and often as foreground to limitless formal vistas. In the French *broderie*, edging plants and continous ribbons became scrolls and arabesques, often arranged on a bed of gravel, everything on a grander scale, and much less intimate than the knot or simple parterre pattern with fewer different types of plant and less emphasis on flowers. The dwarf box (*Buxus sempervirens* 'Suffruticosa') developed in Holland towards the end of the sixteenth century, was the perfect plant for these displays, which became ever more magnificent, with baroque arabesques and curves instead of geometric squares and circles. *Broderie* patterns in flower beds taken from textile designs and architectural motifs united a whole area in quite a different way from the separate knots. Often, like knots, designed to be looked at from above, these schemes were particularly suitable for the grand scale of French gardens, where in a flat landscape, the château dominated its site.

First in Holland in smaller gardens and then in England,

At Ashdown House patterns of box in curving shapes set in gravel are derived from French parterres of the late seventeenth century.

designs were adapted to the terrain. At WESTBURY COURT in the flat fields of the Severn valley a so-called Dutch garden with water-canals has been reconstructed by the National Trust. Simple parterres, using plants available in 1700, are arranged in grass, which is cut at different levels to suggest the long grass of the original orchard, with the centre being close-mown to set off the parterres. (The original orchard has now been replanted with ornamental trees.) On either side groups of small trees and clipped evergreen shrubs are arranged in a quincunx pattern, like fives on dice. At Westbury *Phillyrea angustifolia*, clipped into a rounded dome, is the centre bush; it is surrounded by Portugal laurel (*Prunus lusitanica*). Nearby a simple box parterre in the Dutch style has low box (*Buxus sempervirens* 'Suffruticosa') hedges which define flower beds where marigolds (*Calendula officinalis*) mixed with *Echium creticum*, *Lilium pyrenaicum*, *Iberis sempervirens* with purple-leaved sage (*Salvia officinalis* 'Purpurascens') and golden variegated sage (*S.o.* 'Icterina') grow in a sea of grey-leaved grass (*Festuca glauca*) and *Santolina chamaecyparissus*, which underplants the topiary. In the centre of each bed finials and balls of clipped box give height. This is a very simple pattern, known as a 'cut parterre'; somewhere between a knot and the much more elaborate sort of garden 'embroidery' which was practised in France.

At OXBURGH HALL the Trust has restored the intricate French *broderie*, based on a pattern from a French garden book, first published in England in 1712, but in fact not executed at Oxburgh until 1845. Designed to be seen from a raised terrace walk or from the house, it was described as a *parterre de compartiment*. Today the box edges are renewed and the *compartiments* filled with a permanent planting of *Senecio cineraria* 'Silver Dust' annual and blue-foliaged rue (*Ruta graveolens* 'Jackman's Blue'). Summer bedding plants include ageratums, French marigolds and, in the centre bed, 'Paul Crampel' pelargoniums amidst grey foliage. The box is given a slow-acting fertilizer at the end of the winter and is cut in the summer; rue is cut after the last frost, in May. Annual cuttings of the latter plant are held in reserve, in case of a severe winter.

At ASHDOWN HOUSE, where the Trust took over a Restoration house but no garden, a box and gravel parterre adapted by Mr A. H. Brookholding Jones from a seventeenth-century pattern book was laid out in 1955. Viewed from the windows of the house, the simple scrolls of box and plain dark gravel are the foreground to lime pollards which stretch across the landscape in French style. When it is established in a weed-free site so that the gravel is easily groomed, this sort of simple parterre involves little maintenance, and patterns are easily adapted to suit a smaller space.

In England many early parterres were swept away during the eighteenth century, when surrounding parkland came right to the windows of a house, regardless of whether it was of an earlier period. The National Trust sometimes reconstructs a garden appropriate to a house's architecture when no original records exist.

In Victorian England the bedding system was introduced. In a way this was a new type of parterre design, exploiting the availability of many new tender or half-hardy plants, the extension of greenhouse use and the growth of technical gardening knowledge. Above all, bedding out depended on the cheapness of labour. These bedding displays, often more a meretricious and competitive means of ostentatiously demonstrating new wealth than based on any aesthetic composition, might even be rated by the numbers of plants annually raised according to social rank.

About 10,000 plants might be adequate for a country squire, but an earl or duke should deploy 30,000 or even 50,000. It became a virtue in plants to be tender. In the grandest gardens, after a storm, a band of gardeners would have replaced all damaged plants by breakfast time the next day, adequate replacements being kept healthy in the glasshouse. As well as these massed displays of colour, inspiration came from the Italian Renaissance garden. So-called 'Italianate' parterres in box and coloured gravels became once more the fashion, and were placed on broad terraces. Sometimes a family's coat of arms formed the basis of a pattern; at others, scrolls and feather designs aped those of the seventeenth century. More often the new tender bedding plants replaced coloured gravels between the box.

By the mid-twentieth century these schemes had vanished from most private gardens, as fuel and labour costs made propagation on such vast scales impossible. Municipal parks still cotninue the tradition, massing spring bulbs such as tulips and hyacinths; anemones and tuberous-rooted ranunculus extend the display. Fortunately the Trust is now the custodian of several Victorian gardens, and by using new labour-saving techniques, manages to implement many old schemes, sometimes achieving exact replicas. At WADDESDON MANOR, golden yew hedges frame beds where a fountain of Pluto and Prosperine is surrounded by parterres laid out for Baron Ferdinand de Rothschild by the French landscape designer, Lainé. Plants in the beds were changed twice a year. Today 9,000 tulips and 8,000 wallflower plants are put in each autumn for spring colour; 8,500 pot-grown zonal pelargoniums and 5,000 ageratums, sown under glass in spring, make an impressive summer display. Few private gardeners can attempt this sort of deliberate historical reconstruction. Nevertheless, in many modern gardens, bulbs, hardy and half-hardy annuals and tender bedding plants have become part of the seasonal planting pattern. In fact more bedding-out plants are sold each year than any other type of plant material, yet a coherent planting scheme is often lacking. Much of the planting, whether of bulbs or other plants, is in mixed colours. (Today it is getting difficult to obtain seed of unmixed colour packets, but as nurserymen and seed nurseries exist to satisfy demand it would seem possible to influence what they provide.) Narrow ribbons of wallflowers edge rose beds, followed later by trailing lobelias making a characterless and insipid

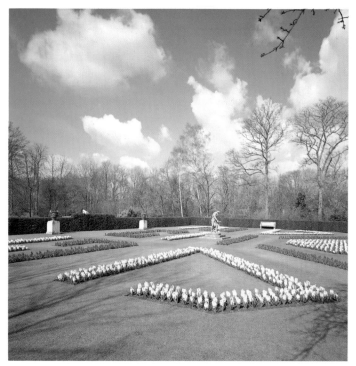

At Anglesey Abbey the Hyacinth Garden, blue and white with scented hyacinths in spring (above), becomes flamboyant with red and orange dahlias in summer (right).

colour scheme. From Waddesdon the aesthetic value of massing one or two colours together in solid-seeming blocks can be learnt. Because of its size, few garden owners can attempt a similar scheme; however, by keeping the relative planting proportions but working on a much reduced scale, it is possible to capture some of its spirit. Growing both annuals and tender bedding plants well needs dedication and most poor results are due to inadequate conditions: the right temperature, the correct compost, potting on at the desirable moment, are all things easier to provide and do on a large scale where one person gives the task their full attention. It is much more difficult to succeed when greenhouse space has to be shared with plants requiring different culture.

At ANGLESEY ABBEY, another grand-scale bedding-out area laid out as recently as the 1930s is a source of inspiration. Four thousand blue and white hyacinth bulbs scent the enclosed Hyacinth Garden in spring. As foliage dies down, orange and deep scarlet dahlias are planted in their place, the whole area enclosed now with a yew hedge: formerly the hedging plant was a form of thuja. Another garden where bedding on a large scale is practised is the restored KINGSTON LACY. Here the parterre in pink, white and purple is reminiscent of a scheme used by the Bankes family in the 1930s.

On the north side of the Elizabethan house of LANHYDROCK, a Victorian-style parterre was laid out in 1851. Originally gravel pathways separated the intricately designed beds all edged with dwarf box (*Buxus sempervirens* 'Suffruticosa'), but now mown grass is more restful and links the area with surrounding smooth lawns. The formal gardens today are enclosed with battlemented walls, an addition made in the 1850s when George Gilbert Scott altered and enlarged the house for Lord Clifden. Originally high walls connected to the superb gatehouse contained garden courtyards typical of sixteenth- and sev-

enteenth-century style, but in the eighteenth century all was swept away and parkland reached up to the walls of the house, until the Victorian alternations once more reinstated a more formal setting.

Round the parterre beds a higher 90 cm (3 ft) box hedge of the specie *Buxus sempervirens* is carefully cut to slope inwards to a 38 cm (15 in) top. This hedge was planted in 1935 to commemorate King George V's silver jubilee. During the war years it was allowed to grow with vertical sides, preventing light from reaching the base, which became bare and woody. The former Head Gardener, Mr Peter Borlase, emphasizes that it took nineteen years to restore the hedge to health and vigour. Now clipping is necessary only once a year; an annual dose of a compound chemical fertilizer promotes growth.

In the beds all plants, except for tuberous begonias which are the non-stop variety, are changed twice during the year. In November the summer bedding is cleared away and the soil dug and manured in preparation for spring bedding plants. The soil is acid (pH 4.5) and the very high rainfall of 130 cm (52 in) washes away nutrients, so there are no short cuts to a careful annual routine of double digging incorporating humus-making material. In the smaller beds trenching is impossible, so the top layer of soil is first placed in a wheelbarrow while the compost is spread; a plastic sheet laid on grass is equally effective and tidy, but the narrow grass paths here do not allow of this solution. Compost at Lanhydrock is made from a mixture of fallen leaves from the woodland garden area, lawn mowings and farmyard manure. Stored in bulky heaps, the compost is turned in winter months when pressure of work allows. Mr Borlase changed plants and colour schemes almost annually. In the winter/spring scheme for one year dark blue and pink hyacinths ('King of the Blues' and 'Queen of the Pinks') were planted in the eight round beds, which resemble Victorian basketwork in shape; each bed of single colour making for the best effects. Darwin and scented lily-flowered tulips interplanted with pansies completed the planting, the colours covering a range of white, ivory, pink, scarlet and yellow, but each bed with a separate single colour scheme. In other years Siberian wallflowers and polyanthus have been used instead of pansies. From 1933 to 1966 all the beds were planted with a carpet of forget-me-nots through which pink, yellow and red tulips grew in very traditional style, but repetition of this kind leads to disease. Mr Borlase continued to use this simple spring planting in another bed on a higher terrace. Forget-me-nots were grown from F_1 hybrid seed to ensure perfectly consistent and even colour throughout.

At the end of May the beds are cleared and replanted. One year fibrous-rooted begonias, petanias and F_1 impatiens grown from spring-sown seed were used. The next summer begonias, blue ageratum, antirrhinum, marigolds, bright red verbena and heliotrope made a change. Again, no colours are mixed in any bed, but actual colour schemes will change from year to year. Plants quickly grow together and except for regular deadheading need little summer maintenance. The parterre remains full of flower until the end of the season.

As in a private garden, the National Trust will try out different schemes and colour combinations, and will only repeat a planting pattern without some variation if there is a strong historical reason. Some gardens such as WADDESDON, ANGLESEY

ABBEY and KINGSTON LACY will have a definite colour scheme for each time of year, but often it is appropriate to use different plants to give variety from year to year.

Although LANHYDROCK has a mild climate, these bedding schemes are suitable for any area, although in the colder northerly regions flowering times will be later, and the danger of late frosts prevents planting out summer bedding until the beginning of June. Gardeners are often strongly tempted to plant out tender spring-sown annuals or other tender plants much too soon, and today some garden centres offer trays of plants in early May. Unfortunately, cold nights, even without actual frost, so damage plants at this stage that they seldom make an adequate recovery, and it is advisable to wait the extra few weeks, allowing the soil to warm up as well as letting all danger of frost pass. In microclimates of larger cities it is possible to plant earlier. Every gardener learns to know his own situation, and can discover small pockets in the garden which remain virtually frost-free.

The most effective planting is often simple. Often colour is badly used, usually because too many different colours are dotted about. In a private garden (if overall space permits) it is easier to set aside areas for seasonal colour; parts of the garden hardly visited during 'out of season' periods. In Trust gardens open to visitors for many months, each area must look its best for as long as possible. As in any planting schemes bedding out must be carefully thought out and prepared for months ahead. Sometimes perennials rather than bedding annuals form the basis of parterres. In the White Garden at SISSINGHURST, some of the beds are rectangular and edged with low box. In spring white lily-flowered tulip 'White Trumphator' pushes through a low-growing evergreen carpet of *Lamium maculatum album*. There are many variations of such a scheme, combining spring bulbs with later-flowering perennials, which quickly hide the dying foliage once flowering is over.

At KNIGHTSHAYES COURT the formal terrace planting is dependent for its success on the use of pale grey and silvery foliage. Pink and mauve flowering plants mix and blend through the carpet of grey. This is not strictly a parterre, as most of the plants stay in the ground as permanent features and do not require any form of winter protection. It is, perhaps, better described as a formal enclosed garden surrounded on three sides by clipped topiary hedges.

This sort of 'formal' planting is useful to contrast with the deceptively sophisticated but informal planting of many of the enclosures at both SISSINGHURST and HIDCOTE. In many beds planting is deliberately dense and weed-suppressing, plants growing into and over each other. At Hidcote, box-edged beds are bright with blue scilla in spring, and hardy fuchsias give summer colour. The Fuchsia Garden at Hidcote is an area enclosed by a 3 m (10 ft) mixed hedged of beech, yew and holly in which two symmetrical parterres face each other. Box-edged beds contain a carpet of spring-flowering *Scilla siberica* 'Spring

The fuchsia parterres at Hidcote are underplanted with spring-flowering scillas.

Beauty' planted tightly between bushes of hardy fuchsias. In March the scilla leaves emerge, followed quickly by three or more stems up to 15 cm (6 in) on which the bright blue flowers are borne. Dying foliage suppresses emergent weed seedlings, but a moisture-retaining mulch is sometimes given towards the end of early summer. The circular middle bed in each section is planted with 70 bushes of *Fuchsia magellanica* 'Variegata', with drooping flower-heads of red and purple and a mass of pale cream-margined leaves on arching 1.2 m (4 ft) branches. In each of the four front beds nearest the central brick path, 50 *Fuchsia* 'Tom Thumb', with cherry-red sepals surrounding mauve petals, make compact bushes, with a height and spread of 30 cm (12 in), hardly rising above the surrounding box hedge. In the beds behind them, the taller *F.* 'Lady Thumb' with its darker flowers is equally reliable.

These hardy fuchsias, flowering from July until October, are sub-shrubs, whose woody stems die to the ground each winter, new shoots coming from the base in early summer. They need little attention except for annual removal of dead wood (usually not done until the spring, since the woody stems protect the crowns in a severe winter). Although pot-grown fuchsias need regular feeding, these open-ground bushes will continue to flower for many season with little attention. They make ideal plants for permanent bedding, with the early-flowering scillas to give massed colour in spring.

ORNAMENTAL FEATURES

The focal point in a garden picture is often something man-made: a statue, an urn, a seat, or a container of plants. Ornaments and container planting have certain properties in common as design features: their appropriateness for their surroundings in terms of style, scale, colour and material, and their positioning at an axial point or against a backdrop where these qualities can be fully appreciated. Ornaments at focal points can be emphasized by architectural perspective. They can be framed by a doorway or flanked by a pair of objects. They can be set into stark relief against a contrasting plain background, perhaps a dark hedge. Equally, but with a subtler effect of contrast, the hardness of a stone urn or wooden seat can be softened by the presence of surrounding loose-textured leaves.

Strategic positioning means that an ornamental feature looks not only right but indispensable to the garden. These criteria can apply equally to a simple terracotta pot of tulips and to a classical stone statue. Either, in its place, should look essential: there is no such thing in good garden design as 'mere' ornament.

ORNAMENTS
IN NATIONAL TRUST GARDENS

Mr Michael Calnan, one of the Gardens Advisers to the National Trust, contributes an appraisal of the objects to be enjoyed in some of the many gardens:

❧ The National Trust's collection of gardens represents almost every period of British gardening history from the seventeenth century onwards, and includes perhaps the greatest collection of garden ornaments ever held in single private ownership. These range from statues, urns, fountains and furniture to temples and triumphal arches – objects other than plants placed deliberately to enhance garden design. They represent the changing fashions, tastes and influences of owners past and present.

The majority of ornaments in Trust gardens are works commissioned or purchased at the time when the garden was made, although mass-produced pieces of high quality are not uncommon. In a few instances modern sculptures and furniture represent the taste of the most recent owners, as at SCOTNEY CASTLE and DUDMASTON.

Throughout the history of gardening and in particular since the eighteenth century, carved stone has accounted for the largest number of garden ornaments to be seen in Trust gardens. No stone weathers better than quarried Portland stone, which takes on delicate shades of green and grey with age and exposure to the elements. Perhaps the finest stone urns are to be seen at WIMPOLE HALL and CLIVEDEN. Stone seats of the nineteenth and twentieth centuries are regular features of formal gardens. Like any stone seat, these tend to be uncomfortable as outdoor furniture, only being endurable on the warmest of days. A good example can be seen at GAWTHORPE HALL.

By the early nineteenth century a substitute for stone manufactured by the firm of Coade and Seely became popular. The composition remains unknown but its weather-resistance was better than that of natural stone. The designs were mostly admirable; a pair of obelisks and six caryatids at ANGLESEY ABBEY are dated 1792. A 'Coade stone' vase can be seen at ARDRESS HOUSE in Northern Ireland. There are also two fine large vases at KILLERTON and statues at BUSCOT PARK.

Today a good range of reproduction ornaments and seats is available, though care should be taken in selecting those that weather well and have not lost any of the fine details of the originals in being cast or carved. Some of the better pieces are those created from reconstituted limestone with a surface texture resembling quarried Portland stone.

Of all the quarried stones used for garden ornaments and statuary, marble had never quite looked at home under our often overcast skies; only under the clear blue skies of its native Europe does it look its best. Furthermore, in our atmosphere pollution dissolves its surface, turning the milky sheen of polished marble to a granulated or pitted surface. Nevertheless the cost of marble statuary today is perhaps the major limiting factor on its popularity. There are still many fine examples in Trust gardens. Mozani's group of Pluto and Prosperine make a central fountain for the south terrace at WADDESDON MANOR. At CLIVEDEN a huge marble fountain sculpture by Ralph Waldo Story depicts the Fountain of Love and marks the turning point in the main drive. Marble was equally popular for seating, especially in the seventeenth and eighteenth centuries. Handsome benches at KNIGHTSHAYES COURT and TATTON PARK remind us of the delicate detailing that it can achieve. The supply of marble features today is almost exclusively limited to originals, which tend to achieve high prices when put on the market.

Terracotta has been used for garden pots from the sixteenth century. Popular external decorative detailing includes the basket weave of which there are good examples at POWIS CASTLE. Glazed pots are at OVERBECKS, appropriate to semi-tropical planting, while traditional pots from the South of France are at ARLINGTON COURT, an extremely handsome early-twentieth-century pair is at WALLINGTON HALL, and pots from Crete are used at PLAS NEWYDD. Only pots which have been well fired can be considered safe for exposure to our climate. Some pots imported from abroad, although of high quality, are not always frost-proof and should be treated with caution if to remain outdoors in winter.

Throughout the history of gardening, bronze has been one of the most widely used materials. The natural deep rich brown patina of this alloy turns to a powdery green on exposure to the elements, a modern phenomenon resulting from atmospheric pollution. A fine nineteenth-century bronze Worshipper and Faun can be seen at HUGHENDEN MANOR, and a pair of twentieth-century bronze nymphs, 'Bondage' and 'Chastity', at CHIRK CASTLE.

A modern group in pure bronze by Henry Moore adorns an island in the lake at SCOTNEY CASTLE garden. Today artificial bronze ornaments can be manufactured from powder mixed with a resin cured in moulds to produce delicately detailed sculptures. Such a process has been used with success at STUDLEY ROYAL in making a copy of a Roman bust of Nero.

Increasing demand for statuary in the seventeenth and early eighteenth centuries gave rise to the use of the moulded lead which, being easily worked, was capable of reproducing fine details. Unfortunately many of these works have been lost owing to the collapse of supporting internal iron frameworks.

A basketweave terracotta pot sits on the stone balustrading at Powis Castle.

These internal frames are generally replaced nowadays by costly stainless steel structures. Lead figures by John Cheere *circa* 1718 of a Shepherd and Shepherdess can be seen at CHARLECOTE PARK.

Lead figures were often painted white to look like marble or stone, or perhaps in naturalistic colours. Conservators nowadays advise the painting of lead figures to ensure the total sealing of the entire surface against water penetration. A fine group of lead sculptures on the terraces at POWIS have been repainted in a 'lead effect' colour, as has a charming group which adorns the walls of the old kitchen garden at WALLINGTON.

Original lead ornaments are hard to come by nowadays, though a number of nineteenth-century reproductions can still be found in auction catalogues and at specialist garden ornament dealers. Few firms manufacture lead ornaments today, though it is possible to acquire good-quality reproductions (or even fibre-glass equivalents) in addition to modern works, which may be more suited to the private garden.

From about 1760 wrought iron was often used for making

A copper container is a foil to scarlet tulips at Sissinghurst.

garden furniture and during the Regency period many graceful seats were produced. Today mild steel is often used as a substitute, although it cannot match the fineness of detail of originals.

Cast iron was increasingly used in the nineteenth century, especially in the mass production of garden furniture, often embodying popular motifs such as ferns, ivy, oak and vine leaves and Gothic or rustic themes. Florid cast iron seats are to be seen at ICKWORTH, CHARTWELL, CLIVEDEN and PLAS NEWYDD, while simpler designs are at KINGSTON LACY, THE ARGORY and ARLINGTON COURT. Cast iron has to be painted to protect the metal. Traditional colours would be various shades of green; black (MOUNT STEWART); blue/green (PACKWOOD); and chocolate. Often seats were painted to resemble a different material of construction (bronze for example). Today's reproductions tend to be manufactured in lighter aluminium alloys and painted white, ignoring this tradition.

Wood, which has always been widely available and is easily worked, was probably the earliest material used for garden ornaments. In Tudor gardens and earlier, wood was used for statuary, fences, *treillage* and, of course, garden implements. Wood carvings tend to lose their finer details with exposure to weathering. For this reason it is as furniture that wood has chiefly been used in gardens for many centuries.

Seats and benches have usually been constructed from a lasting hardwood such as oak, elm and iroko; cedar, although softer, was also popular but is only used now if it can be obtained from a sustainable forest stand. Rustic seats of the eighteenth and nineteenth centuries were often fashioned in yew, pear, larch and apple. Designs in outdoor furniture, particularly in this period, often followed from indoor counterparts, generally drawing inspiration from pattern books and abroad. Styles included Chinese, Gothic, classical and rustic. Good examples of these are to be seen at WESTBURY COURT, TATTON PARK, FARNBOROUGH HALL, WORDSWORTH HOUSE, WALLINGTON HALL, SALTRAM, CHARTWELL and HAM HOUSE. Traditional colours include 'eggshell' (matt) white, grey blue and various shades of green.

Perhaps the best-known seat designs of the early twentieth century are those by Sir Edwin Lutyens. His seats were elegant and always solidly constructed. Reproductions can be seen at CLIVEDEN, painted white (as he often specified). Unpainted seats turn a pleasing silvery-grey with exposure to the elements, as can be seen at CHIRK CASTLE. Today Lutyens seats are still being made and the modern version can be seen at MONTACUTE HOUSE. At SNOWSHILL MANOR Charles Wade used a paint of a powdery blue with a hint of turquoise for all woodwork including seats, tubs doorways and window frames; these are still to be seen, the paint renewed as necessary.

The quality of ornaments in Trust gardens, often contemporary with the house in style and material, is matched by their suitability of scale. Fine design, detailed workmanship, surface colour and texture all contribute to the unity of a garden layout which is set in a definite historical period. Ornaments become part of the architecture of a garden; if in scale and in the right position they are part of the framework and not additional features distributed haphazardly through the garden. The placing of these often exceptional works of art in the great Trust gardens may seem irrelevant to modern gardening. In fact in an age when mass produced ornament can be lacking in detail and harmonious finish it seems imperative for garden makers to take the opportunity to get their eyes attuned to the 'best' in every period; thus developing a critical faculty which they can adapt when choosing something for their own. Unlike ornamental planting schemes which can be more or less copied or adapted on a lesser scale, exact replicas of these bronze, lead, stone and marble embellishments may be impossible. Nevertheless, appreciation of their design and judging how they are placed and contribute to an overall design, leads to a greater awareness of architectural detail and its use in gardens. A fine statue or ornament must compel a glance in passing, implying what Mr Hugh Johnson aptly calls the 'command to look'. Wood is much more easily copied and reproduced, and today garden seats frequently make focal points in place of statuary, their situation chosen either as an invitation to rest, or to stress an accent of design. ❧

──────────*CONTAINER PLANTING*──────────

Much of what has been written in the last few pages relates equally to ornamental containers in which plants are grown – that is, as far as materials, scale, proportion and style are concerned. But two further elements affect the subject of container planting: as well as working well in their context, the plants and the container need to look good together. And finally, the dimension of time plays its part, as the containers perform their various seasonal roles with ephemeral or long-term displays of flowers and leaves.

Where it is traditional, the Trust continues a routine practised in the great Victorian and Edwardian gardens, when bedding-out plants and pots were planted twice a year, for summer and winter effects. Today most gardens are open to visitors for six summer months and sometimes more, so that planning and planting follows the same pattern. Plants for spring display are prepared during the early spring and placed in the containers or beds when conditions are right, often towards the end of May, and when most spring-flowering bulbs or biennials have finished flowering. The summer selection may well include more unusual and tender shrubs and perennials as well as annuals grown from seed that February.

In their heyday some of these grand gardens provided a display only for a very limited period, to coincide with the only time that the house was annually occupied, but preparations were

*In Mrs Winthrop's garden at Hidcote ornamental pots contain
tender cordylines.*

intensive to ensure that enough 'reserve' plants were kept in
readiness in case of unforeseen weather conditions. At WADDES-
DON after a storm *all* the bedding plants used to be replaced for
visitors to admire the next morning. Some Trust gardens, however, stay open the whole year, and, like most private gardens
today, were designed by resident owners who wished for and
achieved an integrated garden, perhaps with separate definite
areas of particular seasonal interest, but which basically 'per-
formed' all through the year. In these gardens, although the
emphasis may still be towards ensuring 'colour' in pots for April,
pansies which perform well during 'open' winter weather may be
combined with small winter-flowering crocus, iris (especially
forms of *I. reticulata*), scillas and snowdrops.

Ornamental containers and ephemeral flowers can add interest, especially at times when parts of the garden tend to be dull.
In a garden which is primarily planned for spring with permanent woodland planting of bulbs and flowering shrubs, pots
filled with summer-flowering annuals, or permanent containers
of later-flowering lilies or other bulbs will extend the season.
Equally, a 'summer' garden can be given earlier interest with

containers planted in the previous autumn with spring-flowering bulbs, pansies and wallflowers. An area with a strict colour theme can have this extended by accompanying containers full of appropriate flower colour.

A predominantly green foliage garden with perhaps grand ranks of topiary can be related to a more human scale by a series of punctuating containers of suitable 'weight' and visual strength. At SHUGBOROUGH, on the main lawn, where the golden-domed yews are a feature, stone troughs are all planted with a summer display of dark-flowered heliotrope, dark blue trailing lobelia and variegated helichrysum – rich sober colours relating to the existing yellows and greens. The plant combination is similar in the east formal garden at BENINGBROUGH, where the colour scheme is blue and white: there a container is planted with standard dark heliotrope, and, this time, with silver helichrysum. Decorative stone vases on the outer terrace at KNIGHTSHAYES are planted to complement the formal enclosed garden. An eighteenth-century lead tank, flanked by a pair of standard wisteria, overflows with the pink trailing *Sphaeralcea munroana*, the silvery foliage of *Helichrysum petiolare* and its smaller-leaved form *Plecostachys serpyllifolia* (formerly *Helichrysum microphyllum*) and heliotrope.

Shrubs or small trees (especially evergreens), perhaps trimmed into topiary shapes, look well in pots, and can be wintered under cover to be in perfect condition when the garden is first visited in spring. At SALTRAM the lemon and orange trees, especially imported from Spain and Italy, are over-wintered in the orangery and brought out at the end of May, exactly as was practised in Renaissance gardens.

Other permanent plants unsuitable for the particular soil of the garden can be given a specially mixed compost in a container. Camellias thrive in pots where an alkaline soil would not allow them to be grown successfully in open ground. They need little winter protection and their architectural form and spring flowers make a satisfactory arrangement of pots grouped in some shady place in a garden.

Both pots and plants become strong design additions to the furnishing of a garden, and increase its range. At TINTINHULL four large pots planted with July-flowering regale lilies are features on the west front of the house. Both stone container and exotically scented lily are part of the garden scheme, the lily growing to flower at eye-level, each group much more imposing than if growing in a flower bed. Some exotics look wrong if given a site next to more ordinary plants in a bed; putting them in a container accentuates their difference and proclaims the artificiality of gardening effects.

At HARDWICK a copper container under the house walls is planted with the dark-leaved *Fuchsia* 'Thalia', the old-fashioned *Pelargonium frutetorum* 'The Boar', which has a vigorous spreading habit and delicate pink flowers, and silvery-leaved *Lotus berthelotii*. The pelargonium, now rarely available in commerce, is a feature also at MOUNT STEWART in Northern Ireland. The lotus has scarlet flowers which appear in the leaf axils of the trailing shoots, and since these grow to 1.5–1.8 m (5–6 ft), the plant needs to be positioned at an adequate height for the stems to clear the ground. It is tender, but cuttings are easily taken and can be over-wintered in a greenhouse where the temperature is just above freezing.

The more ephemeral flowers and leaves of seasonal annuals, biennials or tender bedding plants can be different each year, and can be changed at least twice annually. Quite often the Trust has inherited the care of gardens where specific plants, by tradition, are always used. This historical continuity of planting is exactly the same as in all aspects of Trust gardening. Sometimes over the years an original tree or hedge grows to maturity and changes the aspect of a site, from one in full sun to shade. Then planting is adjusted to the new situation; plants tolerant of shade are substituted for sun-loving annuals.

Fortunately many of these gardens possess a good selection of decorative containers. In many Trust gardens well-designed old stone vases or weathered terracotta pots are already in use and any replacements or additions have to be appropriate in style and material. Nowadays many shapes in different materials are available in garden centres. Old and elegant designs are copied in modern concrete, terracotta, wood and plastic. Unfortunately the best are very expensive. Concrete or powdered stone mixed with cement can be very harsh in texture, but can be improved by frequent dousing in liquid cow manure, to encourage growth of lichen. Terracotta and earthenware made from clay are often reddish-brown when new, and being porous dry out quickly (a glazed surface is easier to clean and retains more moisture); unless they are of good quality and kept dry in winter, they are subject to frost damage. The untextured surface of coloured plastic is glaring and colours are often garish.

It is worth considering scale as well as design and colour. In very small gardens a collection of small pots is less effective than one or two large ones, but good results can be obtained by placing a collection of identical pots together all filled with the same plant to make a massed colour or foliage effect. For ease of maintenance light plastic pots containing the plants can stand inside the more elegant stone or earthenware. At TINTINHULL, again, the tender shrubs for drawing-room ornament are all now grown in easily moved plastic pots, which rest in willow baskets or in stone-glazed containers when indoors. Only the plastic inner pots are taken out of the house for regular watering (the compost now contains Osmocote and there is no feeding needed for the season), much reducing the labour of handling heavy pots and the risk of damaging ornamental ones.

All pot plants growing in the open are subject to greater extremes of climate than if their roots were safely buried in a flower bed. Choosing a site with the right amount of sun, shade or shelter is very important. If roots get too hot in summer all growth will stop, and in winter containers are especially vulnerable to cold winds and low temperatures. In dry weather, and even after rain if foliage is tightly packed together, a daily or twice-daily watering routine is necessary. Today moisture-retentive granules help keep the soil from drying out and lessen the burden of watering. In a private garden an owner may be able to water at weekends; in many of the smaller Trust gardens this is not possible, and plants easily wilt after two days (or three if a Bank Holiday Monday is included) of hot sun and dehydrating wind. Plants which have a setback when newly put out seldom recover to give of their best.

Soil condition, together with watering, feeding and 'growing' the plants well, is vital, and in fact determines how effective are these other routine horticultural tasks. If the soil becomes clogged, water may not drain freely and plants will have their roots permanently in damp stagnant soil; this is a much more frequent cause of poor plant performance than any other. All containers must have plenty of drainage holes and these must somehow be kept open, quickly becoming blocked if in direct contact with soil particles. To make certain of free drainage all pots should always be slightly raised on bricks or slate. There are many schools of thought on the best media for adequate drainage. Coarse drainage materials (in the past, old crocks from broken earthenware vases) are usually put in first, followed by a layer at least 6 mm (¼ in) deep of chippings or gravel, followed by a layer of leaf-mould, moss or chopped-up fibrous turf. Then a compost chosen for the type of plant is added; it should be of good texture, and have the correct balance of lime or acidity. Most planting is done with a formula based on a John Innes No. 3 mix, with adjustments for plants requiring specific conditions. This is loam-based with added nutrients and can be made in the garden. A mixture containing two parts loam, one part peat and one part grit makes a useful planting medium. It is stronger than the No. 1 and No. 2 mixes in which the plant will have been reared from seedling or cutting to the stage for planting out.

If the amount required is small it is easiest to buy a ready-mixed compost, specially modified for acid-loving plants if required. For plants which need very dry conditions an extra proportion of grit is added to improve drainage even in this top layer. Do not store a bought-in compost for many months because the balance and strength of the added nutrients may change and cease to have food value. Soilless composts can also be used. Usually peat-based, these are cheap, light and easy to handle, and very useful in the earlier stages of plant propagation.

When pots are used only for annuals there is no problem about making certain that the soil is always in good condition; if necessary it can be changed with the plants. But most Trust gardens, as with private owners, want to maximize periods when the containers are decorative, so, instead of complete change-overs, planting is mixed, decorative trailing ivies, for example, remaining as permanent features. This means there is no obvious moment to make complete soil changes as some plant is always 'coming on'. During a garden year when any plants are added or replaced, some of the surface layer of soil can be scraped away, and some more mixed compost with artificial or organic fertilizers placed on top. This sort of top-dressing is sufficient for several seasons if adequate drainage has been ensured. Broadleaf P4, a moisture-retentive granule, can be added later and will reduce the need for watering.

All the plants in a container must have broadly similar requirements of soil type, water and feeding. Planting can be of one plant only or can be exactly like a flower bed in miniature,

At Sissinghurst ornamental containers are chosen which are suitable for individual planting schemes.

planned to give a succession of interest with even some permanent evergreen shrub in the composition. A single myrtle, clipped bay or holly gives all-year-round interest and height, while many annuals and biennials with attractive colourful flowers lack individual architectural quality and need to be viewed in a mass. Ivies with interestingly shaped or variegated leaves trail over the edge. In the courtyard at TINTINHULL some of the pots contain permanent planting. The grey-leaved *Convolvulus althaeoides*, a sun-lover from southern Europe, proves suprisingly hardy, and its running roots are contained in a stone pot over the sides of which trail glaucous-leaved *Euphorbia myrsinites*. The euphorbia flowers early with lime-green bracts; the convolvulus bears its single pink flowers through the summer.

Achieving a good container display at the right time depends on a certain amount of strategic planning, and different gardens displays different techniques. Small spring bulbs and corms such as species iris and crocus, although very suitable in ordinary gardens, flower early in the spring, before most Trust gardens are open. A practice in many Trust gardens is to interplant two different types of tulip, each chosen for a definite flowering season.

It is possible to know from experience of a site in a garden the exact week when tulips will open and thus plan ahead to maximize their impact. The first lot, perhaps a group of the Fosteriana hybrids which flower in early April, can be followed in May by Lily-flowered tulips. By the time the first group needs deadheading, the May tulips are already in bud, and their foliage, slightly greyish-green, is at its best. The bulbs are then removed; sometimes they are kept in a trench until the foliage dies down and then dried off, but it is now said that this is unnecessary. Another option is to plant the bulbs straight into a kitchen 'cutting' area, where they remain and are used for house decoration the following season.

If there is enough space, bedding pansies, which flower in winter when the weather is not too severe, make spreading plants whose foliage protects the emerging tulip shoots. It is best to keep some boxes of pansies in reserve in a frame, in case those already planted out (grown from seed sown in the previous July) suffer during a severe winter. Ideally, if pansies are to flower through the winter months, they need to be placed in their pots by the end of September; in practice, because Trust gardens remain open until the beginning of October, it is seldom convenient to throw out the summer bedding so early. Most private owners will sacrifice *some* late-summer display, in order to have flower in the garden in winter.

At SISSINGHURST elegant terracotta pots, which are covered up in winter to protect them from frost, are unwrapped in early spring and planted with forget-me-nots for 1st April; later they are filled with summer-bedding plants.

There is no doubt that keeping healthy plants in pots involves a lot of work. It is only routine maintenance, but planning ahead is very important, especially today when seed packets often contain only mixed flower colours, which may not be appropriate. Without a heated greenhouse, as in many Trust gardens, those annuals which are sown in early spring for summer flowering are difficult to produce. For spring displays it is best to concentrate on biennials, such as wallflowers (forms of *Erysimum cheiri*, syn. *Cheiranthus cheiri*), forget-me-nots and pansies sown the previous summer in open ground, and tulip bulbs. Many of the best 'tender' grey or silver foliage plants which, since they need little moisture, are ideal for growing in containers have to be propagated the previous autumn and kept free from severe frost. In a very favoured microclimate at MOUNT STEWART silver *Artemisia arborescens* and white-leaved cineraria are grown as tall standards, surviving the mild winters, their stems protected in the pots by a sea of blue forget-me-nots. All these 'silvers', flowing over the edges of containers, are the foil to flower colour and a valuable part of annual summer displays in appropriate gardens.

Mr Jimmy Hancock, the Head Gardener at POWIS CASTLE, specializes in growing uncommon plants in ornamental containers. He grows many of the tender perennials and more woody plants, propagated annually from cuttings, which he finds he can put on earlier in the season, as once hardened off in their pots, they will withstand some frost. He writes:

❧ Plants in containers have become a popular feature in our gardens. Gardens today are generally small and paved 'patio' areas give much scope for containers. Throughout the centuries plants in ornamental urns or pots have found favour even in our largest gardens, and were placed and the plants for them chosen with great care. To be a worthy feature in any garden scheme it must harmonize with other features, and should never appear as an afterthought or even perhaps an unsolicited gift which has been placed at random.

CONTAINERS

What about the container itself? In my opinion far too many containers are on the small side and not very practical. A container should have sufficient weight when filled to keep it in place in the strongest winds – this is particularly important when it has to be placed at any height. Containers should be large enough to hold sufficient compost for the needs of all the plants in them for one whole season. They should hold sufficient water to supply the needs of the plants for twenty-four hours, however hot or dry the weather. At Powis we have a good number of Edwardian terracotta pots which fulfil all these requirements. They are still in use and are a great asset to the gardens. When it comes to materials for containers there is little to compare with stone or pottery but pottery is often preferred for larger containers as stone is very heavy. It would be nice, perhaps, to add lead; but most of us have to have wood. The latter can be satisfactory but soon deteriorates unless used with an inner lining.

TABLE 1: POWIS CASTLE
MR J. HANCOCK'S LIST OF LESS COMMON PLANTS OR
VARIETIES WHICH ARE USEFUL FOR CONTAINERS

Plant	Colour	Size	Habit	Season	Aspect
Alonsoa	orange	m	spreading	May/frost	sun/any
Argyranthemum foeniculaceum	white	m	spreading	May/frost	sun/dry
A. maderense	lemon	t	upright	June/frost	sun/dry
Convolvulus cneorum	white	m	spreading	June/frost	sun/any
C. althaeoides	pink	t	twining	June/frost	sun/any
C. sabatius	blue	s	trailing	June/frost	sun
Diascia 'Ruby Field'	pink	s	spreading	June/frost	sun/any
D. vigilis	pink	m	spreading	June/frost	sun/wet
D. rigescens	pink	m	spreading	June/frost	sun
Epilobium 'Dublin' (syn. *Zauschneria* 'D'.)	scarlet	m	spreading	July/frost	sun
Erysimum 'Bowles' Mauve'	mauve	m	spreading	April/Sept	sun/dry
E. 'Moonlight' (syn. *Cheiranthus* 'Moonlight')	lemon	s	spreading	April/Sept	sun/dry
Felicia amelloides	blue	m	spreading	June/frost	sun
F.a. variegated	blue	s	spreading	June/frost	sun
Fuchsia 'Brutus'	red/purple	l	upright	June/frost	sun/wet
F. 'Checkerboard'	white/maroon	l	upright	June/frost	sun/wet
F. 'Mission Bells'	red/purple	l	upright	June/frost	sun/wet
F. 'Mrs Lovell Swisher'	white/pink	l	upright	June/frost	sun/wet
F. 'Ting-a-ling'	white	l	upright	June/frost	sun/wet
F. 'Charming'	red/purple	m	spreading	June/frost	sun/wet
F. 'Eva Boerg'	white/purple	m	trailing	June/frost	sun/wet
F. 'Temptation'	white/carmine	m	spreading	June/frost	sun/wet
F. microphylla	pink	m	spreading	early/late	sun/wet
Gazania 'Cookie'	orange/red	s	spreading	June/frost	sun/wet
G. 'Freddie'	yellow/green	s	spreading	June/frost	sun/wet
G. 'Primrose Beauty'	lemon	s	spreading	June/frost	sun/wet
Heliotropium 'Princess Marina'	purple	m	upright	June/frost	sun/dry
Helichrysum petiolare	silver leaves	l	trailing	June/frost	sun
H. p. 'Limelight'	lime/gold leaves	l	trailing	June/frost	sun/shade
H. p. 'Variegatum'	variegated leaves	l	trailing	June/frost	sun/shade
Lantana camara	orange/red	m	upright	July/frost	sun
L. montevidensis (syn. *L. selloviana*)	lavender/mauve	s	spreading	July/frost	sun
Mimulus aurantiacus	orange	t	upright	June/frost	sun/dry
Oenothera cheiranthifolia	yellow	s	spreading	June/frost	sun/dry
Osteospermum ecklonii	white	m	spreading	June/frost	sun/dry
O. 'Blue Streak'	white	t	upright	June/frost	sun/dry
O. 'Buttermilk'	buff	t	upright	June/frost	sun/dry
O. jucundum	pink	m	spreading	June/frost	sun/dry
O. 'Tauranga' (syn. *O.* 'Whirligig')	white	t	upright	June/frost	sun/dry
Pelargonium 'Mrs Kingsbury'	pink	l	spreading	June/frost	sun
P. 'The Boar'	apricot	m	spreading	June/frost	sun
Plumbago auriculata (syn. *P. capensis*)	pale blue	t	upright	July/frost	sun/dry
Salvia buchananii	purple	m	upright	June/frost	sun
S. chamaedrifolia	blue	s	trailing	July/frost	sun

Plant	Colour	Size	Habit	Season	Aspect
S. blepharophylla	scarlet	s	spreading	July/frost	sun
S. coccinea	scarlet	m	upright	July/frost	sun
S. leucantha	purple	l	upright	Aug/frost	sun
S. patens.	blue	m	upright	July/frost	sun
Senecio cineraria	silver leaves	m	upright	June/frost	sun/dry
Tanacetum densum	silver foliage	s	spreading		sun
Verbena 'Hidcote'	purple	m	spreading	July/frost	sun
V. 'Huntsman'	scarlet	m	spreading	July/frost	sun
V. peruviana	scarlet	s	spreading	July/frost	sun
V. 'Sissinghurst'	pink	m	spreading	July/frost	sun

PLANTING

I have not found it very satisfactory to do permanent planting in containers, except in the case of two plant groups. Firstly, dwarf and slow-growing plants, including alpines, can be grown in shallow stone containers. These will thrive for many years, provided that plant associations are kept well balanced; any plants which tend to swamp others should be lifted as required and thinned out. Secondly, single shrubs can be grown permanently as specimens with ferns, ivies and so on round them. These can be placed in buildings or round the garden during the summer season. If left outside all winter containers, even those made of stone, are likely to suffer frost damage. In a long period of freezing whether the roots of the plants, unlike those of plants growing in the ground, will get frozen solid. In my view it is much more satisfactory, and less expensive to propagate each year and replant containers annually. They can be emptied in November or December and stored safely under cover over the winter.

For this type of planting a wide selection of plants, many of them not fully hardy, can be used and a list is included here. It should be possible to get colour for a period of at least four months, and in some cases six months is possible. I like to have my containers ready for placing in their summer positions by the middle of May. By then the plants should be of good size and growing fast and vigorously, with some flowers already appearing. The weather can be very temperamental at this time of year, so one is looking for a calm settled spell. If the plants have been hardened off properly the frost will have to go down to $-4°C$ (24°F) before doing any noticeable damage. Cold winds are far more damaging, particularly during the first week or so outdoors. After that the breezes and cooler air conditions will have darkened and firmed the foliage, making it less susceptible.

The choice of plants will be determined by size of containers, sun, shelter and aspect of site. You will get more harmonious displays by not overdoing variety; in fact I find I rarely use more than four different types in any one container, and quite frequently only one. For containers to be viewed at eye-level I find fuchsias difficult to better. If restricted to one genus for growing in pots in our climate, it would have to be fuchsias. As they come from several continents they can vary from fully hardy to quite tender, they cover an amazing colour range, and among them are those which perform well in hot dry weather and others which flower well in poor summers. All are capable of five to six months' flowering if treated properly. What else can one ask for?

PROPAGATION AND GROWING ON FOR CONTAINERS
Without facilities, it may be best to buy in plants each year. When dealing with large containers and displays you need space at all times of year. Unfortunately if you have to buy in, the choice of interesting plants is much restricted, unless you can go to specialist growers. Cuttings should be taken as early as possible when there is some good new non-flowering growth. Pelargoniums usually can be taken in August, other plants from mid-September to the end of October as material becomes available. We have, of course, selected many plants because of their ability to flower over a very long period, so it is fruitless to grumble if they continue to flower when we want propagating material. I aim to have any major large plants propagated and potted up before lack of light slows down plant growth, by the end of October if possible. Once potted, they should keep a steady growth, but are only watered when they indicate the need. Very little heat is needed; temperatures will vary from 5°C (40°F) to as low as −2°C (28°F). The greater one's skill as a grower, the more the temperature can drop without harm. With plants kept on the dry side, we had few losses in 1981−82 when temperatures under glass fell to −6°C (21°F).

During the middle of February you will notice the first new growth on many of the plants. Spring has arrived and light has reached a level of real value to the plants. At this stage I start to increase my minimum temperatures, but timing depends on the light and the response of the plants. There can be no rigid rule. There is a difference of about a fortnight between north and south of the country. I am dealing with Midland light values here. As activity grows, propagation is also started again; plants for the smaller containers and a few of the quick growers, including *Helichrysum petiolare* and its cultivars, which can very easily get too large and unbalance a carefully planned arrangement. Potting on quickly follows, and I now do the final potting of my main container plants. There are still two months before they will be put into their containers and during this time they will quadruple in size. I use 1–2 litre pots, so roots are not restricted but will fill the space. For high-quality performance later, this is the most important and vital period. Space in the greenhouse soon becomes a problem, and we now have a large polytunnel to give us extra space. Many plants cope well with the cold once they are growing strongly; fuchsias are among the first to be moved, and make sturdy plants even if temperatures fall to −2°C (28°F). One sees many fuchsias in commerce with soft, drawn shoots, which shows they have had excess heat to encourage quick growth. These plants should be avoided.

MAKING UP THE CONTAINERS

I find the last two weeks in April work best in my system. I make them up in the polytunnel. We use a John Innes based compost, but with a very coarse grade of peat, and the loam also contains coarse particles. We add slow-release fertilizer now, and find no other feeding is necessary during the life of the container planting. By this time the plants begin already to intermingle and growth flops over the edge of the pots. We stake all tall plants at this stage even if they seem sturdy enough: gusts of wind can ruin all the work. Canes will not be visible by the time the containers go out, but new growth should not require further attention. The largest containers which cannot be moved are made up *in situ*, at an opportune moment when it is reasonably mild and there is little wind. A week is long enough to complete this task and I know all will be well. *Fuchsia fulgens* and its forms are our most tender plants; they go out last, in the middle of May.

GENERAL SUMMER MAINTENANCE

If the preparatory work is well done success, whatever the weather, is now assured. There is little work from mid-May to November, except for watering and general picking over flower-heads and removing dead leaves. These maintenace chores are essential and keep the containers looking fresh.

One of the beauties of the complete change made each season is that it gives you a fresh opportunity to experiment and to rectify mistakes. Observe how the various plants compete with each other. Look closely at your colour mixtures, and look at arrangements in other gardens and keep an eye out for suitable new plants. ❧

Containers, filled to overflowing with plants, become part of the architecture at Powis Castle.

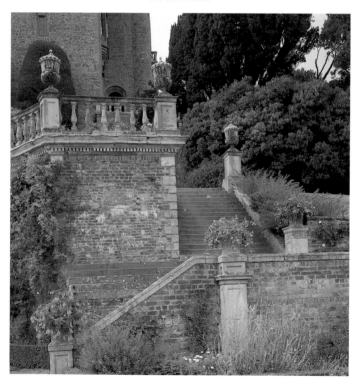

II

GARDEN

FEATURES

BORDERS

In gardening, the term 'border' has not only been used to imply the edging to a garden area, but has also come to be synonymous with arrangements of groups of hardy herbaceous perennials, which are thus often referred to as 'border plants'. The traditonal herbaceous border reached its peak of performance in high summer, clumps of strong hardy perennials all being geared to flower together in July and August. The border usually edged a lawn and was backed by the wall or hedging that enclosed that section of the garden; often, too, double herbaceous borders would edge a pathway or face each other across a broad panel of mown grass. This planting area was just as seasonal as a spring garden or an iris bed, and had little colour or interest in it for the other months of the year. Many of the old gardens had space enough to include such separate areas, which were at their best at different seasons – and could be ignored at other times.

Today, in a small garden, since the 'border' may well be almost the only available planting space, owners seldom wish to confine its season to mid-summer flowering or its range to only one type of plant. Small trees, shrubs, bush roses, hardy and more tender perennials, bulbs, annuals and biennials can all be planted as part of a scheme, each on the right scale and in the right proportions for the site, to extend the season of interest right through the year.

In this practice, gardeners are keeping faith with a condition which persisted through many centuries, often any plant that was reasonably decorative or useful was grown in the border against the house or around the edges of a lawn or courtyard. Many of these hardy plants were native in origin or had been introduced before the eighteenth-century landscape phase swept flowers out of sight. They continued to be grown in smaller manor-house, rectory or cottage gardens during all the years when they were out of fashion in the 'trendsetter' gardens. Even at the height of the Victorian bedding craze, hardier perennials were by custom grown in borders in kitchen gardens, where they were used as cut flowers for the house.

Paintings made by George Elgood at the end of the nineteenth century record borders in gardens of great houses now administered by the Trust, and these show typically 'mixed' planting. Borders were then a delightful mixture of roses, hollyhocks,

mulleins, Madonna lilies, tall annual sunflowers, and, at ground
level, scented mignonette; they were not always massed with the
fashionable annuals. Elgood painted a border in the forecourt at
HARDWICK HALL in 1904. Backed with a high wall on which
climbing roses, honeysuckle and clematis twined, planting
includes a standard rose, macleaya, mulleins and Japanese
anemones, with foreground planting of pinks, tufted pansies and
mignonette. At MONTACUTE HOUSE Elgood painted a bright
border which edged the east forecourt where sunflowers, evening
primroses, border phlox and campanula, pansies and pinks were
all tightly packed together. A large evergreen shrub gives bulk
and solidity but is the only visible concession to the vast scale of
the surrounding architecture. Planting in the borders of these
two great Elizabethan houses at the turn of the century was
essentially similar to that in the flowery cottage gardens painted
by Helen Allingham.

Today at Hardwick many of the same plants are still being
grown but the borders are given depth and density with large
shrubs such as magnolias, clerodendrums and evergreen vibur-
nums, and spreading shrub roses. Sculptured-leaved acanthus,
bergenia, *Crambe cordifolia*, hostas and echinops, planted in
massive groups, match the scale and anchor house and garden
walls to the ground. There are still plenty of flowers from good
hardy perennials, many of them already in garden use in 1900.
Thalictrums, aconitums, macleaya, *Aruncus dioicus* and *Artemisia
lactiflora* perform in season and clematis and roses still climb on
the walls. In the shade of the cedar *Hosta sieboldiana*, with bluish
almost corrugated leaves, is planted to fill the width of the border, making a pattern of rippling waves. At Montacute House
the forecourt borders have been replanted. Badly infested with
bindweed and other perennial weeds, the ground was treated
with dazomet and replanted in 1982 to a theme suggested originally by Mrs Phyllis Reiss after the Second World War. The
creator of the gardens at TINTINHULL HOUSE near by, and interested in colour associations, Mrs Reiss used purplish foliage shrubs
and bright flower colours to tone with the golden Ham stone,
which she felt made paler tints and grey foliage seem insipid.

Garden writers such as William Robinson and Gertrude
Jekyll are often credited with being the orginators of the classical
herbaceous border, but in fact they always used mixed planting.
Even when the herbaceous flower border was at its height in the

early years of this century, their planting was not always strictly confined to perennials: the design structure was often given bulk with permanent shrubs, and the length of season of flowering beauty was extended by bulbs and annuals. Then as now, the most effective border planting would include spring-, summer- and autumn-flowering bulbs interplanted between clumps of spreading perennials to extend both ends of the flowering period. Annuals, biennials and tender bedding plants such as dahlias succeeded each other in drifts or clumps throughout the summer months. The enthusiast kept in reserve pots of lilies, hydrangeas or fuchsias which could be sunk in the border at dull moments.

Then as now, the most successful mixed borders were those where planting appears to be in layers. Starting at ground level, small spring bulbs and early-flowering perennials nestle under the skirts of deciduous shrubs; between the shrubs summer- and later-flowering perennials, biennials and annuals – or even small woody plants – cover the ground with massed foliage but, flower at different levels. As the shrubs grow in width and cast longer shadows as they become taller, these less permanent plants need shifting around: indeed, they need division as part of border routine maintenance, but the whole area may be taken over by the shrubs, which will eventually grow together. On a higher level, a small tree may also cast its shadow over the shrubs and plants in an area, but may contribute height and visual balance, especially when the border is not backed by a high hedge or a brick wall.

Although borders are not the invention of Robinson and Jekyll, their practice and teachings have perhaps altered our perception of them, and it is undoubtedly to Miss Jekyll that we owe the planning – and the appreciation – of a border in the pictorial sense. Borders are often carefully designed to be seen in their entirety from far away across a lawn, but they must retain their effectiveness when viewed from much closer, when the different planes of planting become clear. From a distance the composition blends like a painted canvas; from close to, hidden valleys and shadows appear between and behind the plants. In some cases borders along paths or against walls can be seen only as the viewer walks along them, and in any long stretch of planting,

Summer borders at Powis Castle are among the best in Britain. In a 'hot colour' scheme, orange lilies, dusky purple clematis and scarlet crocosmias are vivid against the dark green yew shapes at the end of the bed.

each new individual group or planting association only unfolds itself to the eye in passing.

However it is seen, the very word 'border' implies something continuous. In any form of decoration a border is an ornamental edging to a usually plainer central part. So a flower border will edge an expanse of lawn, an area of stone paving or gravel, and will often be given a firm backing by a wall or hedge. This background vertical will provide a continuous coloured surface, behind foreground planting. A hedge such as dark yew acts as a foil to flower and foliage colour in front of it, while a stone or brick wall, although equally continuous, often itself becomes covered with growing plants, so that as a curtained backdrop it participates in the colour scheme of the design. These visual effects are accompanied by others of a more practical kind. Hedges steal moisture and nutrients from the plants near by; walls cast rain-shadows and plants at their base often lack moisture.

In border planning the planting is envisaged in its different planes, heights and depths, so that a whole three-dimensional picture is built up. Each individual plant has its own quality, and groups and clumps are put together so that a balanced composition results, an artisitc masterpiece as well as a convincing demonstration of horticultural skill. A whole picture or a series of pictures is revealed, never a flat and level expanse of flower or foliage.

The conventional modern border composed traditionally of hardy perennials will still have the lowest-growing plants at the front, with careful gradation of heights towards the back. Extra interest can be given by making sure that some good foliage plants are brought right to the front, and if lower-growing plants are just glimpsed at the back of others. When planting is more mixed, a small tree, some shrubs, bush roses, bulbs and annuals for foliage or long flowering season require a freer mode of planting, lower-growing plants being suitably placed around the base of a tree or shrub, rather than immediately in the foreground. Spring bulbs show colour under the canopy of spreading deciduous shrubs, extending the season of interest. Perennial plants need to be grouped in clumps of sufficient size to compare with more woody plant material, and must be divided and replanted frequently not only for their own good, but to keep the whole composition in balance and harmony.

If it is possible to walk behind the border using a pathway

between a narrow wall-border or separating the main border from its background hedge, a whole new area of planting is revealed, at the base of taller plants set at the back of the bed. Flower beds, as opposed stylistically to borders, were usually set into a lawn and could be walked round, so both back and front were planted with low edging plants. Traditionally these islands, which might be forms of box-edged parterres or some sort of pattern, would have had 'bedding' plants grouped together all at one height. It is only recently that even these free-standing beds have been treated in a more pictorial way. In many Trust gardens borders and beds on the fringe of woodland, which might originally have been diversely planted, now frequently contain only evergreen shrubs, holly, aucuba and laurel having taken over as the shorter-lived plants died out. These are often made more interesting and lightened by the introduction of paler-leaved deciduous flowering bushes and an underplanting of perennials which not only contribute flower in season but growing tightly together reduce maintenance costs by preventing the weed-germination that would take place in bare soil. Sometimes these plants will be chosen primarily for their foliage colour and texture, usually in tones of green or grey.

It was Gertrude Jekyll's training as a painter that led her to treat her flower beds as a canvas and she developed certain colour 'rules'. She found that the warm bright oranges, reds and crimsons – colours situated next to each other on the rainbow – would also associate most pleasingly in the garden in the same basic order of gradation; the paler 'cooler' colours she liked to plant with grey and silvery foliage plants so that the pastel tints seemed brighter, and she used colour opposites such as blue and orange in juxtaposition to make each colour more telling.

At CLIVEDEN Mr Graham Stuart Thomas designed two long and wide herbaceous borders which face each other across the lawn to the north of the house. Both borders have much the same dimensions as Miss Jekyll's own at Munstead Wood. Stretching north and south 60 m (200 ft), each is 5.4 m (18 ft) wide and backed by high walls where wall shrubs and climbing plants make a backdrop to flower and foliage colours in the borders. At Munstead pale flowers and grey-leaved foliage plants were placed at either end, and there was a careful build up to stronger 'hot' colours in the centre. At Cliveden one border is of strong vibrant colours; the other has misty pale flowers. Nevertheless the 'pattern' of careful graded colour expresses much of Gertrude Jekyll's teaching and practice. She liked to plant her groups as drifts, so that her colour schemes were like a pattern of weaving, rather than in more conventional blocks of triangles where plants in threes, fives, sevens and nines made clear colour divisions and were less likely to blend in the eye as in a pointillist painting.

This practice of pairing beds or borders where one has bright, intense colour tones and another 'quieter', more subtle and muted colours recurs in a number of Trust gardens. An example is at TINTINHULL HOUSE, where two 'colour' borders were planned by Mrs Phyllis Reiss in the years immediately after the last war. Her nephew was killed as a fighter pilot, and the area which had been a tennis court was turned into a garden as a memorial to him.

In the main borders of this Pool Garden, tulips emerge early to flower at the beginning of May and give a hint of the colour theme of each area. In the west (east-facing) border where summer flower colour is predominantly 'hot' – deep yellow, orange, scarlet and crimson – tulip 'Queen of the Night', with subtle velvety-maroon, almost black, flowers sets the tone. Orange summer-flowering tiger lilies (*Lilium lancifolium fortunei* syn. *L. tigrinum fortunei*) push up throught the evergreen leaves of *Iberis sempervirens*, and groups of *L. henryi* with orange-yellow flowers in the late summer grow behind the scarlet *Potentilla* 'Gibson's Scarlet'. Scarlet dahlias such as 'Bloodstone' and 'Bishop of Llandaff' extend the season which starts in June with groups of bush rose 'Frensham', still one of the best performers, and, if dead-headed, ready to give a further burst of flower in late August and September. Other reds include the tender *Salvia fulgens*, which does well in a wet year but performs poorly in drought conditions. Crimson nicotiana were bedded out one year and flowered almost continuously for three months, introducing a 'bluer' pigment into the scheme. Yellow flowers, especially forms of Compositae with daisy-flowers, are used freely, but paler lemon-yellow of *Hemerocallis citrina*, lime-yellow *Alchemilla mollis* and fluffy cream flowers of *Artemisia lactiflora* cool down the whole scheme. A clump of *Sisyrinchium striatum* with cream flowers and architectural iris-like leaves is next to a suckering bush of *Symphoricarpos orbiculatus* 'Foliis Variegatis'. Where the border breaks in the middle and frames steps down to a pink and

*In the walled garden at Mottisfont a central double border is planned to give
its maximum June performance at the same time as the rose collection.*

blue border in the kitchen garden, grey-foliaged *Brachyglottis*
'Sunshine' and *Artemisia* 'Powis Castle' edge the beds.

   In the opposite, west-facing border pastel colours, linked by
grey and silver foliage, predominate. In May clumps of a single,
early tulip 'Apricot Beauty' grow among the later-flowering
perennials, to coincide with the white blossom of a horizontal
branching *Viburnum plicatum* 'Mariesii' across a corner. *Deutzia
gracilis* and the Warminster broom (*Cytisus × praecox* 'Warminster') make a glorious show at the same time. Grey and silver
foliage plants are planted at regular intervals along the front and
pink and mauve penstemons make groups between salvias such
as *Salvia* 'Superba' and *S. pratensis haematodes*. At the back pur-
ple-flowered delphiniums 'Black Knight' grow next to pale blue-
flowered *Campanula lactiflora*. For later in the summer *Aster
× frikartii* 'Mönch', and *A. sedifolius* 'Nanus' (syn. *A. acris* 'N.')
with phlox and tall clumps of *Eupatorium purpureum*. Good
foilage plants such as the spreading *Acanthus mollis latifolius* are
also grown.

Any border plan, unlike a finished canvas, does not present the same picture all through a season – let alone through different years. Each plant assumes many different aspects; some grow quicker than others, altering balance and proportion; flowering time can vary each year, and plants react to weather variations in different ways. The gardener making a border needs not only the skilled eye of a painter to plan the composition but also all the horticultural knowledge possible to ensure that the results are as predicted. In a mixed border shrubs may be single or in groups to suit the scale, but perennials are generally in clumps (hardly less than three of any one kind, and often many more to make an effective 'splurge' of colour) which spread and need dividing every few years. Gardening in this way is a highly skilled craft. In the case of herbaceous plants, which come quickly to maturity to give a peak performance, planning begins at least a year ahead, but a shrub will take much longer to develop its true quality.

Today the range of plants available through hybridizing and breeding is hugely increased, yet many original species are getting increasingly difficult to obtain. Nurseries breed new hybrids or cultivars to satisfy the public's desire for longer flowering periods, for new colours, to make a plant short and sturdy (sometimes at the expense of elegance) in order to save garden staking, or simply for novelty. The cost of nursery work makes it economic to produce only plants which are quick and easy to propagate. Because of historical context many old species and cultivars have been collected and grow in National Trust borders, and several of the gardens have good plant selling areas where these almost 'vanished' species can be obtained.

In a small garden it may not be possible to have separate areas for separate seasonal interest, but as each part of any planting scheme depends for its success on plant association, there is still much inspiration to be gained from the larger garden. A border of spring-flowering bulbs can have neighbouring plants with striking leaves, which bear flowers later in the summer; veratrum, with strange pleated emerging foliage, euphorbias of all classes, *Iris pallida pallida* (syn. *I.p. dalmatica*)with grey sword-like spikes all year, and architectural yucca. Deciduous-leaved shrubs shelter small blue-flowered *Anemone nemorosa* or *A. apennina*, cyclamen species, scillas and erythronium, all woodland-type plants which benefit from the light shade given through the summer months. Tulips, often with fine green or striped leaves, can grow in clumps between hardy perennials, which reach their peak in full or late summer, and little edging iberis and alyssum, flowering in early spring, later contribute pleasant leaves to set off the bright colours of summer. Mid- or late-season lilies welcome some protection for their emergent shoots in spring and grow happily interplanted with any similar low-growing shrub or shrubby spreader.

In larger gardens there can be whole garden areas for just one season. Plants which flower early but have strong or untidy leaves later are particularly suitable for separate garden compartments, which are visited only at one season of the year. Peonies, iris, oriental poppies, delphiniums and lupins, besides winter or spring 'gardens', are all possible. At POLESDEN LACEY, where the large walled garden is subdivided into sections, there is a double peony border, an iris garden and a lavender collection, each reaching its peak at a different time. The great summer border would have plants arranged for display for only a few months, but for that short period all the plants could flower together, simplifying planning. At UPTON HOUSE a collection of asters has been assembled in a 'late' border, and is formalized by the repetition of massive clumps of grass (*Miscanthus sinensis*). At NYMANS a curving border against a yew hedge has very simple planting of bright red dahlias such as 'Bishop of Llandaff', 'Crimson Flag' and 'Breakaway'.

At TRERICE two borders both backed with walls face each other across the west forecourt. Plants with leaves of purple and gold and blue flowers are planned for summer interest. The soil is limy, rainfall is high at about 92.5 cm (37 in) and winters near the Atlantic coast of Cornwall are relatively mild. Both borders are planted similarly, but with adjustments for the difference in aspect. Purple foliage shrubs such as *Cotinus coggygria* 'Royal Purple' and berberis are underplanted with *Osteospermum* and *Argyranthemum*. Golden *Philadelphus coronarius* 'Aureus' and *Spiraea japonica* 'Goldflame' have bright leaves in spring, although these become green as summer advances.

The twining mauve-flowered *Solanum crispum* 'Glasnevin' on the wall flowers at the end of June, later followed by the dark velvety blue flowers of *Clematis* 'Jackmanii'. Yellow flowers are contributed by the winter-flowering evergreen *Mahonia japonica*, which helps to give structure to the border, and the more delicate grey-leaved *Coronilla glauca*, which may flower all through the year. In mid- to late summer the perennial *Anthemis* flowers. Against the wall at the back of the border *Vestia lycioides*, bearing pale yellow drooping tubular flowers has a long flowering season, and the new yellow-flowered form of *Phygelius aequalis* is grouped effectively. The soil is fertile and the only regular feeding is bone-meal in spring. Bushes of lavender 'Hidcote' are along the border, which is 28 m (90 ft) in length and nearly 3 m (10 ft) wide. The border plan is labour-saving, even the delphiniums needing no staking, and only needs attention in late autumn and spring, when shrubs are pruned and herbaceous perennials divided and replanted to make larger groups.

In a lower enclosure to the south, the colour scheme is based on bronze or variegated leaves and white, purple and pink flowers. The architectural sword-like leaves of New Zealand flax (*Phormium tenax purpureum*) with underplanting of *Lamium* 'Beacon Silver' glowing and white in shade, are effective foils to flower colours. The tender *Abelia floribunda* and *Buddleja lindleyana* both have purplish-pink flowers which are carried over a long period, and they thrive against the sunny south-facing wall.

The motive for designing and planting a border is not always the painterly inspiration to manipulate colour in plants in a satisfying visual composition. It may be an idea, an intellectual conceit – although, of course, the plants still need to make a pleasing picture. At WIGHTWICK MANOR, with associations with the Pre-Raphaelite Brotherhood and the Arts and Crafts Movement, borders under a terrace wall are divided by buttresses of yew, and in each the planting is only of shrubs or flowers mentioned in the works of Tennyson, Shelley and Dickens, Kempe (the craftsman and glassmaker), and plants grown at Kelmscott Manor, the home of William Morris. The results are not very visually interesting but the idea is a stimulating one.

At POWIS CASTLE the west border in the Edwardian formal garden is mainly planted with various colour forms of phlox for late-summer flowering. Pink, mauve and white flowers blend together behind an edging of box 45 cm (18 in) high and 30 cm (12 in) across. For the early season onions, including *Allium bulgaricum* (now *Nectaroscordum siculum bulgaricum*), *A. ostrowskianum*, *A. sphaerocephalon*, *A. rosenbachianum*, are grouped with dark blue, pale blue and white forms of camassias and dodecatheons.

At PACKWOOD, famous for yew topiary, there are also some fine borders, which are readily adapted to gardens of a more modest scale. A sunken garden with raised beds of mainly hardy perennials augmented with annuals and tender perlargoniums and a colourful wall border show how close-packed planting of many different varieties, in very small groups, can ensure the good colour effects for many months. The planting style is traditional and distinctive, on the lines of that called by Loudon the 'mingled' border. The former Head Gardener, Mr Corrin, planted in threes, or might even use a single plant of something like catmint; the large species, *Nepeta* × *gigantea*, could stand alone. In the border raised by four courses of brick which make a supporting wall, phlox, golden rod, grassy-leaved crocosmia, heleniums and *Coreopsis verticillata* are interplanted with drifts of dahlias and perlargoniums. Grey-leaved alyssum, a smaller catmint and lavender bushes at the entrance fall over the brick, and are planted at regular intervals to hold the design together. At the back tripods provide a frame for some of the old forms of sweet pea including 'Primadonna' and 'Painted Lady', which are heavy with fragrance. Delphiniums at the back are staked in spring and herbaceous plants are supported by pea-sticking early in the season.

In the wall-border taller plants such as the unusual creamy-yellow *Salvia glutinosa* with coarse hairy leaves and different yellow daisy-flowered plants keep colour going until late in the summer. Tall *Aconitum napellus* in different garden forms with their dark purple hooded flowers complement the bright yellows, while paler mistier blues are at the front. Mr Corrin says the borders are traditionally of a mixed colour scheme. Many of these plants are propagated from the originals used by Mr Baron Ash, who gave Packwood to the National Trust in 1941. He created the sunken garden and central lily pond to add colour to a garden primarily of architectural yew and box.

At BENINGBROUGH HALL a pathway running north and south is flanked by a double border of shrubs (including a large number of Hybrid Musk roses), herbaceous plants and bulbs, designed to give interest from early summer to the end of September. Perennials such as *Crambe cordifolia*, hostas, *Cimicifuga cordifolia* and Japanese anemones have been chosen to contribute good foliage effects even when not in their flowering season. The sword-like leaves of yucca and iris contrast with more rounded soft shapes. On the east the border is backed by a wall of the old kitchen garden, and on this clematis, honeysuckle, roses and an old Teinturier grape (*Vitis vinifera* 'Purpurea') are trained on wires attached to vine eyes to make a backdrop of foliage and flower colour throughout the summer. In the original plans the planting effects were for summer only, the borders coming into flower with the first roses and early perennials such as peonies and irises. Now drifts of tulips have been added to give a colourful display in May, growing beside emerging hostas and alchemilla leaves, and lily bulbs and Japanese anemones prolong the season into autumn. Other plants more recently added include *Thalictrum aquilegiifolium* with fluffy lilac-pink flowers in early summer, and *T. delavayi* which bears its rich lilac, creamy-centred small flowers in July and August.

Mr David Beardall, formerly Head Gardener at Beningbrough, writes about the maintenance programme for the year:

❧ Once the border was established the soil is enriched annually with Growmore and a thick mulch of cow manure (or any available mulching material) is added to improve the texture, keep in moisture through the summer and prevent weed germination. The soil, which is alkaline, is never dug; worms and bacteria do the digging. The leaves of *Prunus* 'Tai-haku' do occasionally show magnesium deficiency and the soil is treated with magnesium sulphate. Otherwise, the tasks for the year consist mainly of pruning shrubs, dead-heading roses, and cutting down herbaceous foliage in autumn or early spring. The Hybrid Musk and Floribunda roses are given an additional 'shaping' when the dead-heading is done after the first flowering flush in June. This keeps them to a reasonable size, especially in relation to the scale of other plants. All the herbaceous geraniums are clipped over with shears after flowering to encourage a repeat performance later in the summer. The deciduous shrubs which flower on the new wood such as *Buddleja* 'Dartmoor' are hard-pruned in winter. When grown among other plants rather than as a specimen this particularly good cultivar with very dark purple flower-trusses and a semi-prostrate habit needs to have its lower branches removed to raise the head. The purple-leaved *Cotinus coggygria* 'Royal Purple' will benefit from spring pruning if foliage effects are required; its typical smoke-bush flowers will then be sacrificed. For maximum leaf colour and size the previous year's shoots are cut back to the lowest two buds. Those deciduous shrubs which flower on old wood, such as deutzia and philadelphus, have their flowering shoots removed immediately after the flowers fade. The bushes can be shaped at the same time. Penstemons flower almost continuously, but need to have their dead flower-spikes regularly removed. Cuttings of these are taken every year in case the winter is severe.

On the wall to the east the climbing roses are pruned in early autumn, carefully tied back to horizontal wires attached to the wall by vine eyes. The large-flowered and late-flowering clematis are pruned towards the end of winter. Also on the wall the semi-evergreen honeysuckle with fragrant whitish-yellow flowers (*Lonicera japonica halliana*) benefits from cutting back in spring, long shoots sacrificed and dead wood and 'ends' removed. ✿

At MOUNT STEWART beds in the Italian Garden to the south of the house are in carefully thought-out colour patterns. The soil is acid and moisture retentive and humidity is, in general, high. Rainfall is 87.5 cm (35 in) but does not approach that of the Cornish gardens, and periods of drought are not unknown. Because of its situation on Strangford Lough, exceptionally mild winters are normal. Nevertheless many of the plants grown in these beds would thrive in a colder garden, and most of the plants are not fussy about a more alkaline soil. To east and west groves of tall *Eucalyptus globulus* give wind protection and make a frame for this part of the garden. From the terrace above, a gap in the tree planting permits a view to the Mountains of Mourne.

Groups of beds laid out in strict colour patterns as formal as a parterre surround a fountain on either side of the lawn. Each planted area is divided into four sections, each of which is further subdivided into three parts. All follow a definite colour scheme to which both leaves and flower-heads contribute in season. This is further emphasized by the foliage of a surrounding low hedge, which has been mentioned before. The hedge marks out a strong pattern and holds the designs together, giving a formal character to a scheme where the main planting is in a free style with the billowing soft foliage growth of herbaceous plants. To the east the predominating colours are bright and 'hot'; to the west grey and glaucous foliage sets off pale flower colours.

To the east a bed of standard and bush yellow roses. 'Whisky Mac' and 'Yellow Pages', is underplanted with scarlet *Potentilla* 'Gibson's Scarlet' and edged with a 45 cm (18 in) hedge of clipped *Erica erigena* 'W. T. Rackliff'.

A companion bed is mainly of perennial plants with creamy-yellow, orange, vermilion and crimson flowers, but is given height with golden-leaved elder (*Sambucus racemosa* 'Sutherland Gold'), which can be pruned back hard each year to prevent it from dominating other plants. In June a delphinium with creamy-yellow flowers and tangerine-coloured *Papaver pilosum* are effective with the glowing young foliage of the elder, and penstemons, including *Penstemon* 'Schoenholzeri' and *P.* 'Rubicundus', both scarlet-toned, begin to flower. Later the recently introduced yellow form of *Phygelius aequalis* flowers beside a citron-flowered montbretia making a cool contrast to the 'hot' colours of bronze-leaved *Lobelia* 'Scarlet Cardinal' and yellow-flowered *Rudbeckia maxima*, both of which need the moisture-retentive soil and high humidity which exists in this garden. The low surrounding hedge is of a dwarf berberis, *Berberis thunbergii* 'Atropurpurea Nana'.

Planting in the third bed is also mainly of herbaceous perennials with flowers of scarlet, bronze, citron-yellow and apricot, with a purple-leaved cotinus (*Cotinus coggygria* 'Royal Purple') as a feature plant. *Monarda* 'Cambridge Scarlet' flowers early with a dark purple delphinium and the even darker carmine-flowered *Paeonia lactiflora* 'Monsieur Martin Cahuzac', while clumps of strong day-lilies, including *Hemerocallis* 'Stafford' and *H.* 'Burning Daylight', have mahogany-bronze flowers in July. Corms of *Watsonia pillansii* (syn. *W. beatricis*) flourish in the mild climate at Mount Stewart and add an exotic note by late summer, growing between clumps of *Rudbeckia subtomentosa*, with black-eyed yellow daises, and the brilliant scarlet blooms of *Penstemon* 'Schoenholzeri', which will continue to flower from mid-summer to October if regularly dead-headed. In gardens with a less favourable climate other watsonias, forms of *Watsonia borbonica* (syn. *W. pyramidata*) mainly with pink or white flowers, can be lifted and stored for the winter. However, *W. pillansii*, its grassy foliage almost evergreen, does not like to be

(Previous pages) In the Italian Garden at Mount Stewart the beds to the west are of pale colours in contrast to the eastern schemes of red, orange and yellow. This view shows variegated phlox, Japanese anemone and Verbena bonariensis.

dried off. This bed is edged round with a low hedge of a golden-leaved cultivar of *Thuja occidentalis*.

On the western fringe of the lawn the eucalyptus trees cast light shade over the beds where paler pink, blue and white flower colours predominate, with occasional strong accent given by the magenta-crimson flowers of the tall *Geranium psilostemon* in June and July, followed by the bright blue spherical heads of *Agapanthus inapertus pendulus* in August. All the 'reds' here have distinct bluish pigment and none of the flaming, almost vermilion touches found in the east beds. The only plants used in both the east and west parterres are the purple-leaved cotinus and, round the roses, the same Mediterranean heather (*Erica erigena* 'W. T. Rackliff') is used for a hedge. The cotinus is a feature to contrast with silvery-grey foliage of *Artemisia ludoviciana*. Standards of the creamy-white rose 'Pascali' give height above 30 bushes of 'Dame Edith Helen', a 1920s Hybrid Tea double pink rose, underplanted with pink-flowering *Potentilla* 'Miss Willmott'. Near the cotinus iris, astilbe, hemerocallis and dicentra contribute foliage shapes, while mauve and pink flowers from thriving perennials succeed each other through the summer. The white form of martagon lily, *Veronica virginica alba* and *Astilbe* 'Bridal Veil' have flower-heads tinted rather than a pure 'laundry-white', to blend gently with the overall colouring. Shining young leaves of the toad lily (*Tricyrtis formosana stolonifera*) are welcome in spring, and their tall stems bear spotted reddish-mauve flowers in late summer. The glaucous-leaved Jackman's rue of the surrounding hedge begins to resent the overhead eucalyptus canopy, but its foliage contribution is hard to replace.

In the third section, hedged by grey-leaved *Hebe albicans*, planting is dominated by the California tree poppy (*Romneya coulteri*), with soft greyish-green foliage and papery white flowers. To extend flower colour until the first cold spell pink-flowered *Dahlia* 'Gerrie Hoek' is planted to make a strong group. *Olearia moschata*, a rare shrub, reflects the microclimate at Mount Stewart. With silvery greyish leaves, the bush grows here to 90 cm (3 ft) and as much across, and is covered in white daisy-flowers in July. Different coloured border phlox and late-flowering Japanese anemones finish the season.

Mr Nigel Marshall the Head Gardener at Mount Stewart, provides a season-by-season summary of the maintenance work in these formal beds.

Autumn and winter work

❧ Certain vigorous plants such as *Veronica virginica*, *Geranium psilostemon*, hemerocallis, kniphofias, border phlox and *Campanula lactiflora* need to be lifted and divided approximately every three years, or they begin to dominate the various colour combinations and groupings of plants. The foliage is cut down prior to lifting. The ground is dug over incorporating garden compost and well-rotted farmyard manure. This is also a good time to remove any persistent perennial weeds such as bindweed or couch grass. After digging the ground should be well firmed by treading with the feet prior to planting. The plants are then divided, usually with two forks back to back. The divided pieces should have three to four crowns; this will ensure nice-sized clumps for flowering in the following season.

This is a good opportunity to make any necessary adjustments in the planting plans, altering shapes and relationships of groups. Also by planting plants in different places over a period of years the incidence of 'replant sickness' is lessened. This applies particularly to roses, which cannot be replanted in the same beds in which they have been for many years. Border phlox also seem to benefit from being moved to a new site every few years.

At this time of year most of the foliage may be cut down and ground generally tidied up and lightly forked over. However, the stems and leaves of tender plants such as fuchsias, penstemons and salvias should not be removed until the spring. This will help to protect the base of the plants from severe frosts through the winter. In addition bracken or other fern foliage can be worked into the ground round the base of the more tender plants. Cannas, dahlias and any other plants with tubers are best if lifted from the ground and stored in a frost-proof shed over the winter. *Lobelia cardinalis* and its various garden hybrids are also vulnerable and best lifted and 'boxed' up, then placed in a cold frame for the winter, where the foliage is kept dry. These plants, completely hardy in their own habitat where winters are much more severe than in Britain, suffer most from alternating periods of cold weather and wet followed by mild spells which encourage premature growth. Further cold will then nip new shoots and weaken the plant's constitution. In north-east America their crowns often remain in frozen wet ground all through the winter and emerge healthy in the warmth of spring. The young basal growths of other plants such as delphiniums will be attacked by slugs during any mild spells in the autumn. This may seem unimportant, but often they lay eggs round the crown of the plant and new shoots are ravaged in the following spring, causing real havoc. Either slug pellets or liquid slug killer should be applied to keep these pests at bay.

SPRING WORK

In the spring work starts when ground conditions allow, and any still outstanding winter tasks are completed as soon as possible. The remainder of last year's foliage may also be removed before any young shoots start to emerge, as otherwise they may get damaged in the process of cutting back. Some plants such as *Aster amellus* varieties, ornamental grasses and kniphofias are best lifted and divided in early spring and not during the autumn. Apply a general garden fertilizer at two ounces per square yard at this time of year and lightly fork it in and generally tidy up the soil. This is a good time to apply a mulch of compost or spent mushroom manure before too much growth appears on the plants. In the past mushroom compost was 'lime'-based and would tend to make the soil more alkaline over a period of years, so that some nitrogen would have to be added, but the composition of growers' compost now normally does not bring this side-effect.

During April and May plants such as fuchsias, lobelias, young penstemons (taken as cuttings the previous season) and salvias can be safely planted out. They will stand the occasional overnight frost if properly hardened off. Dahlias and cannas are best left for a further few weeks until all danger of spring frosts has passed. As growth proceeds certain plants should be either staked or supported with bushy twigs, cut to about two-thirds of the expected height of the flower-stems. For staking strong plants such as delphiniums use 1.5 m (5 ft) bamboo canes, allowing two flower spikes to each cane. Shoots on delphiniums are best thinned out to give good quality flower-spikes. This should be done when shoots are about 23 cm (9 in) in length, allowing seven or eight spikes per each established clump. Each stem will need two or three ties before actual flowering time.

SPRAYING OPERATIONS

Herbaceous plants are not often bothered by garden pests. In some areas capsids can be troublesome and will spoil fuchsias, puncturing foliage and stems and preventing flower-buds from opening. One spray with a systemic insecticide should be sufficient control, if applied when foliage growth is well advanced but before any capsid damage is visible. Delphiniums are often subject to mildew attack, especially in areas of high humidity. This can be prevented by spraying with a fungicide once or twice in the growing season. If lilies (and some other Liliaceae) and peonies are grown, watch for Botrytis, especially in a wet season, as this can ruin the plants. A fungicide will also counteract this, and a systemic insecticide added to the mixture will control the aphids which carry certain virus diseases fatal to lilies in particular.

ROUTINE SUMMER WORK

This consists mainly of removing spent flower-heads on plants to prevent seeding and to allow later flowering. After flowering, forms of anthemis should be cut down to about 15 cm (6 in) to encourage basal growth before the autumn, which is then left on for flower production the following season. August is a good time to lift and divide the bearded iris, *Iris germanica*. This is necessary roughly every five or six years. After lifting, incorporate garden compost or well-rotted farmyard manure into the soil and apply a handful of bone-meal. In gardens where the soil is acid, add two handfuls of hydrated lime per square metre (or per square yard). When replanting select the strong young rhizomes from around the outside of the old clumps. These should not be buried, but planted with the top half above soil level. Heucheras are best if divided and replanted in September rather than in the following spring. Plant the woody rootstock well below soil level to prevent them drying out.

DWARF HEDGES AROUND THE BEDS

Low-growing hedges round the edge of the beds conform with the two distinct colour schemes. At the east end where there are strong flower colours of red, orange, yellow and purple, the hedges are of plum-coloured *Berberis thunbergii* 'Atropurpurea Nana' and a golden cultivar of *Thuja occidentalis*. To the west, where the colouring is much softer, the plants with pink, mauve, lavender, white and cream flowers predominating, the low hedges are of grey-leaved *Hebe albicans* and the glaucous *Ruta graveolens* 'Jackman's Blue'. All the hedges are clipped over twice a year, in spring and mid- or late summer to keep them approximately 45 cm (18 in) high and 30 cm (12 in) wide. Even at Mount Stewart there are occasional losses of rue, which is probably due to the fact that this west end of the south lawn is shaded and overhung by nearby trees which would have been newly planted when the colour schemes were first devised in the 1930s), especially during the afternoons, which makes the plants 'drawn' and young stems and foliage soft and susceptible to cold winters. Being a Mediterranean plant, rue thrives where open exposure to sun will ripen and harden the wood. The cool damp atmosphere experienced in this Irish microclimate encourages excessive growth, and this combined with wet soil conditions, makes such a plant vulnerable to frost.

There are various other problems associated with these 'colour' beds. In original planting plans bergamot (forms of *Monarda didyma*) were used, but did not prove a success in this maritime climate. They suffer from dry spells in summer, and humidity causes mildew. Border phlox, while invaluable for colour display during August, all have to be protected by rabbit netting. Rabbits are a severe trouble but fortunately netting need only be 45 cm (18 in) high and by midsummer it is completely hidden by foliage. It is interesting to note that forms with variegated leaves, 'Harlequin' and a new white-flowered cultivar from the USA, 'Mt Fujiyama', are ignored by the rabbit population and never need protection.

Japanese anemones provide a long season of colour in late summer but are rather invasive. These have to have their roots chopped round with a spade quite frequently to keep them within bounds. It is not advisable to lift them regularly and replant as they take a few years to settle down again after disturbance. *Echinacea purpurea*, with mauve-crimson daisy-flowers on strong branching stems, has also not been a success at Mount Stewart. Unfortunately nurseries usually distribute this plant in autumn when they only do really well if transplanted in spring.

Mrs Norah Lindsay designed the square beds at Blickling Hall in the 1930s.

ROSE BEDS

In the four corner beds of both parterres Hybrid Tea and Floribunda roses are planted to conform with the colour schemes in neighbouring beds. Five standard roses are underplanted with some three dozen of the bush type. In spring tulips, chosen to give a hint of the colour patterns which come late in the season, provide interest in the rose beds. The rose beds are surrounded by hedges of shrubby *Erica mediterranea* (now correctly *E. erigena*) 'W. T. Rackliff', which has dark green leaves carried very densely and white flowers with conspicuous brown anthers. The erica is clipped over annually after flowering and the hedging is kept to a height matching the material used round the flower-beds. ❧

BLICKLING HALL in Norfolk has quite a harsh climate compared to that of Mount Stewart, but many of the same hardy perennials are used in the famous 'square' beds on the main lawn east of the house. Rainfall is much lower as you would expect in a garden in

Colour schemes at Blickling are strict: in the two beds farthest from the house, flowers are predominantly yellow and orange, with a touch of red.

East Anglia, and a moisture-retaining mulch is essential. Although topiary yew specimens mark the corners of each square and outside beds edged with catmint are planted with roses, the rest of the planting is of herbaceous plants only, carefully graded for size and colour. Interestingly, when originally laid out in the late nineteenth century for Constance, Lady Lothian, the parterres, although many more in number and much more elaborate, were filled with hardy plants rather than tender 'bedding' plants favoured in most grand gardens in the Victorian era. By the 1930s many of the smaller beds were swept away and Mrs Norah Lindsay, a well-known amateur designer, prepared plans for planting the remaining squares which we see today. Although roses such as the pink 'Else Poulsen' and scarlet 'Kirsten Poulsen' are original Floribundas dating from 1924, it has not been thought necessary to use only plants which would have been available to Mrs Lindsay. New garden cultivars which prove healthy and flower for long periods are used in addition to older varieties which need more maintenance.

Mr Charles Simmons, the former Head Gardener at Blickling, writes about the planting and upkeep of these beds:

❧ In the early 1930s the fussy and complicated network of small beds and topiary, laid out in 1872, was drastically reduced and simplified, leaving four large square corner beds, now flanked by rectangular island beds of roses and catmint. At each outer corner, and actually positioned in the rose bed, a yew bush, acorn-shaped and about 3.7 m (12 ft) in height, stands in military fashion. After fifty years depressions in the grass still mark the position of many of the smaller beds which were levelled and turfed over at the time. The dense yew blocks shaped like grand pianos were also retained, and these stand aloof on their own areas of grass beyond the four square beds.

In the two beds nearest the house the flower colours are a blend of blue, mauve, pink and white, with a touch of crimson from the rose 'Else Poulsen'. In the two beds beyond the colour scheme is yellow, pale orange and red. Certain plants such as grey-leaved *Stachys byzantina* (syn. *S. olympica*) are used as edging in all four beds, and a single specimen of *Yucca filamentosa* stands at each corner, effectively linking the two schemes and ensuring that they seem part of an integral design. Groups of the double white-flowered *Campanula trachelium* 'Albo Flore Pleno' are also repeated in all the beds. The planting schemes and colour associations for each pair of beds is similar but not identical. For instance clumps of *Eupatorium purpureum*, *Cicerbita plumieri* and pink-flowered lavatera take central positions in both of the beds to the west, nearest the house.

Aconitum napellus is in the middle foreground and *Erigeron* 'Quakeress' is at the edge of both the beds. In the yellow and orange beds to the east *Rudbeckia maxima* and golden rod (an old form of *Solidago* – unidentified) dominate both beds in late summer, occupying the central position, but other plants are repeated in more random positions. Mrs Lindsay understood how colours will appear to change when used in different associations and she never hesitated to use an identical plant with different neighbours to produce her desired effects.

In the beds grading of heights was carefully thought out. The immediate impression is that the soil towards the centre has been raised by 60–90 cm (2–3 ft). In actual fact the difference in soil level is no more than about 23 cm (9 in). In the beds nearest the house height in the centre is obtained by using plants such as *Lavatera* 'Rosea', the large blue-flowered globe thistle (*Echinops ritro*), *Campanula lactiflora* and delphiniums. Sloping away from the centre and providing intermediate height are various veronicas, *Lythrum salicaria* 'Robert' *Astrantia major* and *Salvia* 'Superba'. Towards the extreme outside edge are groups of *Geranium endressii*, mauve-flowered *Stachys macrantha* and silvery-leaved *Anaphalis margaritacea*. In the two beds farthest from the house rudbeckias and tall macleaya are flanked with lower-growing cream-flowered *Artemisia lactiflora* and *Ligularia dentata*. At the edge the forms of the shorter *Rudbeckia fulgida* stand in front of the lemon-flowered *Anthemis tinctoria* 'E. C. Buxton'. These are only a few of the plants used in the four beds and by careful choice of plants which flower successively through the summer the overall picture conveys the defined colour scheme from June to early autumn.

Bordering the west beds are pink and crimson Floribunda roses, 'Else Poulsen' and 'Kirsten Poulsen', their colours blending with massed flowers in neighbouring beds. Catmint (*Nepeta mussinii*) contributes soft grey leaves and mauvish-blue flowers most of the season, cutting back in midsummer preventing it swamping the rose bushes and ensuring repeat – almost continuous – flowering. One year severe winter frosts killed many catmint plants, and these had to be replaced in the spring. The further beds are bordered with Polyantha roses, crimson 'Locarno' and orange-red 'Gloria Mundi', and similar planting of catmint.

Maintenance of these four colourful beds and the long border near by follows a similar annual pattern, and is a procedure which works well. All plants are cut down in November to within 12–15 cm (5–6 in) of ground level, and the beds are raked clean. Because of the density of plants there is no serious weed problem in the summer, although weeds do germinate at the outer edge where there is light and space. Digging is always done in the autumn, but again, can only be done when plants have to be divided or moved, as there is no space even for forking over. Sterilized mushroom compost is spread thickly over the surface of the soil as space permits. Some plants are split and replanted in the late autumn but, in this relatively cold

climate, it is safer to leave division of many until the spring. This also allows an assessment of winter losses. Staking the taller plants is carried out through May and June, as the plants grow, and at Blickling traditional pea-sticks are still used in preference to more modern methods. They are effective and unobtrusive. Another old practice still adopted here is the use of white painted wooden labels. These may last only two seasons, but they seem in keeping with the atmosphere of the garden, and are much appreciated by the many visitors. 🌺

At FELBRIGG HALL, near the coast in Norfolk, a double border runs east–west through the centre of an old walled garden. A box hedge contains the edge and planting is of shrubs only, including a good mixture of old and modern shrub roses, except for a ribbon of autumn-flowering colchicums along the front on either side, inside the boxwood. Much of the original planting was experimental and over the years changes have been made. Lilacs make a formal rhythm along the back of the border, although they have developed some problems.

Planned for minimum maintenance, the shrubs have grown together so that almost no bare soil is visible. Although some winter pruning is necessary (followed after a bad winter by cutting back dead shoots) and an organic mulch given occasionally to help conserve moisture, very necessary in this area of drying winds and a rainfall of 62 cm (25 in), the borders are much less labour-intensive than ones where perennials need dividing and reshuffling every few years, or where pockets of annuals are added to give a long season of flowering colour. The shrubs were chosen to give balanced interest through most of the summer months, some even when not in flower having good textured or coloured foliage. The colour scheme begins with soft colours at either end and works through to strong colours in the centre.

Height and flower given by shrub roses in early summer is followed by strong growing buddlejas, which need hard pruning each February, and will flower on the young wood late in the year. The original plan made in 1977 has been modified as some hebes, cistus, *Brachyglottis compacta* and ericas have proved

(Previous pages) In the other two square beds at Blickling Hall, colours are blue, mauve, pink and white, with a touch of crimson.

unsuitable. *Cotinus coggygria* 'Royal Purple' has been substituted for purple-leaved *Prunus* × *cistena*.

The colchicums (*Colchicum tenorei*) along the front of the border produce their fresh green leaves in early spring and for the good of the bulbs it is essential not to remove the dying foliage until the end of July, when it comes away easily in the hand. Damage to the tip of the bulb may well prevent the stemless flowers from developing for display in September. At Felbrigg the low box hedge partly hides the browning leaves as they die down. A National Collection of colchicums, organized by the NCCPG, is at Felbrigg (see Appendix 1).

Mr Ted Bullock, the Head Gardener, writes both of the routine maintenance of the border plants themselves, and of the more troublesome care of the lilacs behind the border:

� Well-rotted manure is applied only to the roses. A dressing of a balanced general fertilizer is given to the other shrubs in the border in spring. The density of shrubs seem to keep most of the weed at bay, so we only lightly fork over exposed areas. An annual mulch of mushroom compost is applied in spring. Generally I keep fertilizers away from colchicums. It doesn't seem to be necessary where they are grown in relatively clean ground. However, those growing in grass do benefit from an application of Growmore.

The shrub roses are pruned only once a year, and up till now this has proved sufficient to keep the height and relative scales in the right proportions. I should mention that 'White Pet' has not been pruned for some years. We like the effective mass, now approaching 1.5 m (5 ft) in height, at the back of the border. The same rose in the garden at the front of the hall at Felbrigg is kept in check at about 75 cm (2 ft 6 in) maximum by two prunings a year, a main spring pruning and the lighter autumn cut-back, to reduce wind-rocking during the winter.

The lilacs behind the border at Felbrigg were originally obtained from Hilliers, L. R. Russell and Sunningdale Nurseries. Fifteen varieties of lilac were grown at Felbrigg. First planted in December 1973, they were obtained either growing on their own roots or grafted on to privet stock (*Ligustrum ovalifolium*). This was in order to avoid the problem of suckering shoots.

The varieties grown on the privet have not been successful

due to rootstock incompatibility, which becomes apparent after a few years. Whole tops of trees gradually die back and the bush can become detached from the rootstock, especially in the high winds which prevail at Felbrigg.

It is therefore now thought advisable to avoid lilacs which have been grafted on privet and, instead obtain trees growing on their own roots or grafted on common lilac (*Syringa vulgaris*), carefully removing any suckers which do appear by cutting as close as possible to the main roots in summer.

Maintenance of lilacs otherwise is fairly routine. Faded flowers are removed as early as possible. In winter weak thin branches are cut out and old overgrown leggy growth can be cut back to approximately 90 cm (3 ft) from the ground, in order to rejuvenate them.

An occasional spray of liquid seaweed is given during the growing season, and an application of fertilizer is beneficial when the lilacs come into growth in spring. A layer of mushroom compost 7.5–10 cm (3–4 in) thick is applied every two or three years, acting as a weed suppressor and mulch.

One year in the spring the tips of the lilac shoots developed a nasty wilt, which appeared very worrying. Plant pathologists, however, agreed that it was due to excessive moisture, the high humidity causing botrytis. By late in the summer, growth and foliage looked healthy again. ❧

In the walled garden at NYMANS a central grass path has a border on either side in which the main planting is of groups of summer-flowering annuals which keep a good display from the end of June until October. Aligned more or less north and south, the double borders are in two sections, separated by an Italian marble fountain and by topiary yew shaped into elaborate crowns. Growing in rough grass behind the borders, spring- and summer-flowering trees and shrubs give interest and height through the whole season. Buddlejas and the late-flowering shrubby chestnut (*Aesculus parviflora*) become part of the summer scene, joining with groups of tall strong-growing perennials planted at the back of each border to give structure and depth. Many of these perennials have architectural foliage, so that even when not in flower they make a good backdrop. Among the perennials are echinops, macleaya and tall day-lilies. Groups of dahlias, chosen for colour and height, help keep the borders colourful until late autumn.

At Nymans the double borders in the walled garden, mainly planted with annuals grown from seed, are augmented by tall floriferous dahlias.

During the 1980s the groups of annuals were planted in blocks of 20–30 plants, all of which were grown from seed in February. The total number of seed trays exceeded 600, and these, started in heat, were then pricked out with 30 small plants to each box. Fourteen boxes of each plant were divided up between the four borders, three for each and two were put aside in reserve; for no obvious reason annuals can 'miff' off at the pricking out stage or later. Sometimes all plants of one variety do not thrive; at others it may only be some, and the reserve boxes make up the difference. One year all the trays of pure white *Lavatera* 'Mont Blanc' were failures, and **Mr David Masters** filled in gaps with *Salvia patens* with luminous blue flowers and *Hibiscus trionum* with wide white mallow-shaped flowers with deep black centres. Both of these plants have been a success, and, in fact, if there is time for dead-heading, continue to flower over a much longer period than the annual lavatera. Both groups of white and red nicotiana are planted and the larger-flowered *Nicotiana alata* (syn. *N. affinis*) 'Grandiflora' whose white flowers are tinted greenish-yellow. The early-flowering species *N. langsdorffii*, with greenish-yellow flower tubes, has been used to increase the range. Seed of this was obtained from Sissinghurst and, interestingly, appears to have hybridized with some neighbouring plants of *N. alata*, as the tubular-shaped blooms are wider and larger than those of the true species. The taller F_1 hybrid antirrhinums in single-colour packets are getting increasingly hard to obtain.

Planting takes place at the end of May or even the beginning of June. Wedge shaped areas are outlined with a trickle of sand for each group of plants and a label is placed *in situ*. No prepared plan is used, but taller plants such as antirrhinums in a single colour are usually repeated in a regular pattern down the middle of the borders, and the same colour and plant combinations are used in the facing beds. Corner planting groups are also symmetrical. Groups of foreground plants are kept well away from the grass edge so that they will not fall over and make mowing and edge cutting difficult. The general effect seems to be carefully thought out, yet on close examination very variable. This is because the 'key' plants establish a formal rhythm and repetition of colour groups is restful to the eye and gives a sense of satisfactory order. Any plant which grows to more than 45 cm (18 in) needs staking. Fortunately bundles of pea-sticks of hazel or beech are obtained through another Trust property, and 40 bundles of both 2.25 m (7 ft 6 in) twigs and 1.2 m (4 ft) twigs are necessary. The tops of the sticks are bent over tidily in traditional style. David Masters finds that rabbits are a real worry immediately after the plants have been put out, and the area is too large to use netting, which would anyway look unsightly.

In late autumn the annuals are thrown away after any seed required is saved, the dahlia tubers lifted, cleaned off and stored in a frost-free shed, and the ground is then dug over and plenty of farmyard manure dug in. An artificial compound fertilizer, with an NPK ratio of 5.3:7.5:10 and containing chelated trace elements, is also added. There is neither winter nor spring bedding in these borders, which are kept for their spectacular three-months summer display.

TABLE 2: NYMANS: PLANTS USED IN ONE YEAR

Ageratums: 'Spindrift', 'North Sea', 'Tall Wonder' and 'Blue Mink'
Antirrhinums: 'Kim', 'Coronette White', 'Coronette Pink', 'Coronette Bronze', 'Coronette Crimson', 'Coronette Yellow', 'Doublon', 'Leonard Sutton', 'Polar', 'Lyra', Tall Rocket Mixed and Madame Butterfly Mixed

Cleome hassleriana (syn. *C. spinosa*)
Convolvulus tricolor 'Dark Blue'
Godetia grandiflora 'Sybil Sherwood'
Hibiscus 'Sunny Day'
Hollyhock Summer Carnival
Impatiens 'White Tilt', Mixed Tilt
Lavatera 'Silver Cup', 'Mont Rose', 'Mont Blanc'
Nicotiana langsdorffii and *N. alata* 'Nico Red' and 'Nico White'
Petunia 'Red Joy', 'Blue Joy', 'Sugar Daddy'
Perilla frutescens var. *crispa* (*P.f. nankinensis*)
Rudbeckia 'Green Eyes', 'Goldilocks', Gloriosa Daisy Mixed and 'Marmalade'
Tanacetum parthenium 'White Stars'
Viola 'Chantreyland', 'Giant Yellow', 'Prince Henry', 'Blue Heaven'
Zinnia 'Envy'
Groups of cannas and *Lilium* × *parkmannii* were also planted.

DAHLIAS

Cultivar	Colour	Height
'Australia Red'	dark red	1.20 m (4 ft)
'Baby Rose'	pink single	1.50 m (5 ft)
'Baby Royal'	pink single	1.20 m (4 ft)
'Baldre'	orange/pink	0.75 m (2 ft 6 in)
'Cherry Wine'	red	1.50 m (5 ft)
'Cobham G'	bright orange	1.35 m (4 ft 6 in)
'David Howard'	deep orange	1.20 m (4 ft)
'Doxy'	white	1.00 m (3 ft 4 in)
'Edith'	pink/orange	1.50 m (5 ft)
'Future'	light pink	1.05 m (3 ft 6 in)
'Gerrie Hoek'	light pink	1.50 m (5 ft)
'Klankstad Kerkrade'	yellow	1.35 m (4 ft 6 in)
'Kochelsee'	red	1.00 m (3 ft 4 in)
Large Red	red	1.80 m (6 ft)
'Margaret Appleyard'	orange	1.20 m (4 ft)
'Murillo'	pink	0.30 m (1 ft 8 in)
'Nellie Geerling'	red	0.30 m (1 ft 8 in)
'Pink Cactus'	light pink	1.50 m (5 ft)
'Polly Peachum'	dark pink	1.35 m (4 ft 6 in)
'Rothesay Castle'	light pink	0.90 m (3 ft)
'Sneezy'	white	0.30 m (1 ft 8 in)
'Wraybury'	white	1.20 m (4 ft)
'Zonnegoud'	yellow	1.00 m (3 ft 4 in)

BARRINGTON COURT gardens, although attached to a National Trust property, were entirely maintained and run by the Lyle family who lived at Barrington Court from 1923–1991. The Lyles created the series of gardens we see today using designs by Forbes and Tate, the architectural firm already involved in the restoration of the house, but with some planting plans by Gertrude Jekyll. The resulting inner gardens have a strong Jekyllian flavour, with separate areas at their best in succeeding months throughout the summer, and colour schemes carefully graded to an overall plan.

Mrs Christine Brain, the Head Gardener at Barrington Court, writes about the maintenance of borders where annuals extend the length of flowering displays with strict colour themes.

❧ The gardens were planned within the existing walls of some old cattleyards. Four flower gardens were designed with quite distinct permanent plants. Summer and winter bedding schemes increased the length of flowering periods over the year. Through the years two distinct colour schemes have predominated in two separate walled enclosures. In one the colouring is hot and bright, mainly in yellow, orange, red and white. In the other more subtle tints are used, mainly pink, mauve, blue and white. By limiting colours grown near each other to those closely related in the spectrum the eye finds considerable satisfaction, and there are no jarring effects.

The colour plan is adhered to each year, but different plants may well be used. It is not intended to make a garden a 'museum' piece, planted to a strict design, repeated annually, but rather to allow the idea of successful colour combinations to develop further and further. Many visitors return to Barrington to study the colour associations and how they continue to evolve.

SUMMER BEDDING IN THE LILY GARDEN

Against the wall the evergreen *Viburnum tinus* flowers in winter and early spring. On the wall the climbing rose 'Dublin Bay' has rich blood-red flowers and abundant glossy leaves. Permanent plants include *Lilium pardalinum* with orange-red purple-spotted flowers, *Helenium* 'Moerheim Beauty' with bronze daisies, the shrubby *Potentilla fruticosa* 'Katherine Dykes' and in the front plants of *Helianthemum* 'Wisley

Primrose' with small grey leaves and pale yellow flowers. Summer bedding plants are *Dahlia* 'Top Affair' *Rudbeckia* 'Irish Eyes', African marigolds (*Tagetes erecta* 'Moonshot' and *T.* 'Paprika'), *Antirrhinum* 'Orange Glow' and *Nicotiana* 'Lime Green'. These plants cover a colour range of pale yellow through orange to red, with greens and whites occasionally added. Blues and pinks are confined to other areas of the gardens. Although essentially this scheme is 'bright', by being confined to a definite range colour clashes are avoided and the composition is 'easy' on the eye.

RAISING OF SUMMER BEDDING

Dahlias can be either potted and started into growth in a cold frame or planted straight into the ground in late April.

All other plants are raised in a glasshouse with a minimum temperature of 5°C (40°F). Seed is sown in trays of peat-based compost and kept in a propagating case at 10°–18°C (50–65°F) until germination occurs. Trays are then removed to a glasshouse bench where they are grown on until large enough to be pricked off into John Innes No. 1 potting compost. Apart from the cleome and heliotrope, which are potted into 9 cm (3½ in) pots, seedlings are pricked into trays. They are then grown on until large enough to be transferred to cold frames for hardening off before planting out.

Beds are prepared by forking over, giving a dressing of a balanced fertilizer and raking after a firm treading. Plants are put in and watered and slug pellets are scattered near by.

Dahlias will need staking, but all the other plants should be self-supporting, with the exception of the cleomes, which might need some support if in a wind funnel or an exposed position. Antirrhinums, dahlias and marigolds in the Lily Garden will need regular dead-heading to keep them flowering continuously, but hoeing is the only task needed to keep the bedding scheme in the Lavender Walk tidy throughout the summer, from May to September.

RAISING OF WINTER BEDDING

Winter bedding in the Lily Garden consists of 80 plants each of the wallflowers 'Golden Bedder', 'Orange Bedder' and 'Primrose Monarch', and 35 plants each of pansies 'Mount Everest' and 'Coronation Gold'. In the Lavender Walk there are 80 plants of each of wallflowers 'Giant King' and 'Carmine King', 15 *Myosotis* 'Royal Blue' and 35 pansy 'Ullswater'.

All seed is sown in drills in open ground in the nursery area at the end of May or the beginning of June. The plants are transplanted as soon as they are large enough into open ground in the kitchen garden, planted 23–30 cm (9–12 in) apart and with 30 cm (12 in) between the rows. They are grown on until the middle of October, when they are lifted and moved into their flowering positions.

Garden compost and fertilizer is added and the beds are forked over. the soil is consolidated and plants are put in 23 cm (9 in) apart. They are watered and slug pellets are scattered near by. ☘

There are few easily accessible guides to plants which will thrive in the milder counties, and today few nurseries stock plants which are not in general demand. Nevertheless many smaller

TABLE 3: BARRINGTON COURT: SUMMER BEDDING
IN THE LILY GARDEN

	African marigold	Rudbeckia	Antirrhinum	Nicotiana	Tagetes	Dahlia
raising of bedding plants						
sown	4 Apr	5 Mar	8 Feb	28 Mar	4 Apr	
germinated	7 Apr	10 Mar	17 Feb	10 Apr	7 Apr	
pricked off	15 Apr	29 Mar	15 Mar	18 Apr	28 Apr	
outside	7 May	29 Apr	15 Apr	7 May	11 May	
planted	28 June	28 June	28 June	28 June	28 June	
bedding out						
distance apart	23 cm (9 in)	30 cm (12 in)	23 cm (9 in)	23 cm (9 in)	15 cm (6 in)	90 cm (3 ft)
eventual height	30 cm (12 in)	60 cm (2 ft)	30 cm (12 in)	60 cm (2 ft)	23 cm (9 in)	135 cm (4 ft 6 in)
quantity	25	12	40	25	40	3

plantsmen's nurseries can be searched out where stocks of the more unusual and perhaps 'difficult' plants are available. Every garden inside every region will have areas in it with a more favourable microclimate, caused by sheltering walls, overhead canopies or good frost drainage. Some gardeners are able to take the extra trouble necessary to get young plants through their first seasons in the open when they are at their most vulnerable, and protective shields put round them in winter will keep free from icy winds and frost (see 'Practical Maintenance').

It seems right, therefore, to include descriptions of two favoured borders where plants usually accepted as tender and difficult to grow successfully.

At OVERBECKS on the Devon coast, where the climate is exceptionally mild, terraced gardens giving superb views out to the Salcombe estuary contain trees, palms, shrubs and many small plants which will not normally grow without protection. Unlike most of the woodland gardens in Cornwall, Overbecks had

TABLE 4: BARRINGTON COURT: SUMMER BEDDING IN
THE LAVENDER WALK

	Ageratum	Aster	Cleome hassleriana	Heliotrope	Petunia	Salvia viridis	Verbena rigida
raising of bedding plants							
sown	5 Mar	28 Mar	15 Mar	5 Mar	19 Feb	28 Mar	
germinated	9 Mar	30 Mar	22 Mar	13 Mar	26 Feb	31 Mar	
pricked off	7 Apr	18 Apr	5 Apr	1 Apr	15 Mar	7 April	
outside	7 May	7 May	28 May	7 May	15 Apr	28 Apr	
planted	25 June	25 June	25 June	25 June	25 June	25 June	
bedding out							
distance apart	15 cm (6 in)	23 cm (9 in)	60 cm (2 ft)	30 cm (12 in)	23 cm (9 in)	30 cm (12 in)	23 cm (9 in)
eventual height	23 cm (9 in)	23 cm (9 in)	90 cm (3 ft)	30 cm (12 in)	23 cm (9 in)	45 cm (18 in)	45 cm (18 in)
quantity	25	30	9	7	20	25	25

alkaline soil, a pH of 7.5, so rhododendrons and camellias do not flourish, leaving room for other seldom-planted exotics which take advantage of the Mediterranean-type climate. A specimen camphor tree (*Cinnamomum camphora*) overhangs a cliff edge, and *Euonymus fimbriatus* (or possibly the very similar *E. lucidus*) with shining red young spring foliage towers 9 m (30 ft) above beds filled with tender fuchsias, irises, osteospermums, eucomis, fascicularias and both *Puya alpestris* and *Beschorneria yuccoides*. The Australian tree fern (*Dicksonia antarctica*) grows alongside *Astelia nervosa* and the difficult Chatham Island forget-me-not (*Myosotidium hortensia*). American agaves are being encouraged to establish themselves as permanent features.

The mild climate at Overbecks invites the growing of semi-tropical exotics, many with exciting foliage, impossible to grow in most English gardens.

There are so many rare plants at Overbecks that it is tempting to describe them in detail. Instead just one typical border is chosen, where flowers and jungly foliage give a tropical effect.

Mr Tony Murdoch, the Gardener-in-Charge for the National Trust, describes the west Museum Border which lies on the main lawn next to the house. With the warm climate and high rainfall plants tend to grow luxuriantly, so planting schemes cannot remain static. A rock face forms a backdrop to the bed and on it the tender early roses, pink-flowered *Rosa* 'Anemone' and *R.* 'Cooperi', the Burma rose, both types of the Cherokee rose, *R. laevigata*, make a jungle of flower and foliage. The late-flowering *Clematis* 'Abundance' twines among the rose branches, its pinkish red nodding flowers sporting creamy stamens.

At the shady southern end of the border a clump of *Tricyrtis formosana stolonifera* grows in front of the large-leaved *Mahonia acanthifolia* which bears its scented mimosa-yellow flowers in autumn and through early winter. The purple-leaved New Zealand flax (*Phormium tenax* 'Purpureum') makes an architectural background, its huge sword-like leaves contrasting with the delicate lime-yellow tubular flowers of the species *Nicotiana langsdorffii*. In front *Zantedeschia aethiopica* 'Green Dragon' makes a strong group. The half-hardy *Tithonia rotundifolia*

'Torch' from Mexico with orange daisy-flowers grows next to ricinus and tender hedychium species, including red-flowered *Hedychium greenei*. The tall blue echium, *Echium pininana* flowers and seeds itself through the border, above white agapanthus and soft grey-leaved phlomis bushes, which include *Phlomis russeliana* and *Impatiens tinctoria*, canna, the tender *Argyranthemum* (syn. *Chrysanthemum*) 'Jamaica Primrose', the silvery *Astelia nervosa* and the desirable *Kniphofia northiae*, the flower-spikes of which open yellow from buds of coral-pink, between tall grey-green leaves. Towards the house end of the border a clump of pampas grass (*Cortaderia selloana* 'Pumila') carries silky plumes in autumn. Groups of watsonias from South Africa grow luxuriantly throughout the bed, and in this favoured climate survive the winters.

At KILLERTON in east Devon, where the soil is lime-free, the collection of semi-tender plants has been much enlarged under the supervision of the Head Gardener **Mr Andrew Mudge**. Most of this collection is grown in a narrow border which faces the front of the house and is protected at its back by the park wall. The colour scheme is a mirror image of the main herbaceous border which is on a much larger scale and is within view further along the path. Cool colours and grey foliage near the main entrance merge into warm colours at the other end, with the plants blending into each other and lending mutual support in the manner of a traditional herbaceous border. More semi-tender plants are grown against the western wall of the house.

There is a good collection of salvias, which includes *Salvia elegans* 'Scarlet Pineapple', the pineapple sage, *S. discolor* with its contrast of grey leaves and midnight-blue flowers, and *S. leucantha* with buddleja-like white flowers. Argyranthemums range from the grey-leaved *A. foeniculaceum* with flowers like marguerites, to the vigorous 'Jamaica Primrose' which grows to a height of 4–5 ft at Killerton. Osteospermums include 'Whirligig' with its unusual spoon-shaped petals, the yellow 'Buttermilk' and the variegated 'Silver Sparkler'. Amongst many other plants there is a wide range of diascias, cupheas, gazanias, penstemons and helichrysums.

This new bed is an enticing prelude to the luxuriance of the herbaceous borders beyond.

At CHARLECOTE PARK soil is alkaline and dries out easily. The climate is much more severe than that of Cornwall. **Mr David**

Lee, the former Gardener, writes about the border which runs along the edge of woodland to the north of the house:

✣ The 'Shakespeare Border' is situated on the site of an old pleasure-boating canal, which finally fell into disrepair in the eighteenth century. The water-bed was finally filled in with soil, possibly taken from the river's edge when it was being widened, and planted up as a shrubbery with evergreens such as box, holly, phillyrea and yew, and later the snowberry (*Symphoricarpos albus*) from North America, which spreads rapidly in the neutral dry soil. It was left as a shrubbery until 1973 when it was decided to plant it, as far as possible, with plants mentioned in Shakespeare's plays. In 1558 Shakespeare when still a youth had been caught poaching and arraigned before Sir Thomas Lucy, whose descendants finally gave Charlecote to the National Trust in 1946. Heartsease, dog and sweet violet, columbine, burnet, the poisonous hemlock and aconite, saffron and cuckoo flower have been encouraged to spread through the bed.

Before planting, all other plants which had crept in over the years had to be removed, and the existing box hedge running along the west side of the border (*Buxus sempervirens*, not the dwarf form) which had grown distorted and unkempt had to be severely cut back into the old wood to encourage a better shape. After many years of neglect the soil was in poor condition. Both perennial and annual weeds were a problem, and it was important to eradicate ground-elder and enchanter's nightshade before planting any of the perennials. It is extremely difficult to use contact herbicides on a weed such as ground-elder once it is growing thickly round the crown of herbaceous plants without damaging the plants themselves. After initial clearance heavy mulches of well rotted garden compost have been applied annually to improve the structure of the soil, provide nutrients and to help suppress annual weeds. In an old garden seeds of nettles, brambles and others will remain dormant in the soil for many years, only germinating when conditions improve.

The new border is essentially a mixed one, where woody shrubs such as rosemary, lavender, sage and rue mingle with herbs which were of medicinal or culinary use. Other shrubs which were known to Shakespeare, and mentioned in Gerard's *Herball* of 1597, include the cabbage rose or rose of Provence

(*Rosa* × *centifolia*), the damask rose (*R.* × *damascena*), myrtle (*Myrtus communis*), broom (the native *Cytisus scoparius*) and the spiny gorse (*Ulex europaeus*). These are permanent feature plants in the border and give height and solidity. Most of the herbs grown for use before the seventeenth century tend to become woody and grow untidily, giving a border an uncared-for-look, so particular trouble is taken to dead-head spent flowers and to cut back the more straggling shoots all through the growing season. When plants such as wormwood (*Artemisia absinthium*), burnet (*Sanguisorba officinalis*), chamomile (*Chamaemelum nobile*) and forms of pinks – in Shakespeare's time known as gilly flowers – are regularly cut back they make strong bushy plants.

In early autumn flowering stems are removed from all plants where flowering has finished and the reed, if required, has been collected. Plants such as hemlock (*Conium maculatum*), burnet and columbine (*Aquilegia vulgaris*) will all seed too prolifically if they are allowed to do so, and will become as much of a nuisance as any weeds.

An essential part of the management of this border is replacing groups of plants every three to four years. Cuttings from semi-ripe wood are taken from lavender bushes (*Lavandula angustifolia*), rosemary (*Rosmarinus officinalis*), the common sage (*Salvia officinalis*), thyme (*Thymus vulgaris*) and marjoram (*Origanum vulgare*) in August and propagated in a cold frame. Seed is collected from the hemlock, pot marigolds (*Calendula officinalis*), cowslips (*Primula veris*) and oxlips (*P. elatior*), or they are allowed to seed in moderation *in situ*. The seed from double daisies (*Bellis perennis*), the common broom and wild primroses (*Primula vulgaris*) can be sown in seed pans the following spring and the young plants pricked out in rows to be given permanent situations in the late summer. Other plants such as chamomile can be increased by division, best carried out in spring. Thyme and marjoram can also be divided in this way. ❧

Mr Lee also points out that the plants grown in the border do not include *all* of Shakespeare's plants, but only those which might reasonably have been found in English herb gardens towards the end of the sixteenth century. Gerard, of course, lists more than two hundred in his *Herball*.

ROSE GARDENS

The conventional modern rose garden depends on the established regularity of growth, repeat-flowering habit and bright eye-catching colours of the modern hybrid roses. Perhaps fortunately, the Trust in the main looks after gardens where roses are either in separate garden areas, part of a mixed border scheme or have some definite historical association which sets a guide to the type of rose to be grown.

The modern bush roses which need hard pruning each season have little decorative value through the winter months, so, if space permits, are ideally sited behind a hedge or enclosed in a separate compartment where they are visited only in summer. The more vigorous types of bush rose and both old and modern shrub roses fit into planting schemes where other shrubs, herbaceous perennials, bulbs and annuals crowd next to them in happy association. In the third category are rose gardens which represent a particular style, where the roses planted are those that were readily available and fashionable at a definite date. The rose garden can be a complete unit in itself; it may or may not be linked with other garden themes or be in a style appropriate to the house.

Because Trust gardens are usually large it is often possible to fit these rose gardens with an historical context into an existing scheme. Nevertheless there are problems which arise because the visiting public have come to expect roses to have longer and more repetitive seasons of flowering than is possible if strict historical accuracy is maintained. By keeping or introducing architectural motifs with a strong period flavour the Trust has found it possible to extend the range of the rose plants without losing the authenticity of the design. Pale flower colours where pinks and mauves predominate; avoidance of 'salmon' or the more modern vibrant orange or vermilion hues; use of roses with clustered flower-heads rather than large florist's blooms – these are all considerations when planning a rose garden with a Victorian or Edwardian style. A rose garden of the 1930s will have the then new Floribundas such as 'Else Poulsen', its flowers bright rose-pink carried in clusters above glossy bronze foliage. The popular

In the Edwardian Rose Garden at Polesden Lacy old varieties of rose and modern bushes are both used.

Hybrid Tea 'Peace' was first introduced in 1939, the floribunda 'Frensham' in 1946. Most varieties have been superseded by modern roses, longer-flowering and disease-free. Trust period rose gardens are generally a judicious mixture of some old roses which represent the period and style, but with the addition of the more practically satisfying top performers available today.

At POLESDEN LACEY rose pergolas and beds date back to the Edwardian era, when Mrs Greville laid them out as a section within a walled garden. Now a large collection, it remains much as Mrs Greville made it. Some of the roses such as the Ramblers 'Dorothy Perkins' and 'American Pillar' were raised in America in 1901 and 1902 respectively. For no good reason these roses seem now rather despised, but it is still a pleasure to discover them in an old garden. 'Dorothy Perkins' has small double pink clustered blooms; 'American Pillar', more strident, has large single flowers in a vivid carmine pink, with a pronounced white eye. Both have large glossy leaves, which need spraying to prevent mildew.

Elsewhere the Trust has constructed rose gardens or replanted them with roses appropriate to the period of the house or to the style of the garden, which may have been later. An Edwardian rose garden at SHUGBOROUGH matches the period of the terraces and at TATTON PARK another Edwardian rose garden is planted with roses mainly in pale tints. The Trust is restoring Gertrude Jekyll gardens with roses at HATCHLANDS. So far there has been no need for the Trust to attempt to reproduce gardens based on Thomas Robins' paintings of the eighteenth century, where he depicted roses on pillars and palings in very flowery settings, quite remote in style from the prevailing fashion of the landscape park. The nearest approach to an early-nineteenth-century rose garden is the collection at MOTTISFONT ABBEY, covering a wider range than the famous Malmaison roses of the Empress Josephine, immortalized individually by Redouté.

Modern or old shrub roses can be planted as bushes in mixed borders, or in beds of their own often in the latter case with underplanting of suitable herbaceous plants and bulbs. At SISSINGHURST CASTLE the rose garden itself is filled with early Gallicas, Centifolias and newer hybrids and old species, all of which associate well with other plants – pinks, irises, phlox, alliums with spherical heads and grey foliage, colourful herbaceous geraniums and others. Elsewhere at Sissinghurst roses are part of the typical 'cottage'-type planting, playing their part as neighbours to other shrubs or lower-growing plants. They are on walls and cascading out of old fruit trees in the orchard; in the white garden the central arbour of *Rosa mulliganii* dominates the planting scheme at the beginning of July, while white 'Iceberg' roses are set in frames of box to formalize the arrangements.

Mr Graham Stuart Thomas's rose collection at MOTTISFONT now includes 300 different cultivars, and occupies the old kitchen garden, where walls of mellow pink brick are a perfect background to the predominantly pastel tints of the older roses. Mottisfont is an all season garden but the rose collection is best seen in June, with an herbaceous border running up the centre; flowering plants chosen partly to coincide with the main 'flush' of rose bloom also have similar pale colours and nestle between foliage plants of silver and grey.

At MONTACUTE HOUSE a shrub rose border to the north of the broad terrace is underplanted entirely with groups of hostas, their sculptured leaves a perfect foil to the lax growth and arch-ing stems of the rose bushes above them.

At ACORN BANK a border against a south-east wall has been planted with mixed shrub roses, among which foxgloves are encouraged to seed. Roses include an assortment of Rugosas, the single white 'Alba' and the increasingly rare 'Belle Poitevine' with bright almost magenta flowers. Single-flowered Rugosas usually have freely carried hips, so this border is colourful in autumn. Other roses in the bed are the shell-pink Alba rose 'Céleste', the yellow-centred single pink 'Complicata', and a Moss rose 'William Lobb'. The edge of the bed in full sun is car-peted with *Stachys byzantina*.

Roses are difficult to grow successfully in the acid soil and moist clean atmosphere of the south west. At LANHYDROCK in Cornwall the formal box-edged beds on the south terraces within the walled court garden contain bush roses which need renewing every ten years. Some lime is added every year and feeding is given with a fertilizer which contains a higher propor-tion of potash to nitrogen than a normal balanced NPK brand. In this very wet and warm climate nitrogen tends to encourage growth and foliage rather than good flowering. Pruning is done twice, once in the winter to tidy the bushes and make them less subject to root-rock, and again in March to remove any frosted

The walled garden at Mottisfont Abbey contains the National Collection of old roses.

tips. The bushes are cut back very severely. A programme of regular spraying primarily against black spot starts as soon as the roses come into leaf, usually in mid- or even early April in this comparatively mild garden, where spring comes much sooner than in the north or east of the country. Mr Peter Borlase, the former Head Gardener, preferred to change the brand of fungicide used fairly frequently; this and an insecticide are sprayed on at ten-day intervals until the end of the summer. Foliar feeds are also given in the middle of the season and prove very effective.

On the lower terrace triangular beds at four corners are planted with Floribunda-type bush roses including 'Margaret Merril', with creamy-white, scented flowers carried in large open clusters, and green leaves. These beds surround a diamond shape in the centre where pale magenta-flowered 'Escapade' tones down the colouring, and contributes fragrance. On the second terrace a modern rose 'Bright Smile' has replaced massed planting of 'Allgold'. This bush rose is shorter than 'Allgold', and has slender buds which open buttercup-yellow. The foliage is glossy and healthy and is a great success at Lanhydrock.

On the third and highest terrace a rectangular bed of 'Else Poulsen' is surrounded by corner beds of 'The Fairy'. The former, one of the oldest floribundas (1924), has handsome dark glossy bronze leaves and bright rose-pink flowers in good trusses; unfortunately it is rather prone to mildew and is being replaced in several Trust gardens by the healthier and very vigorous Polyantha rose 'Mevrouw Nathalie Nypels' with flowers and foliage of very similar colouring. 'The Fairy' has small double pink globular flowers borne in large clusters, and glossy green foliage, and seldom grows to more than 60 cm (2 ft) but has a useful spreading habit.

Originally at POWIS CASTLE shrub roses were a separate feature on one of the terraces, but the heat in these beds, set against high walls, was found not to be ideal. Recently rose beds have become a successful feature in the lower garden, and are outstanding for the interest and variety of low-growing flowering plants among the rose bushes; plants carefully chosen and massed in groups to complement the colour scheme found in each bed. The more vigorous Hybrid Musk roses (moved from one of the upper terraces) include substantial clumps of 'Buff Beauty', 'Penelope', 'Nur Mahal', 'Wilhelm', 'Prosperity', 'Cornelia' and 'Felicia', all arranged in a bed facing south across the lawn.

At the back of the border runs an English yew hedge, to match the other hedges in this part of the garden. The vigorous bronze-leaved *Heuchera* 'Palace Purple' is planted in groups towards the back. In front, clumps of bergenia, the creeping South African *Diascia fetcaniensis* with delicate pale pink flowers, and dwarf geraniums give foliage or flower interest for much of the year, disguising the base of the rose bushes.

Beyond the end of the vine pergola, still southerly facing, 'Chaucer', one of the English roses bred by the David Austin rose nursery, is underplanted with clumps of *Diascia fetcaniensis*, *D.* 'Salmon Supreme', and *Allium karataviense* with striking foliage and globular flower-heads in early summer. These roses have been bred for fragrance and, unlike most of the older roses, continue to flower all the summer. One of the best is 'The Friar', which has apricot-pink flowers. These shrubs remain about a metre (3–4 ft) in height and spread, and are suitable for the front of wide borders or make a feature bed in a modest-sized garden. The size of the rose bed here is 3.7 by 15 m (12 by 48 ft).

Mr Hancock reports that the soil is enriched with an annual mulch of leaf-mould mixed with straw, grass mowings and farm-yard manure. He says that the fertile heavy soil and a pH of 7 'does' roses well, but a regular maintenance spray programme in summer is necessary to keep the roses clean and healthy.

Along the back of a thick yew hedge another rose bed, this time formally box-edged, faces west. In this planting the colour schemes are bright gleaming yellows and the 'hot' colours of orange scarlet and deep crimson. Here bush roses of Floribunda type are thinned out in late spring. Yellows such as 'Allgold', which keeps its strong yellow tone even as the flowers fade, 'Arthur Bell' and 'Yellow Cushion', with paler yellow fading to cream, move round the spectrum towards the vibrant orange-flame colours of 'Saraband' (semi-double, 60 cm or 2 ft), the ver-milion 'Orangeade', the scarlet 'Eye Paint' (1.2 m or 4 ft) and 'Lilli Marlene', and the deep crimson of 'Europeana' (60 cm or 2 ft). The roses are being underplanted with bidens and *Viola cornuta* Purpurea Group. The latter is easily grown from seed each year, to be set out in May. Another rose bed in more sober colours adjoins to the north and has its flowering season extended by the bronze leaved *Viola cornuta* Lilacina Group and diascia.

At NYMANS, a shrub rose garden is representative of the best of those roses known before the First World War. Trellis arches and metal tripods are curtained with ramblers, and the bushes are underplanted with catmint, geraniums and polygonums, which harmonize with the pale mauves, pinks and creamy yellows. The planting is arranged round a bronze fountain. Another planting of roses at Nymans is simple. Between double curving stone steps a whole bed is filled with *Rosa gallica officinalis*, with hydrangeas to prolong the season. An outer bed is edged with *Euonymus* 'Silver Queen'.

At TINTINHULL HOUSE a pair of rectangular beds, tucked behind and north of 2.4 m (8 ft) yew hedges, is planted effectively with the same rose, its light crimson flowers carried towards the end of June for a spectacular three weeks. The rose foliage is subject to black spot and mildew, so the bed is regularly sprayed with a fungicide even after flowering is over. Earlier in the season, and beginning towards the end of March, when all the roses are cut down to a bud 15 cm (6 in) from the ground, blue scillas make a carpet of flower. The summer snowflake (*Leucojum aestivum*) flowers in April and May, thriving in the damp shade, with a few *Fritillaria meleagris* that have escaped from neighbouring beds.

In many Trust gardens, bush roses and shrub roses are used in mixed borders; shrubs, perennials, annuals and bulbs give a long-lasting display. In the kitchen garden at Tintinhull, where the theme is pink and misty blue, narrow double borders, divided into two sections by a cross-path, are backed by espalier pears which face each other across a stone-flagged path. When first planted by Mrs Phyllis Reiss in the 1940s, the floribunda pink rose 'Else Poulsen' was used interplanted with bushes of August- and September-flowering *Caryopteris* × *clandonensis*. It was found that this bronze-leaved rose is prone to mildew, so recently the Polyantha rose 'Mevrouw Nathalie Nypels' (1919) has been substituted. With equally glossy bronze-tinted leaves, this rose flowers all summer if the dead-heads are regularly removed and it seems disease-free. The bushes are pruned hard at the end of March, and given a good mulch of compost. As they come into leaf a regular spraying programme commences and they are given a sprinkling of Vitax Q4 as buds form and swell. In each of the four borders ten roses flank each side of a 10 m (11 yd) path, in flower beds 1.5 m (5 ft) in width. Between each rose but set at the back of the beds are bushes of the blue-flowered caryopteris and along the front the small catmint *Nepeta nervosa* bears its blue spikes all summer.

Verbena bonariensis with 1.2 m (4 ft) tall branched stems and flat heads of violet has been allowed to seed at random throughout the bed. This verbena, hardy in some gardens, will flower readily in one season from self-sown seed. At the four farthest corners silver-leaved artichokes (*Cynara cardunculus* Scolymus Group 'Glauca') are architectural, and eight pillars are clothed in scented honeysuckle (*Lonicera japonica halliana*), which has to be ruthlessly cut back each April.

Although this rose walk is chiefly dependent on the performance of 'Mevrouw Nathalie Nypels' and the pink and blue colour scheme, the season starts with the flowering of double rows of Single Early orange-scarlet tulip 'Prince of Austria' in late April. Clumps of tulip bulbs fit neatly between the plants of catmint along the front edge, and the grey leaves hide the dying foliage of the tulips.

Climbing roses are another feature at Tintinhull, and **Professor John Malins**, the last tenant at Tintinhull House, described

*At Nymans a collection of old roses has existed since before
the First World War. A profusion of rose arches is
centred around a fountain.*

how he pruned the roses on the brick and Ham stone walls which
partly surround the garden and on the walls of the house itself:

At Tintinhull walls abound and there is ample opportunity
to study the habit of the various roses which are grown on them.
Their height varies from 1.5 to 5.4 m (5 to 18 ft) and it is soon
clear that 1.8–2.4 m (6–8 ft) makes for the easiest pruning. Wall
plants are trained to horizontal wires, spaced at 45 cm (18 in) or
to 5 in square wire mesh. Both systems are made fast to walls
with screws which have a vine eye.

Climbing roses vary a good deal in vigour and the yellow
Banksian rose which produces long and slender shoots in
profusion is the most difficult to prune. Its flowers are borne on
wood which is at least two years old and pruning is confined as
far as possible to the complete removal of older shoots. This
particular plant overhangs a footpath and there has to be some
extra pruning up to 2.4 m (8 ft) and tying in of long shoots
above this, the work being done immediately after flowering.
We find that 'Paul's Scarlet Climber' and 'Guinée' on the west
wall of the house need very little pruning beyond shortening of

*In the kitchen garden at Tintinhull House a double border of pink roses is
backed by espalier pears.*

lateral shoots. 'Climbing Lady Hillingdon' will reach 4.5 m
(15 ft) or more and to reduce this to 3.7 m (12 ft) is the limit of
comfort on a ladder and does encourage flowering at a lower
level, near to the eye and nose. We have three plants of
'Madame Grégoire Staechelin' on the north wall of the house
and they need very little pruning to keep them below 3.7 m
(12 ft) while the rather lax growth is not much disturbed as it
gives support to the frail shoots of *Tropaeolum speciosum*, which
do not climb until the rose's flowering period is over.

Very old plants of 'Climbing Crimson Glory' and 'Climbing
Shot Silk' on a 2.4 m (8 ft) south-facing wall are fan-trained,
avoiding at all costs any crossing over of branches. The laterals
are shortened to three or four buds. With age, the main stems
produced fewer laterals, and then one must hope to find one low
down which can be trained as a replacement.

In this relatively mild climate pruning takes place in the
winter, so avoiding damage to other plants in the border. All
other roses are pruned in February and March. Further action
in the spring is rarely necessary, and never for those grown on
walls. ❧

Rudyard Kipling loved the garden at BATEMAN'S and took a considerable interest in its design. He is responsible for the pear alley already described, yew hedges, and the small formal rose garden which lies in the lower part of the garden beyond a millpond screened with pleached limes. Water from the pond is drawn by gravity to the rose garden's central fountain. Modern roses, 'Frensham', 'Betty Prior' and 'Mrs Inge Poulsen' (the latter not available commercially) have replaced the original Polyantha roses which were available when Kipling planted the garden.

Mr Alan Champion, the former Gardener-in-Charge at Bateman's, describes how the rose garden is maintained today (with updating by Mr Derek Bobin the current Gardener-in-Charge):

The rose garden was planned and planted by Rudyard Kipling. His original plan is on display in his study and is dated 1906.

The roses are of the Floribunda type, now called Cluster roses, but which when planted were called Polyantha. Cluster roses are pruned at about the beginning of April. The reasons for pruning are to allow light and air into the bush and to fight pests and diseases. First of all you should make sure that your tools are in good order. Secateurs are used, but loppers for anything thicker than about 2 cm (¾ in). First remove all dead wood and all crossing wood. This type of rose is cut back by at least a third of the last season's growth to an outward-facing bud. Always make a diagonal cut away from this bud. The bushes should then be sprayed with fungicide.

At Bateman's once pruning is completed the beds are edged with shears, weeded and dug lightly over with a border fork to a depth of a few inches. Care is taken not to dig too close to the rose bushes as this can loosen roots – if a bush starts to rock to and fro this will, in time, kill it. Damage to the roots also causes suckers to grow. These can be recognized by a different growth, leaf and habit to the bushes themselves. Removal of suckers is best achieved by pulling up by hand, wearing thick gloves; cutting only makes them grow more vigorously. After weeding is completed the beds are mulched. You can use pulverized bark, which is very effective and looks good but is expensive. Steamed mushroom compost looks attractive too, but it should not be used continuously on soil unless it is clay, because it can contain too much lime. Ask when buying it what the pH level is; pH 7 or below should be fine.

After this initial work in the spring, the beds are kept weed-free and edged regularly. The roses are underplanted with spring bulbs, including narcissus and muscari.

The roses are sprayed once fortnightly with fungicide. Alternating between two types, after a few months of use, helps prevent resistance to one formula from building up. In between the fungicide spraying they are also sprayed with an insecticide, unless there are a lot of ladybirds present, in which case we leave them to do the work for us.

When in flower the roses are regularly dead-headed which helps to promote more flowers and gives a longer flowering season. This can be done every day but we normally do it once a week because of lack of time. ❧

Although the estate at CLIVEDEN is in essence a large eighteenth-century landscape, there lie within the main design several gardens on a relatively small scale. One such area occupies what was laid out in the 1720s as a circle of yew trees measuring about 60 m (200 ft) in diameter. The land in this circle has, over the years, been treated in many ways; as a bowling green, a tennis court, and later as a rose garden on a formal plan rather like a cartwheel. **Mr Philip Cotton**, the Head Gardener at Cliveden, writes about the rose garden in a wood which Sir Geoffrey Jellicoe designed for Lord and Lady Astor in 1959, and about the adjustments and changes which have been necessary over the years since:

❧ In 1959 the rose garden at Cliveden was laid out on a symmetrical wheel pattern, with an Edwardian feel. It was this formal design that Lord Astor decided to change, and accordingly asked Sir Geoffrey Jellicoe to redesign the garden. While talking to Lord Astor he realized that there was a need for a place within the bounds of the estate where the family could hide from the limelight in a quiet contemplative atmosphere. The resulting proposal was for a 'Glade Garden' into which it was possible to enter 'as into the centre of a cabbage or a rose', hidden in the surrounding woodland. The scheme was for beds contained within irregular sinuous curves which flow gracefully into one another to create six beds of different sizes with paths between. The main 'circular' path was to pass at intervals under delicately constructed, wooden, painted arches, clothed in clematis, honeysuckle and roses. A statue of Hercules is placed at the centre of the design, and is a focal point as seen from the entrance to the garden.

By 1989 this design, planted almost entirely with old and modern shrub roses, was suffering from weak and unhealthy growth which we felt was due to the build-up of pathogens in the soil affecting the vigour of the plants. This phenomenon, 'rose sickness' is well known where roses, or indeed any monoculture, has occupied the same soil for many years. It was decided, therefore, that we should take steps to improve the vigour of the roses, and to improve the feature if possible. The design occupies approximately half an acre, but the action we took is just as appropriate for a much smaller area.

In the late 1970s a great deal was done to thin the surrounding woodland, which had grown very dense, to let in more light and encourage air movement to combat black spot and mildew. An experiment was made to enhance the shape of the rose beds by planting ground cover amongst the roses. *Ajuga reptans* 'Jungle Beauty', *Veronica spicata incana*, *Viola riviniana* Purpurea Group, *Geranium endressii* 'Wargrave Pink' and *Dianthus* Highland Hybrids were used, but we found that it was difficult to keep the plantings weed-free in the heavy soil. It also made fertilizer application difficult. *Lysimachia nummularia* 'Aurea' (golden creeping Jenny) was also used, but we found that the colour did nothing to enhance the yellow rose blooms above. After about four seasons we abandoned the idea. All gardeners learn from their mistakes!

At that time the planting in the surrounding perimeter beds was improved by introducing indigofera, exochorda, weigela, eucryphia, cytisus, ceanothus, acers and many other plants. This extended the season in the garden, for the shrub roses, although many are repeat flowering, do tend to have a short season. These shrubs were planted, using the surrounding circle of yew trees as a backdrop. The yews were part of the early eighteenth-century design, and as such have been preserved by pruning back the existing trees and planting anew where gaps have appeared. Now, some fifteen years later, we are again beginning to see the circle more clearly.

We felt that the Jellicoe beds should sit more happily in the surroundings, so we adjusted the width of the surrounding lawn to approximate to the circular design. We could not make it accurate because of the fine holly, which has *Rosa* 'Bobbie James' sprawling through it, being in the way but a reasonable compromise was reached, and 'Bobbie James' flowers magnificently, still.

Rose sickness, however, became more serious, and we tried sterilizing some beds chemically with dazomet [not available retail]. When sterilizing with this chemical we have to be careful that the gas released does not contaminate the surrounding lawn, so a trench is dug 40 cm (16 in) deep all around the edge of the bed, and the vertical side of that trench is lined with polythene sheeting, the trench is backfilled, and the same sheet then laid over the surface after the chemical is incorporated in the soil to a spit deep, and the surface sealed by watering and rolling. A noticeable improvement in the vigour of the roses followed this treatment, but sadly, it lasted only two or three years. We also tried the effect of changing the soil entirely to a depth of 40 cm in a rose bed. Again, we achieved an improvement which lasted a similar time to the dazomet treatment.

In order to add interest early in the season, we planted early-flowering bulbs in drifts through the beds. *Tulipa praestans* 'Fusilier', *Narcissus* 'W. P. Milner' and *Muscari* 'Blue Spike' gave a wonderful effect. These alterations maintained the rose garden in a reasonable condition through the mid 1980s, but later in the decade the rose had again become weak in places and an increase in muntjak deer resulted in the young spring growth of many of the plants being eaten to the ground for two years. Clearly it was time for drastic action!

There was obviously no point in doing anything to the garden before taking steps to exclude the muntjak and rabbits, and the existing fence of rabbit wire was not sufficient. So we looked for something better. The search led to a catalogue of the late 1800s where a pleasing design in 'wirework' was depicted, and a visit to a local churchyard where some of that very fencing remained convinced us that it would be both rabbit and, if extended in height, deer-proof. A firm who had the necessary skills were tracked down, and two pairs of gates with flanking panels of the decorative design were ordered. As much of the fence would be hidden in the shrubbery, and the design of fence was expensive, we economized by using cheaper netting wire where it was not seen. All this was erected by our own maintenance man during the summer of 1991, and there is no longer any damage from the creatures – providing the gates are kept shut!

The fencing was the first stage in a planned major refurbishment of the rose garden. Next we had to tackle the rose sickness. We also took the opportunity to refer to Sir Geoffrey Jellicoe's original plan, and to ensure that the National Trust were doing justice to this, this being the only example of his work in a Trust garden. This prompted a visit to Sir Geoffrey, who vividly remembered the discussions he had with Lord Astor as a result of the commission, and gave us valuable information on his perception of the form the garden should take. One important element of the original design which was missing was the hard surfacing of the path passing under the arches, in either brick or gravel, and we decided that, especially as increased visitor numbers wear the turf, this should now be laid in gravel. We also, with Sir Geoffrey's agreement, added a spur from the entrance (a 'stalk to the cabbage',) also to take the wear on the lawn, and to lead in to the design. So that the design should remain crisp and practical we edged the path with steel strip, following the curves drawn on the original plan.

It appeared from the behaviour of the roses in the past five years, which grew far better immediately after sterilizing or changing the soil but within two or three years gradually deteriorated, that disease organisms were present in the subsoil, and reached by the root systems during that time span. So deeper treatment was necessary. As the soil in the beds (Cranleigh loam, imported in 1959) was of a very heavy silty consistency, being putty in wet weather and rock in dry periods, we took the opportunity to remove it all. Nearly 300 tonnes were dug out and replaced by a more workable loam.

When the beds were empty of topsoil, and the shapes had been corrected with reference to the original plan, The heavens opened! A group of advisers from the Royal National Rose Society, with us to discuss the methods of steam sterilization, suggested that waterlogging may be having just as much bad effect on the growth of the plants. Cliveden is a garden of gravel soil overlaying chalk, but in random places there are beds of clay under the gravel which hold water and cause bad drainage.

Our excavations revealed that one such clay bed occurs under the rose garden. Our attempts to sterilize the subsoil at that time proved impossible because of the wet conditions, and that had to be postponed.

This was a marvellous opportunity, however, to install a drainage scheme. We used perforated rigid plastic pipes laid in something like a herringbone pattern, as far as the shape of the beds would allow, which conducts the excess water to a distant soakaway in the gravel hillside. As the soil is generally so free-draining and is on a hilltop we have to irrigate frequently in the summer months. So, in spite of the peculiar conditions in the subsoil, we also provided irrigation points in the beds while we had the opportunity. We now have the perfect conditions for cultivation; a well-drained soil with water available when needed, just as in the case of a pot plant.

By the spring of 1993 the beds were refilled with good loam, the path was surfaced with Witney gravel, turf re-laid where necessary, and the three cast iron seats were returned to their original positions on the path, just as Sir Geoffrey had intended. For the 1993 season we felt that the beds should have the opportunity to settle down before the permanent planting was introduced. So, for the summer months, a bedding scheme was designed in colours ranging from white to pink and purple, using blocks of *Lavatera* 'Loveliness', cosmos (mixed), cleome, *Nicotiana alata*, and for the lower front groups, *Senecio cineraria*, *Salvia farinacea* 'Victoria', and *Antirrhinum* 'Sonnet White'. The planting plan was marked out on the surface of the beds in sand to indicate the position of each group of plants, and by late May all the young plants were establishing well. We deliberately omitted any fertilizer application, because we were not looking for rank growth. Even so, the wet season combined with the free root run in the new soil produced staggering results, with lavatera and nicotiana reaching to over two metres. But the overall effect was well received.

In 1994 we saw another bedding scheme, with slight differences. Then by the autumn and winter we introduced some permanent planting. The plants were chosen to provide two main flushes of bloom in June and early July and again in late August and September. It was provided largely by roses, but also using herbaceous plants and bulbs. The planting was low in the centre of the garden and high at the sides, as intended by Sir Geoffrey Jellicoe in the first instant, and fragrance was important. The colour scheme ranged through purple, pink, white, cream and pale yellow, with some mauve. ❧

At TATTON PARK an inner garden, almost surrounded with walls, is known as Her Ladyship's Garden. A tea house set in a wall with access to a tennis court beyond, looks over the enclosed area where pool, pergola and rose beds are remote from the rest of the garden. Tradition had it that gardeners had to finish work in this area before 10 a.m. in Edwardian times, so that Anna, the last Lady Egerton, should not be disturbed. Stone steps lead down to the pool and a low balustrade and wall, over which climbers such as *Rosa mulliganii* (formerly known as *R. longicuspis*) clamber, separate the garden from the thickly planted Tower garden beyond.

The rose beds have recently been planted in pale pastel colours very much in Gertrude Jekyll's style, although she rarely used the salmony tints such as those in 'Margot Koster', which was not introduced until 1931. Two symmetrical 9 m (30 ft) square areas are planted in different patterns. In one to the east an outer bed almost surrounds the entire square, leaving a stone paved path for access to a central sundial. The first bed is planted with 180 bushes of the fragrant white-flowered 'Katherina Zeimet'; the second and smaller bed with 'Margo Koster'. Both these roses are Polyantha pompons, with small rambler-type flowers held in close clusters. They are low-growing and compact and flower through most of the summer. The planting is in irregular lines, the bushes spaced at approximately 45 cm (18 in) apart.

In the western section the garden is divided into eight segments, each individual segment massed with equally small, compact roses – 'Baby Faurax' with violet almost blue-tinged flowers, or 'Cameo' with china-pink small double blooms. There are about fifty plants in each bed.

In both sections standard bushes of 'White Pet' are arranged symmetrically to give height and interest. This rose, an 1879 introduction bred in America, is busy with double white well-formed petals. Round the edges and breaking the harsh line of stone paving glaucous-leaved dianthus make an elegant and neat ground cover, about 30 cm (12 in) in width, reminiscent of some of Miss Jekyll's plans for rose gardens made in the first 30 years of this century. The dianthus supply the fragrance lacking in these roses.

At SHUGBOROUGH a rose garden was constructed by the National Trust in 1966, just below the main terrace west of the house. A Victorian design includes roses swinging as garlands on ropes between pillars, trellis-work arches and pyramids for roses and clematis. The period flower-colouring is in a range from white, pink purple to dark red, but does not include any flowers, with a more modern 'salmon-pink' tint. At first only roses which were available at the end of the nineteenth century were used, but more recently, to get better performance in this cold soil and poor site, healthier bushes and modern roses with a longer flowering period have been added to the scheme. In the main beds towards the centre, beds of the Polyantha rose 'Mevrouw Nathalie Nypels' face each other diagonally across a sundial. With semi-double china-pink flowers carried all season and healthy foliage with bronze tints to the young shoots, this massed planting is matched by two beds of 'Cardinal Hume' (1984), a rose with larger fragrant deep purple flowers. Blue clematis flower on arches above a bed of the modern Floribunda rose 'Olive' (1982) with flowers of ox-blood red.

Bush forms of 'White Pet' grow under standard 'Ballerina' with shell-pink clustered heads, and 'New Dawn', 'Mary Wallace' and 'Violette' link the outside framework. 'Zéphirine Drouhin', the thornless rose, and its sport 'Kathleen Harrop', with clear pink flowers, both find a place. Rugosa roses, both 'Fru Dagmar Hastrup' and 'Roseraie de l'Haÿ' surround 'Jacques Cartier' and are wonderfully resistant to disease and very free-flowering.

HERB GARDENS

Perhaps because the earliest gardening books were herbals, where plants were described for their medicinal or culinary use rather than for their ornamental flowers or leaves, herb gardens not only have a poetic and historical attraction but seem important because they are useful. Herbs seem evocative of fragrance and pot-pourris, faintly ecological as so many of them are original 'unimproved' species, and if used infrequently today for cures, are still a vital ingredient of the cookpot. Today when privately owned gardens are mainly small a herb garden remains a popular feature.

In Tudor gardens (and earlier walled monastery gardens) the herbs were grown with the root and leaf vegetables, and each herb needed a separate plot to avoid confusion when harvested. Herbs were necessary not only for flavouring dishes but for curing and 'scenting' to disguise disagreeable odours. In these early herb gardens no attention was paid to attractive forms of growth, and the knot of ornamentals was in a separate part of a garden. In a modern herb garden plants from both areas are included. Rosemary, santolina, thymes, hyssop and germander (*Teucrium × lucidrys*), essential ingredients of the knot, are included for their aromatic foliage, and quite often are used to make low surrounding hedges or patterns in beds, separating herbs and protecting them (and their fragrance) from drying winds.

In the eighteenth century, when flowers were banished to a distant walled kitchen garden, herbs went with them, and it was not until the first years of this century that interest in their ornamental possibilities was reawakened. One of the most successful herb gardens, and one which has proved a lasting influence, is that at SISSINGHURST CASTLE, a property of the Trust since 1967. Here Vita Sackville-West (Mrs Harold Nicolson) not only gardened but also wrote articles about her gardening interests. She helped popularize the idea of making a herb garden an ornamental feature, and giving it a garden compartment of its own.

At SCOTNEY CASTLE Mrs Christopher Hussey and Lanning Roper together made a herb garden in a sunny area inside the ruined walls of the originally fortified medieval castle. Designed in a circle, the planting includes many herbs that would have been essential when the castle still housed a community which on occasion would be isolated from the outside world. Sage, including the ordinary culinary *Salvia officinalis* and its golden and purple-leaved forms, fennel (*Foeniculum vulgare*), marjoram (*Origanum vulgare*) and its silver and golden cultivars, and thyme all have highly aromatic leaves. Among this basic planting polyanthus give colour in spring, and any bare earth is covered during the summer with heliotrope 'Princess Marina' and scented-leaved perlagoniums.

In the mid-1970s the original herb beds at HARDWICK HALL were extended by the Trust into a large herb garden. In the formal layout, hops, both the green *Humulus lupulus* and its golden-leaved cultivar *H.l.* 'Aureus', are grown on tripods as draped pyramids to give height and form, at the corners of the beds. Only plants likely to have been in the original Elizabethan garden are grown. Divided into two sections, each with a square central bed surrounded by a gravel path. with further beds of herbs on all four sides, the garden grows mainly culinary herbs and a pamphlet describes their uses.

Mr Robin Allan, the Head Gardener at Hardwick, writes about maintaining the herb garden:

✣ We deal with spreading roots by digging out the excess, which are then potted up to sell to the public. Soapwort and wall germander are typical examples. Herbs need little feeding and at Hardwick a general fertilizer is only given when plants are put out and at seeding time.

Some of the seed is raised under glass, including parsley, sweet marjoram, basil, and tobacco. Some plants are allowed to seed *in situ* and are thinned out into a row in spring; orach, with bronze-purple leaves, opium poppies, and marigolds. Some plants we do not allow or are reluctant to let seed over the garden. These include angelica and good King Henry. We cut off the flower-heads of some plants in August, partly to keep them tidy but also because those such as comfrey and sweet Cicely will sometimes flower again.

The hop shoots need constant cutting back as they invade the borders. Juice from the cut stems will make a brown stain on clothing (only visible after washing) and can cause severe blistering to skin. We constantly suffer from flea beetle on young seedlings of borage so now we grow on the young plants in a cold frame until they are large enough to withstand any attack. In autumn when we cut down the plants we find that sheep shears are often very effective. ✣

The paths in the herb garden are of crushed limestone, rolled in and very hard. In summer they become very dusty; dust which the constant traffic of visitors' feet distributes over the plant leaves. In winter frosts tend to lift the surface and lime sticks to boots. Nevertheless, the paths blend in very well, remain neat and are not rough or noisy for walking or wheelbarrows.

In other Trust gardens, herbs occupy areas of a kitchen

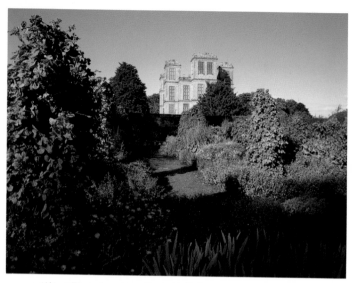

*(Above) The herb garden at Hardwick Hall was redesigned in the 1970s.
Many herbs are prolific seeders and have spreading root systems.
(Right) An open sunny site by the ruined Scotney Castle provides a bed for
mixed planting of herbs and perennials.*

garden. At GUNBY HALL culinary and medicinal plants surround
a bay tree, and at FELBRIGG HALL in Norfolk where the Trust
has restored the kitchen garden, a hot sunny south-facing border
backed with a high wall is used for growing herbs, which thrive
in the hot dry climate of East Anglia.

The herb garden at ACORN BANK was begun in the 1960s, but
mainly developed in the 1970s to replace a small vegetable garden. A special feature is the Trust's largest selection of herbs and
medicinal plants, including a large variety of aromatic-leaved
trees and shrubs as well as the usual perennial herbs. Annuals
such as calendula, chervil, borage and basil are encouraged to
seed freely, and height is given to the beds by quince trees and
damsons.

Mr Christopher Braithwaite, the Gardener at Acorn Bank,
writes about the conditions in which the herbs are grown:

❧ The herb garden contains culinary and medicinal herbs
grown in three different beds, separated by gravel paths. Most

are woody shrubs or perennials but annuals such as calendula, chervil, borage and basil are encouraged to seed freely. Some, in fact, such as thornapple (*Datura stramonium*) and poppy resent being transplanted even as seedlings. Against the south-facing wall, in the past heated with flues to protect fruit blossom from late frosts, the bed is hot and gets baked in summer. The central bed is half-shaded but the bed along the south-west wall is in dense shade cast by canopies of quince and damsons. Many plants used for medicinal purposes, among which are many British natives, require rich soil and good drainage rather than the full sun associated with the aromatic-leaved Mediterranean-types. Fortunately at Acorn Bank, on the site of the old kitchen garden, soil is deep, light and loamy and slightly alkaline, and remains rich and fertile. Only the shaded bed where moisture-loving plants include trilliums, veratrums and ferns is given even an annual mulch. ❧

Chris Braithwaite finds that the thirteen different varieties of mint, and soapwort and danewort (*Sambucus ebulus*) are the most invasive, spreading by underground roots. He finds that by planting annuals around them, rather than other perennials, he has a chance to discourage the creeping rootstocks at the end of the season, and thus prevents them from spreading through the bed. Mints do best if allowed a free root run and are seldom happy if grown in drainpipes or containers sunk in the ground. Each year he keeps some of the young rootstock and cuts of the older central crowns on one side or the other.

Most of these plants with fragrant leaves come from warm Mediterranean-type climates, where they thrive in well-drained sunny positions. Many prefer alkaline soil and few need rich feeding. Herb gardens are at their best in the early to mid-summer, inevitably becoming blowsy and overgrown later. Many different designs for herb gardens exist, some based on an historical concept. Others evolved as it became obvious that plants with such 'wandering' qualities needed firm control and separating by paving of brick or stone, hidden strips of slate or metal, and low-growing hedging plants. For marking a frame or pattern box, lavender, sages, rosemary and santolina are ideal, usually needing to be clipped only once annually. If a taller dividing screen is desirable, yew or holly will provide a dark background to the predominantly pale leaves and pastel flower colours, or roses with scented leaves (hybrids of *Rosa eglanteria*) can be trained on wires to make a barrier. The evergreens tend to grow too tall and they take away the essential light on which these sun-living herbs depend, but even yew can be kept as low as 90 cm (3 ft) if pruned very regularly.

Other perennial herbs are also used for tracing the outline of beds. Violets, chives, London pride (*Saxifraga* × *urbium*) and pinks (cultivars of *Dianthus*) are suitable. Because each individual plant is not always top-grade, a bold design and some sort of repeated planting theme in beds of defined shape is advisable when the separate herb area is planned. Herbs can be divided up into types for different uses. Some are for cooking and flavouring. Some are for medicines and pot-pourri. Some are particularly suitable for the site. Gardeners with botanical interest like to grow herbs for Compositae, Labiatae or Umbelliferae, while in other gardens the plants may be for dyeing or even may have traditional astrological significance.

Of course herbs do not have to be grown in separate areas. Even in Trust gardens herbs are scattered between vegetable rows, are found suitable homes among good perennials, or carpet soil or paving with matted growth. Angelica, fennel, lovage, bay, bergamot, rosemary, rue, various sages, sweet Cicely and thyme are all excellent ornamentals worthy of a place in the garden, without consideration for their more utilitarian qualities. In the warmer gardens bay trees and rosemary bushes are used architecturally, and bay can be shaped like topiary. At WESTBURY COURT clipped bays act as buttresses to the walls each side of the *clairvoyées*. In other gardens bay trees in pots are clipped into formal spheres or pyramids. Rosemary makes a corner plant, its woody branches straggling over steps or pavement. Bergamot (*Monarda didyma*) actually prefers the rich manured border to the sunny well-drained sites. With scarlet flowers in the type, or with the pink flowers of some of its cultivars, it is a useful addition to a mixed border. Rue (*Ruta graveolens*), and particularly the cultivar *R.g.* 'Jackman's Blue', is a valuable Mediterranean foliage shrub, its grey-blue leaves a foil to bright flower colour or blending with metallic 'silvers'. At Westbury Court the purple-leaved *Salvia officinalis* 'Purpurascens' make patterns in the simple parterre. Thriving in hot sunny well-drained beds, these shrubby sages quickly grow woody, and if part of a formal foliage scheme, needs renewing every few years. Angelica (the

biennial *Angelica archangelica*), the stems of which are preserved for cake decoration, fennel (both the common *Foeniculum vulgare* and its bronze-leaved cultivar *F.v.* 'Purpureum') and lovage (*Levisticum officinale*) are architectural foliage plants of ornamental value in any part of the garden. Angelica is useful in a new border, which lacks 'body' in its first season, and can later be abandoned. Fennel seeds freely and as the seed-heads are attractive is often allowed to multiply while lovage tends to spread quickly by underground roots. The rampant double soapwort, *Saponaria officinalis* 'Rosea Plena', or bouncing Bet, needs its rhizomatous roots controlled by deep slates or sheets of corrugated iron. Restricted in this way at Westbury it is a useful and colourful addition to borders of plants all grown and known before 1700. Carpets of thyme are fragrant when trodden and are ideal plants for paving cracks. Forms of *Thymus praecox arcticus* (syn. *T. drucei*) make creeping mounds, and coloured-leaved cultivars of the lemon-scented *T.* × *citriodorus* will carpet the ground in light shade.

WATER

All great gardens of the world make use of water as an element in their designs, each country adapting its many qualities to particular climate and needs. Eighteenth-century landscapes with water such as those of FARNBOROUGH, PETWORTH, STOWE STOURHEAD, STUDLEY ROYAL and WEST WYCOMBE, where naturalistic lakes reflect sky, trees and classical buildings, are today in the care of the Trust. For many people these parks, and others privately owned, are the epitome of English garden design, where scenery has become linked with emotional response, the sites and source of poetic imagination, and their preservation more vital than any other gardening style. But the Trust has not only been influential in preserving landscapes where water is on a grand historical scale; more recently it has rescued and restored important almost forgotten and derelict gardens, where the element of water is dominant. At WESTBURY COURT, in the flat countryside bordering the estuary of the

(Previous pages) The border in the enclosed Herb Garden at Acorn Bank. The herbs are for culinary and medicinal use, and include many native plants.

Severn, late-seventeenth-century water canals have been dredged, their walls rebuilt, parallel lines of yew hedging (with holly topiary) replanted, and the surrounding garden restored with plants of the period. At ERDDIG, water canals are reflecting mirrors for lime avenues, but have only very recently been restored to their contemporary appearance. In England these gardens are among the few which remain of this style (many other or earlier formal water gardens were swept away during the eighteenth century) and their faithful restoration enables historians and modern gardeners to trace the influences of fashion on the use of water in the garden.

At CLAREMONT an early landscape garden complete with lake and island was given to the Trust in 1949. The property, associated with Vanbrugh, Bridgeman, Kent and Brown, has a green amphitheatre carved out of the hillside, overlooking a lake and island. Completely overgrown with small trees and cherry laurel, the amphitheatre was reseeded and the lake dredged. Interestingly, the mud and rubbish taken from the lake bottom was 'campshedded': close-driven posts of elm were placed in the water behind which the spoil was dumped. These have now been replaced by steel piling with a wooden facia. The size of the lake, was reduced by a metre or so around the edge, topsoil added, and grass was sown to consolidate this new bank. This commonsense approach can easily be copied when cleaning out any pond or lake, provided the edging makes naturalistic curves.

SHEFFIELD PARK, a great landscaped arboretum has eighteenth- and nineteenth-century lakes which reflect the exotic trees planted on their banks. A 7.5 m (25 ft) waterfall of Sussex sandstone and clay, with no retaining cement, connects the lake areas; it has been carefully restored, and planting at its edge is suitably naturalistic.

Water in gardens is not always represented by an expanse of still reflecting surface, stimulating the mind to contemplation (the double meaning of 'reflection' suiting the eighteenth-century interest in man's inner life as well as alluding to water in a landscape). Moving water awakens the senses by its constant movement whether from fountains which fill the air with sparkling drops and murmuring sound (which by association suggests coolness), or natural or man-made cascades of rushing water, slow-moving streams or narrower fast-running rivulets. The essence of all water garden design lies in appreciating these dual qualities, and using them to evoke moods as well as visual satisfaction. Any expanse of still water increases the feeling of space, reflecting the sky, the changing patterns of sunlight, and moving shadow and cloud. In Britain's atmosphere reflections fade away into misty distance, giving gardens a mysterious quality seldom realized in hotter countries where water appears dark in contrast to bright sunlight. By planning and manipulating the level of water and the angle of vision, Le Nôtre, in seventeenth-century France, extended his garden dimensions by exact reflections; under grey changeable skies these effects are less predictable. The great landscape lakes reflect the surrounding woodland and, as at WEST WYCOMBE, classical temples seem to float on misty water. The fluidity of water provides contrast with the stability and immobility of architecture, its depths providing tranquillity and a living place for fish, and a still surface a reflecting mirror for swooping swallows.

In many gardens now owned by the Trust water is not only used for display but provides a site and setting for growing a wide range of aquatic and moisture-loving plants. Sometimes these gardens have been made where natural streams could be shaped and dammed to provide the still water around which plants could thrive. It is the skill of the plantsman which determines appropriate planting beside the naturalistic lake, such as STOURHEAD or SHEFFIELD PARK, or the more domestic ponds at UPTON HOUSE or ARLINGTON COURT. The water garden at CLIVEDEN, complete with restored Japanese summerhouse has been cleared in part of plants which choked the surface, and surrounding beds simplified with moisture-loving plants in broad sweeps of each sort. At HIDCOTE, in a garden renowned for its series of enclosed 'garden rooms', a further area of stream and open woodland allows informal planting.

In gardens where water seems to be merely ornamental, it often has a secondary, more utilitarian purpose. The formal lily pond, itself kept filled by channelled rain-gutterings or main water supply, bubbles up as a water receptacle for storage and can be dipped into for hand-watering.

In the history of gardens the earliest were the oasis enclosures of the Middle East, set in harsh desert surroundings, where water was canalized for irrigation as well as to express man's symbolic progress through life. Fountains, out of fashion in the landscape period for being too contrived and artificial, were

At Westbury Court late seventeenth-century canals have been restored.

originally designed to clear the water surface of insects rather than to please, and their development as garden ornament in classical and then Renaissance times was a secondary function. The use of water as 'jokes' came from sixteenth-century Italy and demonstrated ingenuity and a grasp of hydrostatics. At DYRHAM PARK, the formal ponds and cascades remain in the garden west of the house, but the original formal garden on the east side was very much larger with cascades and water canal. It included a rustic sitting area where the unwary could be doused by the turn of a water cock. Moving water moistens and cools the air (perhaps less important in British gardens than in hotter climates) and in Victorian times fountains were back in favour, providing a chance and reason for monumental statuary.

In a small modern garden water pressure (or an electric circulating pump) makes it possible for sparkling water drops to fill the air from a simple concealed jet. Large holes give single water spouts held together by surface tension, while a network of tiny perforations makes a haze of mist. Sometimes the effect we see today is not the original intention. For instance, a fountain jet originally designed with large holes becomes clogged and instead produces a fine spray. At TINTINHULL the fountain has changed its performance in just such a way, and is not easy to clean out, but its subtler effect is also pleasing.

Even the smallest garden where there is no room for any expanse of water surface can safely introduce some water feature. A small electric pump can force upwards a huge jet of water, giving both movement and sound, and, if falling into a surrounding pool, an ever widening series of ripples. Piped water through a hole in a wall can run over a decorative surface or drip over a ledge as in an eighteenth-century grotto, taking up little space yet breaking the silence with its continuous murmur. Monumental sculptured fountains such as the Victorian one at the end of the avenue of limes as the house at CLIVEDEN is approached, or the earlier statue fountains at WADDESDON, may seem to have little relevance for the modern gardener, but the largeness of their scale reminds one how necessary it is to fit any feature into an appropriate space. From visiting these great gardens it is possible to acquire a feeling for the relationships of size which later becomes instinctive. A garden designer is manipulating and making use of space in his basic plan, long before he uses his horticultural knowledge to furnish the garden with plants.

Like all garden features water must be planned appropriately, its scale and relationship to the rest of the garden as important as how it itself is shaped or used. The nature of a garden site generally determines what sort of water is suitable. National Trust gardens, reflecting taste and fashion covering all periods of garden development, give inspiration and guidance. Lessons absorbed from larger gardens, which may be supreme examples of style, simplify decisions in smaller garden areas. Sometimes in a small garden, as at SNOWSHILL, the pleasant gentle sound of dripping water is sufficient to convey an impression of coolness. At TATTON in the Edwardian rose garden steps descend invitingly to a stone balustraded swimming pool combining ornament with use. The raised mirror pool at HIDCOTE was also originally designed for practical purposes as the family swimming pool, a pleasant reminder that often the greatest National Trust gardens were originally for living in as well as for display. Now the circular design where surrounding hedges make dark reflections has become an architectural feature in this famous garden.

——————————— *FORMAL WATER* ———————————

Formal water proclaims artificiality; tanks, canals, rills and pools are contained in geometric shapes, straight lines and curves edged by stone parapets or paving, sometimes steps leading down to the water level, the surface of which gives the best reflections if it is as high as the surrounds. These water features can be near buildings, often constructed on a level terrace, the main feature of a sunken garden open to the sky, or reflecting light and shadow in some secret garden corner. In some gardens water lies as a formal geometric mirror, between grass panels and intensive border planting. At BODNANT a long rectangular canal set in green lawn reflects the eighteenth-century Pin Mill, which faces the raised green theatre at the far end. In the Pool Garden at TINTINHULL, on more modest scale, the rectangular tank 17.5 by 3.7 m (19 by 4 yd) stretches south from a modern summer-house built as a memorial just after the Second World War. Red- and yellow-flowered water-lilies link the dominating 'hot'-coloured border to the west with pale primrose and pastel tints to the east. At KNIGHTSHAYES tall yew hedges surround a centrally placed pool where a silver-leaved weeping pear (*Pyrus salicifolia* 'Pendula'), three stone seats and a statue add to the visual effect. Sometimes stonework alone is linked with a natural river by balustrading high above or by a water-gateway where steps lead to a landing place. At CHARLECOTE PARK Victorian balustrades, recently restored by the Trust, frame curving stone steps descending to the slow-moving Avon (the river was diverted by Brown in the 1750s), as romantically as in any Claudian land-scape, where departing travellers are embarking from the steps of classical buildings. The Trust have plans to restore a simpli-fied version of the elaborate parterres which would have been first revealed to a visitor approaching appropriately from the river. Moving water, canalized, at BUSCOT PARK descends to a lake by low falls and under a bridge through a series of narrow and widening geometric pools, quiet reflection contrasting with constant gurgling sound and movement, just above or below. The designer Harold Peto aligned his formal water garden to stretch down the high hill on which the house stands, carrying the eye across the lake towards a classical temple on the further side.

Aquatics, plants physiologically adapted to airless soil, thrive at varying levels in shallow or deeper water, their leaves and flowers floating on the surface in the summer. Some such plants even have air-ducts which carry air from the water surface to the roots deep below. Sometimes the roots of plants find sites in the mud on the bottom of a pond, but they are more usually planted in containers placed on bricks or masonry ledges. Water-lilies (*Nymphaea*), and cape pondweed (*Aponogeton distachyos*) spread horizontally to contrast with the vertical shapes of irises, rushes and grasses.

True aquatics will only flower and thrive in still water, and cannot survive changes in current and changes in water depth through the seasons. On the other hand, many plants such as Japanese iris (*Iris ensata*, syn. *I. kaempferi*), *I. laevigata* and its variegated cultivar, and the so-called hardy arum lilies (*Zantedeschia aethiopica*), which dislike a position in moist soil where in winter roots become surrounded by frozen water, will survive very low temperatures if roots are safely below surface level.

Ornamental pots containing plants not suitable for growing in water are arranged near the water's edge. Venus' fishing rods (*Dierama pulcherrimum*) a bulbous plant preferring moisture-retentive soil, droops its grassy leaves over reflecting water and is a feature at TINTINHULL. There, its hanging bells in pale almost white to purplish pink tints, are draped over a lily-pond in the predominantly white-flowered Fountain Garden.

When choosing a site for a pool remember that full sunlight encourages algae, but that few aquatics will flower in shade. The formal pool has to become a happy compromise between planting with 'spreaders' such as water-lilies which prevent light reaching into the water depths, and the maintenance of clear areas of reflecting water. Ideally at least a third of the water surface should be clear. All aquatics are oxygenating plants but the most effective in controlling algae are those with very rapid summer growth, which by consuming carbon dioxide and mineral salts, help to filter and clarify the water. Once a balance has been reached, pool gardening does not involve constant attention to spread and density of plants, but most aquatics will need thinning and replanting every few years. The more formal the garden the more essential it is to spend some time removing

At Buscot Park moving water, descending to a naturalistic lake below, was canalized by Harold Peto. Quiet reflections contrast with movement as geometric pools broaden and narrow.

unsightly dying leaves. In a hot summer many large flat water-lily leaves wither and have a very unkempt appearance.

Ornamental fish can only thrive if they have enough oxygen so care must be taken not to clean out the most vigorous oxygenators. If fish appear to gasp, running water from tap or hose pipe will quickly restore a balance. Most plant life produces enough food for fish, bit it is often recommended to give some food before the winter, so that the fish build up a reserve of fat. When ponds become completely frozen across, air-pockets should be made by thawing small circles with hot water; on no account break hard ice as this can be dangerous to aquatic life.

Plants would grow most luxuriantly if the bottom of the pond were covered with suitable soil, but the results would quickly become a tangle of unsightly growth. It is much better to use some form of perforated container, plants then becoming confined to their allotted root area, and easily lifted when soil needs renewing or roots need dividing. Broad-based stable wooden crates with low sides, perforated plastics made specifically for the job, or even hessian sacking containing root balls can all be used. Rich, heavy loam is ideal, but do not add peat or organic fertilizers which encourage algae and pollute the water. The use of weed-killers in ponds is now strictly controlled, which makes it all the more important to choose plants well and wisely at the beginning of a scheme. Over-vigorous water plants can quickly get out of hand, taking over from and killing less stalwart neighbours, and totally spoiling planned effects within a few years.

The lily terrace at BODNANT is dominated by two old cedars, to the north the glaucous-leaved *Cedrus libani atlantica* Glauca Group has sweeping skirts which almost brush the surface of the central pool, and on the south side the more sober dark green cedar of Lebanon (*Cedrus libani*) casts its shade. These two great trees, planted in 1876, had already begun to dominate the steep slopes below the house at Bodnant when the terraces were completed in the years before the First World War. As a result steps and balustrading are aligned not on the house as might be expected, but in such a way as to allow the cedars to give symmetry and balance to the whole architectural scheme.

The lily pond, on the third of a series of five hanging terraces, is reached from steps at the side, and yew hedges are cleverly placed on the outer edge so that the view, even from a higher level, cannot reach into the Pin Mill canal and long herbaceous borders below, but only out to the Welsh hills beyond the garden perimeter across the valley of the Conwy river. Thick planting of evergreen oaks to the north, and deciduous trees to the south of the terrace, further increase a feeling of being in a remote secret part of the garden and, more practically, protect this planting area from cold winds.

The lily pond is a basic rectangle, 33 × 16.5 m (110 × 55 ft), but on its western edge a complete semi-circle, with a radius rather less than half the width of the pool, completes the outline. The design is such that the whole facade of the house above is reflected in the calm surface of the water, and planting of water-lilies and other aquatics is planned to ensure a wide central patch of clear empty surface, with the rafts of floating lilies to either side. The water is 1.5 m (5 ft) deep, its surface almost 20 cm (8 in) below the overhanging coping of large York stone slabs with which it is edged, and the water, fed from the hills above and channelled through a series of canals and basins, is constantly renewed and fresh. An overflow outlet releases the surplus water into the long rectangular pond on the canal terrace below. A round raised pool, with rustic stonework and a shell basin, at the back of the terrace, built against the high retaining walls, allows water to feed the pool along a narrow stone-edged rill, and the constant sound of running water is cool and refreshing.

Much of the planting is done in brick containers on the base of the pool, but plants such as water-lilies which need shallower water grow in wooden receptacles on raised brick supports. On the western edge a stone ledge 60 cm (2 ft) below the coping stone allows more shallow planting to a depth of about 25 cm (10 in) of water, and it is here that the graceful stems of clumps of *Cyperus longus* give some vertical accent in contrast to the floating lily rafts and the horizontal water surface. On a corner a vigorous clump of native flag iris (*Iris pseudacorus*) with vertical sword-shaped leaves and yellow flowers in early summer give interest, but the main planting is hardy water-lilies, placed in varying depths of water to suit the types. The pattern of planting is dominated by the eight squares of lilies in the deepest water. Some have glossy green leaves, others have purple-bronze foliage. The water depth is rather more than that usually recommended in text books, and flowering tends to be later than when plants are in shallower water which heats up early in the season.

The flowers are mainly crimson and pink and include the most brilliant red of *Nymphaea* 'Escarboucle', *N.* 'James Brydon', with maroon leaves and rose-crimson blooms; and *N.* 'Colossea', which bears flesh-pink flowers. There are also some white, cream and yellow-flowered lilies, but these are less striking; planted near the water's edge, they allow the eye to be drawn towards the brighter reds at the centre, flanking the space kept empty for reflections. Each of the main squares which in summer has a spread of approximately 3 m (10 ft) is occupied by 15 plants.

Contrary to what is often said, the climate at Bodnant is quite harsh, and in most winters the temperature falls to as low as −12°C (10°F) and ice 15 cm (6 in) thick forms on the pond. The lowest temperature recorded is −14°C (7°F); combined with a wind of gale force 8, this created a great chill factor, hence causing much damage. In summer during periods of extreme heat algae can build up, but rainfall is high (an annual average of 100 cm or 40 in) and periods of drought seldom prevail long enough for this to cause serious problems. Water remains clean and sweet due to the constant movement and replenishment, but if for some reason the natural water reservoir supply is temporarily suspended, evaporation is very rapid. Fish in the pond are attractive golden orfe and they were selected because they are hardy and have a streamlined shape. They survive periods of a few weeks or more when the water has a 15 cm (6 in) crust of ice; cold is not a problem as long as enough oxygen is trapped under the ice.

Oxygenating weed is kept at a low level in proportion to the numbers of fish and volume of water, since the constant supply of running water provides the fish with sufficient oxygen. In a still pond more of this vegetative plant would be necessary. Water-lily leaves provide shade and keep the fish cool even in periods of excessive summer heat.

The pond is cleaned out approximately every three or four years, in April, before temperatures increase enough to start growth. The bottom 22.5–30 cm (9–12 in) of mud is cleared (and used as a mulch on neighbouring flower beds), the base and sides repointed where necessary and water-lilies and other plants divided and replanted.

Mr Martin Puddle, the General Manager and Head Gardener, treats the operation with military precision. In his family he is the third in succession to hold this position; his grandfather

Frederick Puddle, coming from Yorkshire in 1920, was succeeded by his father Charles, from whom he took command in 1983. Experience and continuity is thus remarkable, and tasks which might be daunting to a newcomer now become routine. Over the years it was established how important it was that the thick rootstock and long tough lily roots should never be allowed to dry out, so the maximum time allowed for the entire cleaning programme is eight days.

Eight men are part of a team, one being in charge of the lower water outlet, where a filter prevents fish being washed away. The plug over the lower outlet is pulled out at 3 a.m. and the water is emptied slowly. As the level is lowered, fish are caught by hand or scooped up in buckets, great care being taken not to allow the bottom mud to cloud the water, and make location difficult. When the level at the lower end is about 15 cm (6 in), fins of the last 50 fish are just visible and they can be easily caught. All the fish are immediately put into other pools, where water-temperature and conditions will be similar. After the fish have been removed the sludge has to be excavated by wheelbarrow and shovel; no heavy machinery can be allowed in or on the edge of the pool. The plants are taken up and covered by plastic bags to prevent evaporation.

The whole surface is brushed in one direction, washed down with hoses and scrubbed with hard bristle brushes before drying out so that any necessary repairs to the base or sides can be effective. Frost and melting ice have usually caused minor leaks and crevices. The large square brick bases are then lined with turf sods, upper surface downwards, and the containers tightly packed with fine loam, given bulk with small chopped turf. The soil is beaten down with wooden hammers, and rammed so firmly that no air pockets can remain, which might later fill with water and 'float' the soil up. The lilies are then split with forks and knives, and are carefully replanted in the top 10 cm (4 in) of soil using a hand-trowel. The pool is filled gradually and the golden orfe returned, breeding rapidly to increase their numbers. Oxygenating weed does not need replacement but appears naturally.

Most National Trust water features were made before plastics existed, and there are expensive maintenance bills when concrete linings crack and edges leak under pressure from an expanding sheet of ice, or from movement of subsoil. Restoration of water canals at WESTBURY, where containing sides were of brick, needed skilled masonry pointing, and few owners today would use materials such as brick if starting from scratch. Actual construction of a formal pool today is relatively simple and inexpensive using modern diggers, and some sort of plastic or fibreglass liner (although these are seldom available in large geometric shapes) is often cheaper and easier to install than traditional concrete. Swimming pool experts now usually use liquid concrete forced rapidly through a tube. Both laminated PVC and butyl synthetic rubber last for many years, and are easily repaired if accidentally punctured. The flexible type of plastic sheet, with folds at the corners can be draped in an excavated hole and its overlapping edges covered with soil and stone or modern composite paving.

INFORMAL WATER

In the eighteenth century the contours of parkland were reshaped to create hollows where rivers were damned and widened to make placid expanses of water in which surrounding woodland and classical temples were reflected. When not fed by natural rivers these lakes had densely planted sides which curved out of sight to hide the furthest shores. In the same way, but on a much reduced scale, the smallest garden pond will simulate reality, and must lie at the lowest point of a garden site to which water would flow of its own accord. The most fortunate owner may have, if not a broad river to be adapted into the landscape, a stream where moving water can be dammed to make quieter pools or canalized to make narrow rills. Rock garden pools can be constructed between slaps of rock making miniature cascades and faster currents, where water broadens out to allow bog and moisture-loving plants to thrive in the damp soil at the edge, and alpines, secure in a well-drained niche, get their roots down to water.

At SIZERGH CASTLE a storage lake feeds a string of rock pools below. Made in 1926 from local Westmorland limestone, the rock garden covers a quarter of an acre, and lies in a hidden trough to the east of the house. Although planting round the edges is planned to look natural, the area is not part of a wider landscape, and except for the use of local stone, bears no relationship to the bleak countryside beyond the park. Originally Japanese maples, small conifers, alpines, and moisture-loving perennials were planted by the pool and today, surrounded by trees, it houses the best collection of hardy ferns in the country (see p.187). Many of the conifers have had to be removed and others have grown to tree size, and the planting covers a wide range of interest. Tall pines which provide shelter from wind cast shade at the back of the pool, and spreading dwarfer conifers and maples make pockets of light and shadow nearer the pond edges, increasing the planting possibilities. This sort of gardening is very labour-intensive and requires a sound knowledge of which plants need moist or comparatively dry conditions. The planting patterns should appear to be natural, some plants making drifts in clefts of rock, others thriving beside the water's edge and following its contours and cambered sides. In some areas dense planting excludes many weeds, but some of the more unusual small plants and ferns need to be constantly handweeded. Also there must always be a continual reshuffling of plant groups to adjust the balance between the 'rompers' and those naturally less vigorous.

Round the water giant-leaved skunk cabbage, both the American *Lysichiton americanus* with yellow flower spathes and the white Asian *L. camtschatcensis*, thrive between groups of primula including *P. japonica* 'Miller's Crimson' and the later-flowering *P. florindae*. Higher on the banks groups of spreading tellima, geranium, epimedium (both *Epimedium rubrum* and *E.* × *versicolor* 'Sulphureum') and *Campanula poscharskyana* are interrupted by ferns among which are hart's tongue (*Asplenium scolopendrium* Crispum Group, syn. *Phyllitis s.* Crispum Group) with goffered edges to the fronds, and the lady's fern (*Athyrium filix-femina*). A pendulous eastern hemlock (*Tsuga canadensis* 'Pendula') weeps above patches of bronze-leaved *Astilbe* × *arendsii* 'Fanal', golden grass and *Asarum europaeum* with shining kidney-shaped leaves. A white-flowered pulmonaria makes a good clump in spring, near the rarer *Glaucidium palmatum* with flowers of violet-lavender. *Oenothera fruticosa glauca* (syn. *O. tetragona*) contributes dark foliage early; later crimson buds open to clear yellow. Tangled mats of saxifrages cling to the limestone rocks, including *Saxifraga umbrosa primuloides* 'Walter Ingwersen'. A group of ostrich plume ferns (*Matteuccia struthiopteris*) is architectural, with hostas, veratrum and sheets of blue omphalodes under a spreading Japanese maple. Rodgersias and day-lilies make large clumps in the moist soil while brunnera and bergenia are massed in drier conditions under a fine specimen of *Pinus wallichiana*. A clump of the now increasingly rare native oxlip, *Primula elatior*, shows the interest of the Head Gardener, Mr Malcolm Hutcheson, in conserving native flora. Willow gentians (*Gentiana asclepiadea*) have seeded everywhere; clumps of royal fern (*Osmunda regalis*), summer snowflake (*Leucojum aestivum*), corydalis and dicentra spread in natural groups. This garden has developed over 60 years; the wealth of botanical interest to be found can be maintained only with constant supervision.

A walk to the east of the third lake at SHEFFIELD PARK has been named the Queen's Walk to commemorate the Jubilee of Her Majesty Queen Elizabeth. Part of this walk is across a swamp, a silted area of lake where alders and other trees had grown into a jungle. A track was cut out and branches of trees cut into lengths which could be lifted by four men using two rope slings. The branches were laid end to end on each side of the proposed path, marking its width. Smaller branches and top growth twigs were packed in between, and then 'plastered' with thick mud and allowed to settle for a few weeks. The surface was then levelled and covered with Sussex hoggin, a sort of quarry rubble containing a high proportion of clay. When laid and rolled, hoggin makes a surface almost as hard as concrete, and will last a long time. A slight sloping camber allows rainwater to drain off.

At SCOTNEY CASTLE garden a moat surrounds the ruins of a fortified castle, which lies in the steep-sided valley below the Victorian house. A dramatic view from the bastion above frames the castle ruins in surrounding trees. Fortunately at the time of the building of the new house by Anthony Salvin advice on the garden was sought from William Sawrey Gilpin, nephew of the Rev. William Gilpin, the author of *Picturesque Tours*, rather than from W. A. Nesfield, brother-in-law of Salvin himself, who loved to design formal Italianate parterres on flat areas near a house. As a result the gardens made in the hanging valley above the old castle and moat are a supreme example of 'picturesque naturalism'. Round the water planting has been enriched with large-leaved exotics and hardy natives, all of which could have been recommended by William Robinson or Gertrude Jekyll. Fortunately both Mr Christopher Hussey and his wife fully understood the true 'romantic' spirit of the place, and Mrs Hussey still manages the garden with the Trust, who acquired the property under Mr Hussey's will in 1970.

A view of the pond made in the 1960s in the walled garden at Wallington by bringing an underground stream to the surface.

On descending from the bastion, the water garden is seen to be in two parts. A small island in one section, previously covered in ponticum rhododendron, was cleared and a statue by Henry Moore (a gift from the sculptor in memory of Christopher Hussey) placed in the centre. Planting near the statue is very simple, yellow and white rhododendrons, and ferns. Drifts of *Primula japonica* 'Postford White', with flowers whorled round the stems, grow by a white-barked birch (*Betula utilis jacquemontii*), a thicket of evergreen *Lonicera pileata* and the creeping grey-leaved willow (*Salix repens*), and a patch of *Persicaria affinis* 'Superba' (syn. *Polygonum affine* 'Superbum') drops down to the water edge. Near by tall swamp cypress (*Taxiodium distichum*) take advantage of the moist conditions, their fresh bright green foliage turning dusky shades of pink in autumn.

Elsewhere round the moat's edge the leaves of gunnera, *Iris pseudacorus*, rodgersias and royal fern make architectural shapes, while king-cups (*Caltha palustris*), forget-me-nots, polygonum and astilbes give flowers in season. There are groves of rustling bamboo and giant lilies (*Cardiocrinum giganteum*) are grouped in the shade. At Scotney plants romantically frame the old castle ruins, which give a domestic perspective to the wooded landscape beyond. The garden is designed to produce a series of pictorial views, where vegetation, water and centrally placed buildings build up a balanced composition, each dependent on the other.

At WALLINGTON the mean temperature for January is 0°C (32°F), but most of the kitchen garden slopes south and east so that water and frost drain away downhill. Many of the waterside plants which do so well at TRENGWAINTON also thrive here, although flowering in the north is probably three weeks later, and the summer growing season (the weeks in which the soil is warm enough for plants to grow and all danger of ground frost is past) much shorter: hence the wood of some plants does not harden sufficiently to withstand the winter. The stream in the kitchen garden at Wallington ran through an underground culvert until 1962, when the Trust brought it to the surface in the upper part of the garden and made a feature of its banks, planting with alpines and small shrubs. The sides of the stream are built up with concrete so plants do not benefit from moisture at their roots. Planting is therefore mixed, since good drainage allows for a wide range, although as much as possible plants are chosen which look appropriate beside water. The stream runs down the centre of the walled garden in a conduit (known locally as a 'cundy'), and recently water from it was used to make a natural-looking pond where aquatics float and the margins are covered with bog plants. **Mr Geoffrey Moon,** then Head Gardener, gives the account of the making of this pond:

✤ When it was decided to make a new pond in a corner of the garden at a low place we did not know exactly where the cundy was located. We knew that parts of it were inside the walled garden because at three places it was open to the sky with steps down so that water could be scooped from a little chamber for watering plants. The cundy carries water from an outlet where the lake in the wood outside the walled garden overflows; in parts it runs under woodland and a field and in parts under the garden.

When we came to excavate the pond in the chosen site we hit right on top of the cundy. Because it is 1.2 m (4 ft) high and 90 cm (3 ft) wide with a curved top it was impossible to get the required 1.5 m (5 ft) for the deepest part of the pond without removing the cundy over this part. This was done and 5 cm (2 in) diameter pipes laid out side by side as a substitute. The water supply pipe was laid in a trench from the nearest open place in the cundy, 10 cm (4 in) plastic pipes being used; a small circular 'well', 60 cm (2 ft) in diameter and 1.5 m (5 ft) deep, was built over the pipe end. This was made of stone, the water filling from the bottom and splashing noisily out of a spout at the top into two small ponds set at lower levels; then into the pond proper. A similar stone well was built as an overflow in the deepest part of the pond with a short pipe into it at the base, fitted with a hand-operated valve for draining the pond, and a pipe leading back down into the cundy.

Sand was laid over the bottom of the excavated area to a depth of 15 cm (6 in) and a butyl sheet in one piece laid out over it. It had to be adjusted to size on site by cutting off the surplus at the narrow parts of the pond and putting in folds and tucks to get it to follow the curves. Plastic bags filled with sand were used at intervals round the edge to hold the sheet in position. The water was turned on and the pond filled; each day the sand bags were lifted and the sheet adjusted so that the pressure of water carried the butyl sheet over the contours of the base and sides of the pond. When the pond had been filled for about a month and was nicely settled, the edges of the sheet were cut again more neatly to size, enough being left to turn about 60 cm (2 ft) into a trench 15 cm (6 in) from the edge of the water.

Two-thirds of the pond is planted with a narrow border around the edge, and the other third, where water and lawn meet, is left so that people can walk right to the water's edge. Plants were placed in the water and in the border; the area around was levelled to match the water's surface and sown with grass seed. After a short time the appearance of the site changed from that of devastation to order and visitors began to walk down to see our handiwork. However, this happy state was not to last. Came the autumn rains and the pipes under the pond were too small to carry the volume of water. Pressure built back into the cundy and the joint between pipes and cundy fractured, causing water to burst through under the butyl sheet, which lifted up so that the pond emptied out and caused a flood lower down the garden. This caused a lot of disturbance to the plants in the pond and in the borders round its edge and it took some considerable time and labour to reinstate them.

The following summer the water surface was progressively obscured with spirogyra, the floating green blanket which grows rapidly in sunlight and despite strenuous raking and chemical treatment it persisted. Came the autumn and again floods fractured the joints under the sheet which was badly torn and had to have patches glued to it. The plants in and around the water had again to be replanted. At this stage we seriously considered abandoning the pond altogether – filling it with soil and making it into a lawn. It was decided to make one last attempt to solve the problem of flooding. We dug exploratory trenches outside the garden wall and found the cundy; from here we excavated and laid big pipes to conduct the flood water away from the pond and down to the River Wansbeck which runs near by. This operation was successful and pond and plant settled down and took on a natural effect.

In 1973 we planted in the water submerged aquatics including *Callitriche stagnalis*, the water starwort (*Ranunculus aquatilis*), *Crassula aquatica* and the Canadian waterweed (*Elodea canadensis*). Floating plants were *Hydrocharis morsus-ranae* and the water soldier (*Stratiotes aloides*). Unfortunately the elodea has grown too successfully and has become a pest, choking the water and harbouring blanket weed. It proves very difficult and costly to remove and impossible to eradicate. The most successful water plants have been the white water-lily (*Nymphaea odorata*) and the yellow-flowered *Ranunculus lingua* 'Grandiflorus'.

Round the edges of the pond we had some problems hiding the butyl sheet which tended to be visible above the water line. This problem was solved by raising the water level 7.5 cm (3 in) by adding stones to the top of the outlet 'well', and by planting with large-leaved plants in the borders so that they would grow right down to the water's edge. Here the most successful are the umbrella plant (*Darmera peltata*, syn. *Peltiphyllum peltatum*), the giant rhubarb (*Rheum palmatum rubrum*), *Rodgersia aesculifolia*, *Ligularia stenocephala*, *Iris pseudacorus* 'Variegata' and the grassy *Cyperus longus*. Where the bank is very steep a shrubby willow (*Salix fargesii*), with stout reddish stems and attractive buds, is decorative in winter. To break up the rather regular outline of the inlet 'well' we have planted the low horizontal-growing laurel *Prunus laurocerasus* 'Zabeliana', which sends out shoots across the stone work.

At Tatton Park, behind the half-moon bridge, a symbolic Japanese garden was constructed in 1910. A moss-covered glade is half-shaded by Japanese maples, and ferns clothe the sloping banks.

In some spots in the borders we have planted the spiny *Berberis wilsoniae* to deter people from walking on the borders to reach the water's edge. In other places for the same purpose we have used bent hazel sticks as hoops, inserting both ends into the ground.

Twenty-four fish, golden orfe, were put in the water and prove to be a great attraction for the 90,000 people who visit the garden every year. 🌿

Today with modern excavators, electric pumps for raising and recycling water and suitable 'liners' or shaped fibreglass containers an informal water garden can be constructed relatively easily. It is all the more important to make sure it is an appropriate feature in any particular garden. Obviously, to appear natural, all artificial edges must be concealed by plants, water or soil: a hint of plastic or fibreglass destroys the natural effect aimed at. Surrounding banks should not be too steep for ease of planting or for access. Gertrude Jekyll, writing at the turn of the century, recommended a substantial ledge beside a pond. Conditions for different sorts of plants have to be planned. Bog plants are like aquatics and need soil permanently saturated and no drainage; their roots are specially constructed to need little oxygen. The swamp cypress (*Taxodium distichum*) as it grows to tree size, throws up 'knuckles' in order to breathe. Other plants love and need moisture, but the soil must also drain freely and it may be difficult to keep the conditions just right all through the year. It is obviously easier to make a 'bog' than provide a damp bed where with open porous soil, it becomes too dry in summer or too water-logged in winter. if the water table is high it may be necessary to raise soil level; if drainage is too good plastic sheeting will hold additional water, and some holes can be cut in it to allow excess to escape. When an artificial pond or stream is made it is difficult to ensure the right growing conditions; concrete edges or soil beyond a container will receive no benefit from the nearby water supply. Suitable moisture-loving plants will not thrive, and other planting looks inappropriate and unnatural beside water.

If space is restricted it is hard to make a water feature that seems to have occurred naturally. Just as planting in or near a formal pool is controlled and architectural, designed to complement and enhance the geometry in a restricted space, a 'natural' pond or lake provides a setting for groups of moisture-loving plants, which appear to grow as they would in nature in the transitional moist area between the water and higher, drier ground. Interesting exotics can be interspersed with indigenous plants which further enhance the natural aspect. Many of these plants which thrive in a temperate climate have large textured leaves, and their luxuriant growth gives a semi-tropical jungle effect, intensified by the smooth contrasting water surface. Gertrude Jekyll's recommendations here are still valid today, and have influenced National Trust gardening styles: 'It is as well as a general rule, in planting wild places . . . to keep exotics nearest to the home end, and to leave the native plants for the further part of the wild.' Giant gunnera, rheum and rodgersias contrast with the spikes of indigenous flags (*Iris pseudacorus*) and its startling variegated cultivar (*I.p.* 'Variegata'). Astilbes, *Aruncus dioicus*, hostas and ligularias are solid perennials which can be planted in broad masses. In acid soil drifts of Asiatic primulas give colour in spring, and in neutral or limy conditions the July-flowering

Primula florindae contributes sheets of yellow. Plants growing on the margins of ponds should be allowed to grow freely and planting should look as unplanned as possible.

At CLIVEDEN the Trust has replanted much of the water garden, using larger areas of each plant group to suite the scale. Enlarged from a duck pond in 1893, the curving stretch of water surrounds a magnolia hillock, reached by a stone bridge where William Waldorf, later the first Viscount Astor, placed a Japanese summerhouse which had been exhibited in the Paris Exhibition of 1867. As in many so-called Japanese gardens of the late Victorian or Edwardian eras, planting was exuberant, making use of the many moisture-loving plants which were then available, rather than concerned with the deeper philosophical and symbolic meanings of the genuine Japanese water garden, such as that constructed in 1910 for Lord Egerton at TATTON PARK outside Manchester. At Cliveden clumps of small-leaved rhododendrons and azaleas make a solid background on the contoured sloping banks, giant king-cups (*Caltha palustris*), flowering also in spring, grow below at the water's edge. Later Asiatic primulas, moisture-loving iris, astilbes, hemerocallis and finally purple loosestrife provide flower and leaf interest through the rest of the summer season.

At TATTON a wide pond called the Golden Brook surrounded by dense woodland, including dark spires of conifers, many of them Japanese species, is densely planted to the edges, azaleas and rhododendrons overhanging and reflected in the water contrasting with the large leaves of *Gunnera manicata* grouped by the pool's edge. On an island that is approached by a half-moon bridge a Shinto temple overlooks the Japanese garden, complete with the Master's tea house on a small central island. Here in a sunlit glade planting is simple and restrained, the moss-covered ground making a gentle carpet beneath spreading Japanese maples. In Japan there are more than 40 different mosses which are recommended in gardens. On the banks at the sides which rise steeply to frame this pocket of sophisticated planting, clumps of the native British royal fern (*Osmunda regalis*), also found growing wild in Japan, and the evergreen *Gaultheria shallon* from North America make a dense thicket.

The garden was built about 1910 by labour especially brought from Japan to erect the Shinto temple. The design incorporates many authentic scenes and is typical of a wealthy lord's garden.

The success of design and layout of a Japanese garden with its intricate rules is perhaps finally proved by the quality of overall peace and natural tranquillity that it creates in the contemplative beholder.

STREAM GARDENS

Quoting Miss Jekyll again: 'A natural running stream, especially if it flows fast over a shallow pebbly bed, with sides either naturally near the water-level or purposely made so, is one of the very best settings for beautiful plants. It can often be so arranged that the path shall cross it from time to time, either by well-set stepping stones or by a simple plank or log bridge. But it is most desirable, especially in places that have a natural character . . . that a wise restraint should be observed about the numbers of different plants that are to be seen at a glance.'

Trust stream gardens with plant associations that can be copied, or adapted easily to a smaller scale, are those of DUNHAM MASSEY, SHEFFIELD PARK, SPEKE HALL, WALLINGTON, and TRENGWAINTON in the mild climatic conditions to be found in Cornwall.

At DUNHAM MASSEY, after clearance of brambles and nettles, the stream-side Bog Garden has received massed plantings of waterside and shade-loving perennials. Mr Peter Hall, the Head Gardener, described the work done in this area of the garden. The banks of the stream had suffered from years of neglect when the Trust took over the property. The 'spring-fed' stream runs more or less from east to west and the south woodlands of oak and birch are still being gradually cleared and replanted. Old hollies, gaunt and disfigured with age, grew along the northern wall, and in many cases have needed rigourous cutting back to force successful rejuvenation. On the southern, more gently sloping, stream edge a few good moisture loving plants remained, surviving between seedlings of oak, birch and rowan and old tree stumps. Brambles infested the whole area and as the ground was cleared and later dug, trailer loads of old brick were discovered and had to be hauled away. Although some of the best specimens of oak were retrained to provide a canopy, most of the tree seedlings were removed. Stumps were excavated and the brambles cut down and cleared away.

The stream itself was cleared out with a mechanical digger, and the sloping banks graded and smoothed down. The ground

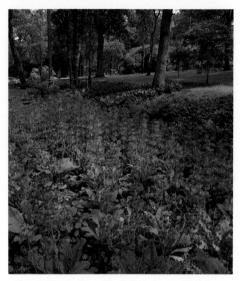

*Streamside planting at Sheffield Park – an old drainage
ditch has been opened up, dams constructed to give
contrasting areas of still and moving water, and hardy
plants make drifts to give flower and foliage interest.*

was first covered with leaf-mould and grass-cuttings from the
lawns, and farmyard manure was incorporated as the soil was
dug and levelled. Following a soil test the area was dressed with
a balanced compound fertilizer and magnesian limestone was
added to increase the lime content (the soil is very acid, as low as
pH 4.2), to supply magnesium and to release other nutrients and
make them available to the plants.

Most moisture-loving plants thrive in light shade and at Dunham, oak, which is relatively 'benign', provide just the right conditions to prevent the soil drying out excessively in periods of
drought, although manures and composts are used as a mulch in
more open sections. This reduces water loss from the sandy soil.

The new planting plans laid emphasis on foliage form, shape
and colour as well as on the more fleeting seasonal flowers. Along
the edge of the stream, existing clumps of giant gunnera were
reinforced with rheum, lysichitum, *Iris pseudacorus, I. laevigata*
and *I. ensata* (syn. *I. kaempferi*) cultivars, and drifts of the royal
fern (*Osmunda regalis*). *Meconopsis* × *sheldonii* provides one of

many bursts of colour during the season – its rich blue poppy flowers are outstanding in late May. A drift of *Salix elaeagnos*, decorative with its rosemary-line foliage, white Rugosa roses and the low-growing evergreen *Berberis candidula*, with shining leaves conspicuously white beneath, mark the corner and screen the stream and its planting from the entrance to give surprise. Herbaceous astilbes, ligularias, cimicifuga and lythrum are planted in wide clumps, and hostas and striped grasses give foliage interest. Along the path edge alchemilla, *Geranium macrorrhizum* 'Ingwersen's Variety', with scented leaves, pulmonaria and hostas thrive where the soil is drier. Since planting, the native bluebell has become invasive and, for this particular problem, digging out by hand is essential. Mare's-tail is a perpetual weed and needs careful spraying with glyphosate. Wiping with an impregnated glove proves practical and effective in preventing the herbicide touching other plant foliage. Other weeding is done by hand, but the soil is occasionally forked or cultivated with a hoe. Most success is achieved by mulching and maintaining a dense covering of foliage to prevent weed ingress.

At SHEFFIELD PARK water is on a very grand scale with Capability Brown and later lakes forming a landscape where native and exotic trees are planted. Nevertheless, some of the details at Sheffield are worth considering for adapting to gardens on less magnificent scales. The rocky falls between two lakes have been repaired with sandstone slabs from the Forest of Dean, which better resist the wear of water and frost than the Sussex stone originally used for its construction in the early years of the century (by Pulhams, the creators of the Wisley rock garden).

To the south of the main garden and lakes, and just beyond the rectangular gentian beds, an area containing many good conifers such as *Abies procera*, *Cephalotaxus fortunei*, *Picea likiangensis* and *Pinus pinaster* had become overgrown with brambles, bracken and sycamore seedlings. Fallen trees lay on the ground. In 1980 the former Head Gardener started a clearance operation, a task mainly confined to winter when time was available from the other more urgent maintenance jobs. During the work an old drainage ditch was discovered and this, with planting along its banks, has made an attractive stream garden. The bed of the ditch was widened and dug out, dams were put in to make contrasting areas of running and calm water, and to give the continual sound of water gently dropping to lower levels. The wood was used from sweet chestnut made water-tight with blue-clay purchased from local brickworks. Once the ground was cleaned and prepared the stream margins were planted with moisture-loving hardy plants to provide foliage interest and flower colour through a long summer season. The hardy arum *Zantedeschia aethiopica* thrives in shallow water and mud. Bulbs of summer snowflake (*Leucojum aestivum*), a British native, make drifts, and interplanted ferns give interest when flowering is over. The giant lily *Cardiocrinum giganteum* from the Himalayas has its emerging shoots shaded and protected by more ferns and is planted in soil richly prepared with well-rotten manure and leaf-mould.

There are many good groups of hostas which include *Hosta fortunei* and *H.f. aurea*, *H.* 'Honeybells', the latter with fragrant flowers inherited from *H. plantaginea*, but with faintly blushed lilac colouring instead of pure white, held above undulating leaves. The very similar *H.* 'Royal Standard' flowers late and has equally fragrant white blushed lilac flower-heads, on 90 cm (3 ft) stems above broad heart-shaped rich green leaves. *H. rectifolia* 'Tallboy' also has lilac flower-spikes, held on 1.2 m (4 ft) stems above heart-shaped fresh green leaves, and is one of the most rewarding and spectacular hostas. Hostas combine beautiful leaves with scented flowers and are effective in massed planting. Although normally quite hardy, they are slow to increase; any division necessary for named forms yields only few plants after a couple of years. The current Head Gardener, Mr Nigel Davis, likes to increase the stock before planting so that he can keep his groups in the right scale and proportion.

Drifts of Asiatic Candelabra primulas such as *Primula pulverulenta* with tiered flowers in pink and mauve spread in the deep acid soil, and plants can be split up to make new groups. *P. bulleyana* has more striking orange flowers. Seedlings of the drumstick primula (*P. denticulata*) are encouraged to mingle between other plants. Mr Davis is also making a collection of varieties of Siberian iris (*Iris sibirica*), which with vertical grassy foliage and tall stems topped with flowers in different blues are planted in the moist soil along the stream edge. Plants planted 30 cm (12 in) apart quickly grow together and make effective ground cover.

At TRENGWAINTON, too, the stream originally ran underground, but it was brought to the surface and planted by Sir Edward Bolitho in 1897, more than sixty years before the Trust received the property. Here, near Penzance, rainfall is high –

often as much as 115 cm (46 in) annually – and the climate is exceptionally mild. High humidity and warmth make perfect conditions for Asiatic primulas and blue meconopsis, yellow skunk cabbage from America (*Lysichiton americanus*) and white from the Far East (*L. camtschatcensis*), and large-leaved rodgersias, many of which were introduced to gardens only in this century, and would have first been grown experimentally in these ideal conditions.

The stream runs down beside the main driveway to the house, and is overhung by a mature planting canopy of old ash, beech and sycamore which was opened up to start the woodland garden in the early years of this century. The Monterey pine (*Pinus radiata*), the Monterey cypress (*Cupressus macrocarpa*) and, since the late 1960s, new windbreaks of Leyland cypress (× *Cupressocyparis leylandii*) have been added for extra shelter as well as for their value as evergreens. As in many seaside gardens (and Trengwainton is only a few miles from the Cornish south coast) wind, and in this case prevailing wind from the south-west, is a major problem. At a lower level the rampant bamboo *Yushania anceps* (syn. *Arundinaria anceps*) was planted to make wind-filtering screens to protect a collection of fine rhododendrons and other good acid-loving shrubs, which would thrive in the mild climate, especially if given a good start. Planted to the southwest of the stream which carries peaty water through a farmyard higher on the slopes of the hill to the north-west, the bamboo also provided shelter for moisture-loving perennials which are placed in great drifts to match the shape of the winding streambed. At some points the banks are steep, at others the bed broadens out so that plants grow at waters' edge, and take advantage of the boggy soil. High humidity suits many of these plants and growth is lush. Near the stream spreading tree ferns (*Dicksonia antarctica*), the even finer-leaved *Woodwardia radicans* and strong spreading clumps of *Blechnum tabulare* flourish well between groups of hydrangea, olearia, rhododendrons and azaleas, together making a textured green backdrop through the seasons for the massed flowers of primula, crocosmia, astilbe, day-lilies and spires of white *Cimicifuga racemosa* in later summer.

In the past many of the bamboo plants have flowered and died, and when clumps have been removed it has been possible to extend the stream garden into a new area to the south-east,

The stream at Trengwainton runs at the edge of
woodland. Planting is luxuriant. In the mild Cornish
climate high humidity and warmth provide the
perfect conditions for exotic waterside plants.

away from the edge of the drive. A pair of the evergreen *Podocar-*
pus salignus frames a view downstream to this newly opened section of woodland. Cascades have been made with flat local stone
which quickly become moss-covered. As light is let in seedlings
of brambles, nettles and docks start to germinate, and these are
sprayed with triclopyr. *Primula pulverulenta* seeds prolifically
and the elegant *Stipa arundinacea* (syn. *Apera arundinacea*) with
soft reddish-brown arching stems and grassy flower-heads
places itself in strategic sites. A new bed has been made in the
woodland for the Chatham Island forget-me-not (*Myosotidium
hortensia*) which needs a very mild climate and plenty of seaweed
mulch. Its bright blue flowers above shining leathery leaves are
worth every horticultural effort; the tender crowns with emerging shoots are protected from rabbits by wire netting.

Further upstream planting is mature and thick clumps often
need dividing and splitting. The moist mild conditions also suit
weeds such as ground-elder and the equally invasive creeping
buttercup (*Ranunculus repens*). Mr Peter Horder, the Head

Gardener, who has been at Trengwainton since 1970, finds that
with today's shortage of much skilled help, his team will
tackle stretches of the planting every few years, rather than
attempting to keep the soil clean throughout the beds; this
is especially true in an infested patch where plants are weak-
growing.

Many of the plants by the steam have striking foliage which
contributes as much to the beauty of the whole effect as the more
fleeting seasonal flower-colour.

Plants include: *Aruncus dioicus*, astilbe, the double and single
king-cup (*Caltha palustris* and *C.p.* 'Flore Pleno'), *Cimicifuga*,
Crocosmia, including the bronze-leaved *Crocosmia* 'Solfatare'
and groups of scarlet-flowered *C.* 'Lucifer', moisture-loving
euphorbia such as *Euphorbia griffithii* 'Fireglow' and red-
stemmed *E. sikkimensis*, *Fascicularia*, many different hedychi-
ums with strongly scented late-summer flowers, hemerocallis in
variety, *Persicaria affinis* 'Superba' and a drift of *Persicaria
campanulata* (syn. *Polygonum capitatum*). Early spathes and later
giant leaves of *Lysichiton americanus* make bold waterside
groups, with effective foliage of rodgersias, darmeras and
variegated glycerias. A clump of *Zantedeschia aethiopica* 'Green
Jade' has grown to 1.2 m (4 ft) in height. *Iris sibirica*, *Libertia
ixioides* and groups of pampas grass in front of healthy bamboos
such as *Fargesia nitida* (syn. *Arundinaria nitida*) add foliage contrast. *Sanguisorba obtusa* has elegant pinnate leaves and bottle-
brush flowers of soft pink in August after many of these plants
have already finished their display. There is a good collection of
kniphofias covering a long flowering season.

Mr Peter Horder writes about the maintenance of the
stream garden:

During the winter we embark on ground preparation of
preselected areas for replanting. The soil is well forked over to
ensure the area is free of perennial weed before applying well-
rotted farmyard manure 10–12 cm (4–5 in) deep. A quantity of
carefully cleaned soil mixed with leaf-mould or peat may be
brought in to top up the areas, then gently firmed according to
the moisture content. A second firming will be given after
raking in a basic general fertilizer prior to planting out primula
seedlings in February and March. The splitting and replanting
of subjects such as astilbes, day-lilies and irises is done between

March and early spring when weather and soil conditions are suitable. Clumps are divided, old rootstocks discarded and the stronger divisions replanted a foot or so apart.

Established plantings will benefit from a light dressing of bone-meal during a moist spell in April. During the flowering season which follows we rogue any Candelabra primula seedlings which have strayed into the wrong group. We favour bold plantings of one variety for maximum effect, just as drifts and blocks are made in the planning of a good herbaceous border. By this time, weeds – hopefully only annuals – are appearing and an early clean through will save a lot of work later in the season. By June and July there may be empty patches where perennial weed is growing strongly enough to be eradicated by weedkillers. Creeping buttercup, couch grass and ground-elder are treated with glyphosate; the deeply rooting horsetail with ammonium sulphamate. The treatment is repeated if necessary in August. These areas must be thoroughly cleared before preparation for planting can be done during the winter. Where perennial weed is found growing among herbaceous plants, they are lifted, split and cleaned before replanting may be carried out.

In mid- to late summer, when water-levels are at their lowest, we repair any leaking water courses and cascades. The water-level is controlled by damming higher up the stream and a grey-black colouring powder is added to the cement so that the alterations are not visible. In the damp climate moss soon forms on the new stonework, especially if liquid manure is brushed on to it a few times. On one side, between the stream borders and a line of shrubs, is a narrow undulating strip of dry shaded ground where little grows well except weeds. Here the area is sprayed with paraquat probably twice in the summer to form a moss-covering. Our stream garden benefits from being fed naturally with liquid manure from the home farm above, but although good for the plants and ensuring lush growth, this can be a problem. A mass of pungent slurry accumulates in the wider pools, especially where there is insufficient moving water, and has to be raked downstream or removed with a shovel. It is too concentrated and thick to be spread around any plant material. While working on the stream-bed it is possible to reduce any rampant growth of plants such as yellow monkey-musk which have invaded the water-courses.

During August and September seed of the Candelabra primulas is collected as it ripens and is sown as soon as possible after gathering. This ensures maximum germination. This is also a good time of year to look at the various plantings along the steam and make notes of any flowering plants which clash in colour with neighbours, and need regrouping in the following late winter or early spring. Most years when the ground is moist, soft or recently cultivated, we have trouble with moles and slugs. Traps and baits have to be used as the creatures soon eat the roots and leaves of the primulas and weaken the root systems of plants around their tunnels.

Dead-heading of flowers through the summer is kept to a minimum; many plants such as astilbes have heads which turn to lovely bronze shades, giving added value during the winter months. In the autumn as well as taking the leaves of beech and sycamore off the main stream, we clear the thickest accumulations from adjacent borders. Then we return to our notes to reflect on the current successes and failures in the stream garden and to plan for the following year. ❧

F E R N E R I E S

It is rare today to find separate garden areas put aside for fern cultivation, yet any north-facing bed which has a reasonably moisture-retentive soil and pockets of dry-stone walling makes an ideal site for hardy ferns (many of them native) or their cultivars. Indeed, in an old neglected garden, ferns can be survivors when other fussier plants have been choked by rampant weeds or died from neglect. In fact ferns will also thrive in more open situations and contribute their delicate lacy foliage as ground cover in the light shade of deciduous shrubs and trees. Some of these natives reach the garden by wind-borne spores. One of the commonest is hart's tongue (*Asplenium scolopendrium*, syn. *Phyllitis scolopendrium*) which will find a place at the base of any wall in sun or shade. Almost evergreen, young fronds are shining and smooth and the only attention it needs is the removal of unsightly leaves in early spring. Many cultivars are 'crested', forms where the point instead of tapering becomes puckered and frilled; others have waved undulating margins. The native soft shield fern (*Polystichum setiferum*) and its cultivars, tolerant of bright sun and heat, will grow in pavement, its roots cool beneath the stone. *P.s.* Acutilobum Group grows to 60 cm (2 ft), with pointed dark green divided fronds, and at NYMANS a fine group of *P.s.* Divisilobum Group, with graceful dark green finely divided leaves, thrives on the edge of a shady bed in the lawn beyond the house.

For the enthusiast the best collection of ferns in any of the Trust gardens is at SIZERGH CASTLE, where they thrive in the rock-pool garden made for Lord Strickland in 1926. This is part of the NCCPG Collection (see Appendix 1) of four genera. Today many of the dwarf conifers and maples planted at that time have grown to spreading dimensions, and the ferns grow in rocky niches between clumps of low-growing small perennials and more delicate alpines. Many have already been mentioned in the chapter on water gardens. Unusual forms of the more common polystichum include the sword fern from North America (*Polystichum acrostichoides*). The rare *Asplenium scolopendrium* Crispum Group, a hart's tongue with undulate goffered fronds, grows beside the lady fern (*Athyrium filix-femina*). A fine group of ostrich plume ferns (*Matteuccia struthiopteris*) is found contrasting with the broad heavy foliage of neighbouring hostas and veratrum. Forms of the native male fern (*Dryopteris filix-mas*) and a dryopteris from Japan, *D. erythrosora*, superficially seem to have little in common except for being of the same genus. Fortunately the Head Gardener at Sizergh, Mr Hutcheson, has labelled most of the ferns so it is possible to learn.

The best-known fern in British gardens is the royal fern (*Osmunda regalis*), another native from damp acid bogs, and thriving along stream edges and by ponds. It is a feature by the lake at TATTON PARK and in the quarry at STANDEN, the leaves colouring to a rich tawny brown in autumn. This fern is surprisingly tolerant of lime, but must not have soil which dries out in summer. Rarer forms of it can be seen at SIZERGH. A maidenhair fern, *Adiantum pedatum*, introduced from North America in 1656, has glossy black stems and the young foliage is a delicate pinkish brown, later turning a bright green in summer and remaining attractive as the leaf browns and dies in winter. It looks exotic but is reliably hardy; it is more likely to die from scorching sun than from low temperatures. Ferns certainly prefer partial shade and some degree of humidity, and grow best in good friable loam. Many will only thrive if the soil is acid, and some need calcareous soil.

Other hardy natives such as *Dryopteris filix-mas* and the more delicately made *Athyrium filix-femina* will thrive where soil is moist, and usually seed freely and need no special attention. The Japanese painted fern (*Athyrium niponicum pictum*, syn. *A. goeringianum pictum*) has glaucous grey lacy fronds and is very desirable, not difficult to grow if it can be obtained.

One of the reasons that ferns are not grown more often is a general lack of knowledge about how to look after and to increase them. Perhaps also the Victorian fern craze of the 1850s has led gardeners to believe that all ferns need the closed humidity of a Wardian case or fern house, while, in reality, many are hardy natives. Ferns do not flower; they produce spores, usually on the undersides of their leaves. These spores drop off, take root, but do not become ferns themselves; instead they produce the seed from which new ferns grow. To save and germinate these spores watch carefully until spore marks become brown, and then collect them in clean paper. Sow them on compost, cover and keep moist and wait for the prothalli, the small heart-shaped growths which have both male and female organs, to appear. As fern fronds develop, pot on into suitable containers. In fact many hardy ferns can be increased by division with a sharp spade, a quicker and easier method than collecting and sowing spores, but only possible if the fern is growing in a bed rather than in the cracks of a wall. When replanting after division the rootstock or rhizome should not be placed too deep; those in the wild generally sit on the soil, pushing down fibrous roots for nourishment. Some ferns such as hart's tongue and the lady fern will produce bulbils on the old fronds; these can be sliced off and pegged down in peat boxes.

Less hardy ferns introduced from abroad grow in Trust gardens on the south Devon coast and in Cornwall. At GLENDURGAN, TRELISSICK and TRENGWAINTON clumps of *Blechnum chilense*, with broad arching much-divided fronds, grow near the tender Australian tree ferns (*Dicksonia antarctica*) which are also to be found at PENRHYN CASTLE, and thrive under the woodland canopy. If happy, this fern tends to spread rapidly and, given a protective mulch, it will survive in quite a severe climate. Coppery when young, the pinnate leaves become dark green and leathery in summer, and often remain so through winter months, needing little attention except for cutting away the old fronds as new growth begins. The walking fern (*Woodwardia radicans)* has arching 1.8 m (6 ft) lighter green fronds, at the tips of which are buds which take root in the right conditions. In places near the stream at Trengwainton it has almost made a colony. In the colder climate of Cheshire artificial heat is necessary for these plants: at TATTON PARK in the recently restored Fern House built by Paxton in the middle of the nineteenth century, both *Dicksonia antarctica* and *Woodwardia radicans* are a glorious sight. Smooth green leaves of agapanthus arch in front of the ferns and behind, clinging to the walls, the little creeping fig (*Ficus pumila*) makes a leafy curtain.

A Victorian fernery has been completely restored at KINGSTON LACY in Dorset. In semi-shade winding paths run between raised beds contained by dry-stone walling. In each bed separate groups of hardy ferns grow in new topsoil. This fernery also houses a National Collection of *Anemone nemorosa*. At CRAGSIDE ferneries are one of the features of the formal garden, laid out in the high Victorian style, which was acquired in 1991.

ROCKERIES

A true rock garden, envisaged as a site for growing small mountain plants which need good drainage and simulated mountain conditions, is expensive to make and labour-intensive to keep. Today a modern alpine gardener is more likely to give these small colourful flowering plants the conditions they crave by building raised beds or 'screes'. The soil is specially prepared for those plants which come from limestone mountain ranges or for those which come from areas of non-calcareous rock. The soil is contained by dry-stone walling, railway sleepers, blocks of tufa (or peat for raised peat beds), and outside troughs, all of which can be wholly or partly protected in winter by glass or polythene lights. The alpine enthusiast will have a greenhouse with temperature and ventilation adjustment to provide almost perfect growing conditions.

Some of the earlier rock-work creations were bizarre attempts to simulate the landscape from which these plants derived. From a visual as well as a practical point of view it became apparent that rock-work was among the more difficult types of garden scenery to design and execute successfully. At Lamport in Northamptonshire Sir Charles Isham built a north-facing rock garden in 1848. Its south front was a vertical wall over 6 m (20 ft) high; its north face a steep slope with miniature crevices, rocks and chasms simulating an alpine hillside where dwarf conifers, ferns and ivy were grown, but few flowering alpines would thrive without the intense light of their own habitat. Stone gnomes were the forerunners of today's plastic dwarves. In the second half of the nineteenth century an amazing landscape was constructed at Friar Park, including a miniature Matterhorn and glaciers.

Many of these early attempts were haphazard as sites for growing plants, only occasionally acknowledging the special needs of alpines. (Just as often they were frankly intended as landscape features, designed to evoke the sublime and awesome effects of mountainous terrain.) These mountain plants need to be both dry and freezing in winter (usually covered with snow). The temperate lowland garden is in general too damp and too mild, and average garden soil is often slow in draining and too rich in nutrients. At the beginning of this century the greatest rock-garden expert was Reginald Farrer, and his advice on construction and alpine growing still has much to offer today. He recognized that many other plants from all regions of the world would benefit from the same garden conditions as were required by plants from the Alps. He stressed the importance of so constructing a rock garden as to make it look as natural as possible. His famous dicta on 'almond puddings' (spikes and pinnacles of limestone as at Friar Park), 'dogs' graves' (puddings with stones laid flat), and 'devil's lapful', where cartloads of bald square-faced boulders were dropped about anywhere, are often quoted. In the twentieth-century rock garden, rock should be tilted backwards into the slope, with the largest surface to the ground, all nooks filled tightly with soil (so no questing root could find a vacuum and starve), and only a half or less of the rock showing above soil level. In the Alps and similar terrain, moisture is abundant yet sharp light grit allows good drainage: a foundation layer of clinker (or similar materials), topped up with stone chippings and a light sprinkling of loam and soil creates comparable conditions. More alpines die of defective drainage, water freezing round their crowns in winter, than from any other cause. To further simulate conditions of a natural mountainous habitat an underground water-pipe with minute perforations could be set at least 30 cm (12 in) below the soil, and water introduced.

Although Farrer recommended that a rockery should appear as a natural feature at the edge of a shrubbery, he also stressed the importance of sun and wind, and that shade should come from the rocks and not from overhanging trees. Over the years since some of these great rockeries were constructed, trees and shrubs have grown and much of the area is heavily shaded. Fortunately, although the small alpine flowers no longer thrive in these conditions, other plants such as ferns and the dwarf rhododendrons are in their element.

Nevertheless, where the Trust has inherited a craggy Victorian rockery – even of the kind deplored by Farrer – its policy is to conserve it in the spirit in which it was made rather than to convert it to the modern taste. At CRAGSIDE in Northumberland Lord Armstrong created, at the end of the last century, one of the greatest rockery–pleasure grounds ever made in these islands, partly by using the natural outcrops and partly by skilful construction to create the effect of tumbled disarray on a gigantic scale.

The scale of most of the rock gardens in Trust properties is much too great for easy adaptation to a garden of restricted size. Yet in many of the gardens a rockery area has evolved for reasons not strictly to do with providing conditions for growing alpines successfully. Sometimes a rockery has been established in the quarry first excavated to provide building stone for the house, as at COLETON FISHACRE, STANDEN, KILLERTON and SCOTNEY CASTLE. John Coutts, Head Gardener at Killerton between 1900 and 1909, before he left for Kew where he later became the curator, was responsible for clearing the quarry of old cherry laurel and planting interesting alpines and acid-loving small plants, suitable for shade. Today the quarry garden has been restored and replanted with a mixture of sun-loving cistus, helianthemums and ceanothus. At STANDEN the rocky dell behind the house where ferns thrive in shade beside a pool is called the Quarry Garden and was made when the sandstone hillside was quarried to provide stone for the house.

Most gardens in the hands of the National Trust are those which have been acquired as the surroundings of a house of historical importance; in a few cases the garden itself has been of such interest that it merited preservation regardless of the house itself (indeed, in some cases such as at SHEFFIELD PARK, house and garden are now separately owned). In either case the Trust inherits a duty to keep the garden as nearly as possible as it was in its heyday, both for historical continuity and also quite deliberately to stress the history of garden design and plant introductions. As in all old properties, different layers of history become interwoven, successive generations of owners imposing the gardening fashion of their time on what was there before. The Trust has constantly to balance opposing interpretations of style against increasingly high cost of upkeep and the need to preserve a garden as an example of its period. Rock gardens are very labour-intensive to create, especially when they are made from stone specially imported in to the garden, and the Trust policy is rather to restore old ones than to create new features. The Trust cannot afford to expend countless man-hours in growing 'tricky' plants which need special conditions, but vast drifts of ground cover quickly lose scale with existing rockwork or even hide it. It is a question of selecting plants that are neither fussy nor invasive, but are fairly dense and weedproof. Their scale and character should be appropriate for their site, and they should contribute variety and interest.

Fortunately among Trust properties are some with important rock garden areas which were developed just at the turn of this century and reflect the contemporary style and affluence. At WADDESDON MANOR a natural outcrop was moved and used as the basis of a rock garden, built of artificial 'Pulhamite' stone by the famous Pulham firm from Bishops Stortford. At SIZERGH CASTLE in the 1920s T. R. Hayes from Ambleside used local Westmorland water-worn limestone to construct the rocky pool garden mentioned earlier. At HIDCOTE MANOR local Cotswold limestone, unearthed when the garden was being made, was used to make a natural-looking rock bank, thus increasing the range of plants which can be grown, but not restricted to alpines. At ARLINGTON COURT a raised bed acting as a retaining wall links two different levels in the terraced Victorian garden and is attractively planted with heathers and cistus. Filled with suitably draining composts, this type of rock bed, far from interrupting the coherence of design, unites separate garden areas.

At ROWALLANE in Northern Ireland the most spectacular of all Trust rock gardens has been made over the glacier-smooth natural outcrop of whinstone. Here where rock was never far from the surface, cartloads of acid topsoil were added to make planting pockets for Asiatic primulas, silver-leaved New Zealand celmisias, erythroniums, gentians and meconopsis. Small-leaved rhododendrons, heathers, philesias and other acid-loving shrubs give bulk and winter shapes as well as flower-colour later.

Mr Mike Snowden, the Head Gardener at Rowallane, talked about the problems he inherited in an old and established rock garden, and how he continues to tackle them. Planted at the beginning of this century by Mr Hugh Armytage Moore, this rock garden had by the 1970s become infested with perennial weeds. Ground-elder, bluebell and the white wood anemone (*Anemone nemorosa*) grew densely and the soil had become a seed-bank, so that any disturbance brought fresh germination, even when roots and bulbs had been removed. All the plants were taken up, their roots were washed free of soil and they were then stored in a nursery area. New growth of weed-leaves was then sprayed, using a hooded sprayer to prevent drift on to some of the shrubs which were retained *in situ*, with glyphosate, a contact herbicide which works through the foliage to the roots of a plant. Because effects are not immediately apparent, Mr Snowden uses a dye in the mixture so that it is clear which leaves have been sprayed. Later he uses a Croptex glove, impregnated with weedkiller and dye, to touch individual weeds which still recur.

After a couple of seasons the ground was clean enough to start replanting. Hand-weeding is done where residual weeds still appear, but is a relatively simple task. Formerly when weeding was done often only the 'tops' could be pulled off, because of fear of disturbing the root system of neighbouring plants, and much of the good topsoil disappeared over the years to the compost heap. Originally Mr Armytage Moore both excavated the rock, delving down between the natural outcrops where soil was deep enough for planting, and imported additional soil to fill up rock crevices. He also placed a rock or two to fortify a new pocket of soil. Nevertheless the rock garden remains a natural phenomenon, and the bare rock surfaces are as they were when the land was grazing pasture, which still exists just beyond the garden perimeter. The local name whinstone (also used in the north of England) indicates an acid soil where gorse (*Ulex europaeus*) naturalizes. The rock is exceptionally hard, having been exposed during the most recent glacial period when softer limestones were pushed aside. The dramatic effect of the rock outcrop had also become blurred by an accumulation of overgrown 'dwarf' conifers, many of which have now been removed.

*In the rock garden at Rowallane,
New Zealand daisy-flowered
celmisias are a feature in the early
summer.*

In replanting there is no 'drawing-board' plan. Rather, groups are instinctively placed to make the right patterns, and plants given just the depth of soil in which they will do well. No plan on paper could indicate the deep declivities and contrasting areas of shallow soil, or even areas of sun or shadow. Different faces of rock shade sections where Asiatic primulas and dwarf rhododendrons do well, and daphnes and potentillas will flower to extend the season. At the base of the rocks wide groups of self-seeding primulas and monocarpic meconopsis are a distinctive feature. Heathers have been collected on the face of the rocks which look to open countryside, and at the lowest end more dwarf rhododendrons, pieris and ground-covering gaultherias grow tightly together, allowing little space for smaller plants. Pockets of soil in the centre are planted with more unusual plants, and, if necessary, Mr Snowden varies the pH of the topsoil to suit individual types. In places the soil is deliberately maintained as neutral where small herbaceous geraniums will flourish but gentians, maianthemums and celmisias like the acidity. Mulches of leaf mould are applied when possible, but Mr Snowden points out that today mushroom compost, which used to be based on alkaline ground limestone, now contains gypsum and will not make the soil more alkaline. He advises storing it for a year and not using it fresh. Falling leaves are a problem among the rocks, collecting in crannies, and Mr Snowden uses a leaf-blower extended with a length of plastic drainpipe to blow the leaves off the smaller plants and from under heathers.

III

GARDEN

WALLS

A ny wall, whether it is the side of a building or a boundary or compartmental wall, offers a third dimension in planting to serve as a frame or backdrop to the garden proper. The presence of a wall has an effect on local conditions and both extends and limits the choice of plants in its vicinity. Subdivision into separate enclosures and compartments, many of them walled, paradoxically gives even large Trust gardens a great deal in common with many ordinary domestic private gardens. The majority of town gardens, for example, are rectangular in shape and much of the planting is on the walls of any adjacent buildings. A town gardener, therefore, may draw much inspiration from wall planting schemes found in the larger Trust gardens: aspect and suitability, which dictate planting policies and plant choice, may correspond, even if the scale is widely different.

In decorative terms, wall planting falls into three categories. there is the 'architectural' planting, when foliage plants act visually as buttresses or grow in a bed at the base of a wall to link the buildings to the ground. There is the more ornamental theme (a Jekyll favourite) of softening hard masonry lines with a curtain of foliage. There is the practical role which walls play as supports for espaliers, for example, demonstrating that function and decoration are almost inseparable in gardening. Finally, and more generally, walls and walled enclosures provide shelter and protection for plants, often extending the planting range of the garden.

Walled gardens in classical times developed as an extension of the house, the enclosure being used as an additional room. The walled courtyards round many houses are still treated in this way, and are linked both with the architecture of the house and with the life-style of its occupants. Originally walls were for security and all gardening took place inside them. Gardens attached to ecclesiastical foundations grew mainly culinary or medicinal herbs during the Middle Ages, but gradually areas were set apart for places for retreat, the *hortus conclusus* where arbours and scented flowers offered refreshment. The Renaissance-type gardens of the seventeenth century were still based on a series of enclosures, as evidenced by William Lawson's plan first published in 1618 (but reprinted several times to 1683). The garden, divided into six compartments, provided spaces for completely individual gardening themes, with mounts at each corner from which the countryside beyond could be surveyed. In this sort of garden style raised walks and mounts allowed glimpses of the world beyond the garden walls, but glimpses to be snatched only from the security of an enclosed space. It was not until the eighteenth century that the idea of the garden being part of the greater landscape became accepted in England. Walls were relegated to making enclosures for the functional areas of the garden. By the end of the century, elaborate walled kitchen gardens, often placed some distance from the mansion, were established for fruit, vegetables and for cut flowers and pot flowers for the house. They often also contained decorative flower borders. Those on the grandest scale were run as factories, with a team of gardeners, each one with an allotted role in seed-sowing, fruit and vegetable cultivation and the management of hot-houses. Here tender pot plants were kept in winter and cuttings from the tender bedding plants were housed for the twice yearly change-over in Victorian schemes.

The Trust has inherited many such large walled gardens, which were built to provide for the great house and the numerous servants attached to it. Today fruit and vegetables are uneconomical to produce when employing paid gardeners, and few actual kitchen areas are open to public view. The sloping vegetable area at UPTON PARK still grows its early crops and there are vegetables to be seen at BARRINGTON COURT, FELBRIGG HALL and CALKE ABBEY. At BUSCOT HOUSE the old walled garden has been restored and replanted with trees, covered walks and borders. In several cases walled gardens have been largely converted for economy into ornamental orchards with climbing plants on the walls, for example CLUMBER PARK, LACOCK ABBEY and OXBURGH HALL. At GREYS COURT there is a walled small ornamental, vegetable garden. The transformation of the walled kitchen garden at MOTTISFONT ABBEY to house the National Collection of old (pre-1900) roses is mentioned in Part II. Elsewhere there has been an even more abrupt change of usage within the walled areas: at BASILDON PARK, CLIVEDEN and MONTACUTE HOUSE the walled gardens proved to be conveniently sited for car parks.

By the end of the nineteenth century, in a return to the spirit of the Renaissance, architects again saw the ornamental garden as an extension of the house, designing a series of outdoor rooms divided by walls and hedges. This framework provided the perfect setting for 'cottage-type' informal planting, where hardy plants as advocated by William Robinson and Miss Jekyll were used to furnish the rooms abundantly and to soften hard lines of clipped hedges and of masonry.

WALL PLANTING

In a walled garden the vertical surfaces covered in climbing and trailing plants displaying ornamental flowers and foliage or more utilitarian espaliered fruits become curtained backdrops to planting in the beds beneath. When a garden is a series of enclosures in this way, the second side of the wall provides further planting space, but with distinct differences in aspect on either side, offering conditions to suit a different selection of plants. the gardener needs to take into account the special growing conditions that may prevail near any wall: perhaps a favourable microclimate where plants whose hardiness is doubtful will be able to thrive; possibly problems of wind turbulence, rain shadow or increased alkalinity. Plants can be chosen to suit the site. South-facing walls provide sites for tender sun-lovers and bulbs which need hot dry soil. The north side of a wall suits shade-lovers, although if the prevailing wind is south-westerly, the wall often acts as a rain shadow and the soil can be very dry at the base. The soil at the base of a wall also tends to alkalinity since mortar chippings add lime. In full sun this sort of poor soil suits plants such as the Algerian iris (*Iris unguicularis*), and many South African bulbs revel in the heat. The shady side provides a site for the ferns that do not need a lot of moisture, and for plants such as Lenten roses (*Helleborus orientalis*), if plenty of humus-making organic material is added. East-facing walls which receive the early morning sun should not be planted with spring-flowerers, since frozen buds will be damaged by the quick thaw after a night of frost: camellias and tree peonies are obvious examples.

Exploiting to the full the planting potential of a walled enclosure – such as an old kitchen garden – can be a plantsman's paradise, especially when the garden is in one of the more favoured regions. Even in colder inland northern and eastern areas differences of aspect expand the planting possibilities. At BENINGBROUGH HALL, for example, the old walled kitchen garden has been redesigned in a relatively labour-saving layout, with a refreshingly uncluttered atmosphere. It is now sown with grass

*In a border at Felbrigg spring peonies and summer lilies extend the
season of flower under a brick wall. Box hedging hides the
untidy base of the lilies as they come into flowering.*

and is used for events and as an informal play area for visitors. A
central alley is formed where the original espalier pears which
once lined the path are now trained to meet as archways. Against
high walls ivies, climbing hydrangeas, vines and hops with
golden leaves (*Humulus lupulus* 'Aureus') are systematically
arranged. Trained into fan-shapes, they act as flat green butt-
esses in architectural symmetry along the walls. Figs grow in full
sun on the south-facing top wall and a glossy-leaved cherry laurel (*Prunus laurocerasus*) occupies the shady corners. White
painted seats are arranged in a regular pattern. Outside the bottom wall plants which prove tender in this east Yorkshire garden
have been given a protected site: facing south, bay, ceanothus,
choisyas, jasmines and *Actinidia deliciosa* (syn. *A. chinensis*) take
advantage of reflected heat from the high walls.

At ROWALLANE the walled garden formerly used only for
kitchen produce, fruit and as a nursery area for young plants
going later into the woodland was gradually filled with exotics by
Hugh Armytage Moore and over the years has developed into an
interesting ornamental area. Herbaceous borders with shrub

roses and fuchsias, a blue and yellow garden and fine shrubs have grown into tall specimens against the walls. Until recently a *Cupressus torulosa* 'Cashmeriana' with blue-grey foliage carried on pendulous branches survived in a corner. Large hoherias, many magnolia and hydrangea species, *Pileostegia viburnoides*, the climbing *Schizophragma integrifolium*, *Drimys winteri* and *D. lanceolata*, *Itea ilicifolia*, and tender escallonias all grow here. Now mature, these plants, many of which are evergreen, have to be pruned hard, or in time their canopies will completely shade the planting beds below, where meconopsis, double-flowered colchicums and *Celmisia holosericea* from New Zealand give a good display. A National Collection of penstemon cultivars is now held here.

Incidentally, the walls date back to the 1860s, when they were built by the Rev. John Moore, who had recently bought the property. He devised a unique method of plant support, incorporating bands of projecting tiles pierced with holes to which to tie the plants – originally conventional kitchen-garden fruit but nowadays ornamental shrubs. These tiles are now getting old, but some replacements have been obtained in a modern version of Kilmarnock glazed bricks. Elsewhere at Rowallane special wall ties are used which are forged in a smithy near Lanhydrock.

At PENRHYN CASTLE in North Wales the sloping walled garden at some distance from the castle has a formal parterre on the upper terrace, and the walls give extra shelter to the tender plants that grow well there: spring-flowering *Clianthus puniceus*, lemon-scented verbenas, *Pittosporum eugenioides*, *Vitis vinifera* 'Purpurea', *Drimys lanceolata* (syn. *D. aromatica*) and smaller plants such as a selection of osteospermum. There are mixed borders at the base of the walls. Other good plants include fre-montodendron, *Solanum crispum*, various ceanothus, *Corokia virgata*, *Smilax aspera maculata*, and by the entrance gate for its scent in spring, *Azara microphylla*. In shade the coral plant (*Berberidopsis corallina*) produces its deep crimson flowers in late summer, and *Distylium racemosum*, with glossy leathery leaves, has petalless flowers in April.

At COLETON FISHACRE in the milder west-country climate near Dartmouth, where the woodland garden slopes down to the cliffs above the sea, the walled garden gives extra protection for tender plants. **Mr David Mason**, describes the planting:

❧ The garden at Coleton Fishacre was begun in 1925, while the house was being built for Rupert D'Oyly Carte (whose father Richard was the famous impresario). The architect, Oswald Milne, was a pupil of Lutyens, and both house and garden architecture show a strong Lutyens influence, which often leads visitors to wonder if Miss Jekyll was responsible for the planting. Not so; the landscape architect Edward White (who among other achievements was involved in the design of the rock garden at Wisley) was in some way that is not clear from the archives concerned with the initial design of the garden; Lady Dorothy D'Oyly Carte herself was largely responsible for the actual planting. The garden diary she kept shows a progression from fairly commonplace familiar shrubs and trees to a more adventurous approach, as, no doubt, she began to appreciate the climatic and edaphic potential of the site.

As in any coastal garden, the first requirement was shelter, and while the massive belts of pine were still small the garden was very exposed to violent sea winds. In these early days the walled rill garden, with its typically Lutyens central watercourse, must have been almost the only part of the garden sheltered enough for very tender plants. This symmetrically designed garden slopes gently, so that the narrow stone-lined rill drops over a series of small falls, filling the little garden with the sound of water. It is in effect three-sided, with walls facing roughly south, north and east. The north-facing wall, shady yet warm, offers ideal conditions for plants of Chilean origin, and both *Mitraria coccinea* and *Berberidopsis corallina* do well and flower freely. Camellias, too, appreciate these conditions – all too well, as they have grown far too large and have to be severely cut back. They provide additional shelter for a newly planted *Jasminum floridum*; other north-wall plants include *Lonicera tragophylla*, *Aconitum hemsleyanum*, with *Dicentra macrocapnos* scrambling through shrubs and displaying its beautiful yellow pendant flowers.

The upper, south-east-facing wall is occupied by two vast wisterias, to which has been added *Datura sanguinea*, *Cestrum elegans*, *Lilium lancifolium* and *Abutilon* 'Cynthia Pike' – a harmony of soft colours in the yellow-orange-red range.

The long south wall was originally the home of *Mandevilla suaveolens*, now surviving, and thriving, only on the house walls, and of *Wattakaka sinensis* with a campsis and an enormous *Feijoa sellowiana*. In place of the mandevilla is planted *Araujia sericofera* and the beautiful Chinese *Buddleja lindleyana*, both growing strongly. Other uncommon plants include the Australian *Hibbertia aspera* and *Melaleuca ericifolia*, the Mediterranean *Coronilla valentina glauca* 'Citrina', and from New Zealand *Clianthus puniceus* with its red parrot-bill flowers in spring. Several unusual hedyciums including 'Tara' and 'Stephen' are scattered under the shrubs taking advantage of the wall's shelter.

The symmetrical beds on either side of the rill are planted in soft pastel colours with an unusual collection of predominantly half-hardy perennials including *Argyranthemum* 'Sark' and 'Wellwood Park', a floriferous single pink; *Osteospermum* 'Silver Sparkler' and 'Carrington Katrina'; *Salva leucantha, S. uliginosa*, and the low-growing, soft-orange *S. oppositifloria* for the front of the border. Adding contrast are the silver-foliaged plants, such as *Gazania* 'Green Beauty' and *Senecio cineraria* 'Ramparts'. In the centre of the beds is a clump of *Canna iridiflora* with its large green leaves and soft plum-pink flowers hanging above the massed plantings, with the lilac blooms of the Mexican *Dahlia merckii* in attendance. ❧

Further west, in Cornwall, the walled bays at TRENGWAINTON, which were originally built for fruit and vegetables, now overflow with rare tender plants. Wall shrubs, climbers, bulbs and perennials, many from the southern hemisphere and introduced only in this century, have grown large and present an exciting collection to the plantsman. These walled areas and sloping walled vegetable beds (see below) were constructed in 1820 to allow the maximum heat from the sun's rays striking the 45-degree slope to stimulate production of early crops; today those in the lower garden walled area are planted only with ornamentals. Mr Peter Horder, the Head Gardener, points out that over the years many of the trees and shrubs have grown to shade sun-loving tender perennials, so since 1980 these have been moved into an open central section of the inner gardens, part of a new scheme of development. Here the collection has been augmented with a wider range of tender, and above all, later flowering subjects, which contribute interest when spring and summer displays are over. Mr Horder adds that the earliest planting of ornamentals dates from 1910 and includes *Podocarpus salignus*; *Magnolia campbellii mollicomata* was planted in 1926. However the majority of the planting, now mature specimens, has been done since the 1940s. He finds that although sheltered from winds, these walled areas are frost pockets, 15 degrees of frost having been registered on a few occasions since he became Head Gardener in 1970. When planting, care is taken to site tender plants in the higher beds and banks, preferably where the morning sun does not reach the buds while the frost is still on them.

It is hardly possible to include a full list of the interesting plants at Trengwainton, but the names of a few will stimulate interest.

Climbers include *Trachelospermum asiaticum*, a cultivar of the Chilean lapageria, *Lapageria rosea* 'Flesh Pink', *Berberidopsis corallina*, *Pileostegia viburnoides* and *Senecio scandens*. Asiatic magnolias include the *Magnolia campbellii mollicomata*, *M. nitida* and the related *Michelia doltsopa* with fragrant multi-petalled white flowers. Evergreen olearias from New Zealand, Tasmania and the Chatham Islands include *Olearia furfuracea*, flowering with daisy-heads in August, forms of *O. phlogopappa* and particularly the hybrid from Tresco, *O.* × *scilloniensis*, and *O.* 'Henry Travers' (*syn. O. semidentata*) with lilac daisy-flowers in June. *O.* 'Zennorensis', a hybrid of the rare *O. lacunosa*, which also grows here, and *O. ilicifolia*, which thrives on shady banks in the woodland at Trengwainton, has remarkable sharply toothed leaves and stalks covered in brown tomentum. *O. virgata lineata* has wiry linear leaves carried very densely to give a grey cloudy effect, and although seldom seen is one of the hardiest of this ornamental genus.

Evergreen shrubs given the benefit of wall protection include *Abutilon* 'Kentish Belle', *Buddleja lindleyana*, *Cassinia leptophylla*, *C. l. vauvilliersii albida*, *Cestrum elegans*, *Cleyera japonica* 'Fortunei' with marbled grey-green polished leaves, and *Rhododendron maddenii crassum* and *R.* 'Fragrantissimum'. Ginger-plants include *Hedychium densiflorum* and *H. greenei*, and echiums such as the tall *Echium pininana* seed freely. *Rhaphithamnus spinosus*, a shrub rare in the British Isles but which flourishes at Tresco in the Scillies, has turquoise flowers and fruits.

Callistemons, clethras, tender escallonias and eriobotrya, *Dodonaea viscosa* 'Purpurea', eucryphias, fuchsias and myrtles combine to give the effect of semi-tropical jungle.

In the new garden beyond the inner wall, an *Acacia cultri-formis* has been trained back against the wall where it benefits from the extra heat. Tender salvias, *Hedychium forrestii*, *H. gardnerianum* and *H. thyrsiforme* (normally grown in the heated greenhouse), kniphofias, *Lobelia tupa*, white and blue-flowered agapanthus and the large strap-leaved *Wachendorfia paniculata* all do well. Various species of eucomis give interest in late summer, and the sword-shaped leaves of New Zealand dwarf phormiums provide a permanent architectural element. Over the corner of an old rock garden an impressive clump of royal fern (*Osmunda regalis*) has formed a massive root system. A red sedge (*Uncinia rubra*), and golden-variegated *Hakonechloa macra* 'Aureola' give leaf colour.

The National Trust found no garden existing at MOSELEY OLD HALL when it acquired the property in 1962: the partly walled enclosure at the front of the house contained only an old holly standing by the front door, and some of the lilacs which are seen today. Since the future Charles II sheltered at Moseley after the Battle of Worcester, garden features on a period theme were chosen as the basis for the reconstruction. In various parts of the garden contemporary style is manifested in the wooden arbour, knot garden and other features described in the appropriate places in this book.

In the recreated walled garden, box specimens clipped into finials and spirals which rise from the grass are typical of the seventeenth-century passion for topiary. In two rectangular beds groups of *Hypericum androsaemum* with bright red berries are surrounded by low hedges of germander (*Teucrium* × *lucidrys*). Lilacs and old shrub roses occupy the corners and give height, and honeysuckle clambers on the walls. Only plants that Charles might have found here in 1650 have been used in the borders, which were replanted in 1984.

Walled enclosures often have problems from wind turbulence. Wind, perhaps funnelled through a narrow opening, strikes the solid masonry and bounces off again making strong currents which are very damaging to plants in the vicinity. Moving air tends to rise above or go round any obstacle in its path, increasing its speed close to the highest point or at the sides. On the lee side of a wall there will be more shelter, and turbulence produces swirling effects which can pull climbers down or rock established plants. Thick dense hedges will have almost the same effect as walls; the ideal barricade filters and diffuses the strength of the wind, providing sheltered areas on the lee side, where the speed of the current is much reduced. For gardening the optimum reduction of wind speed and turbulence is provided by screens with a ratio of about 60 per cent solid material to 40 per cent space; obviously it is difficult to measure density of hedges, but the general principle is easy to grasp.

A small walled garden such as that of the Chapel Garden at CASTLE DROGO, first designed and planted by Dillistone in the 1920s, is particularly vulnerable to wind currents. The sunken garden under the west walls of the house is reached by narrow entrances down steep granite steps. The house with its main terrace is situated on the eastern edge of Dartmoor above a precipitous slope to the river Teign, where it is exposed to the full force of south-westerly gales. Some of the original planting of evergreens remains, but in 1985 rose and lavender beds were renewed and the small lawn completely reseeded. The beds were treated with dazomet against rose replant disease. A glossy-leaved *Magnolia grandiflora* 'Exmouth', with *Garrya elliptica*, is trained back on strong wires against the stone, and there is a very large *Camellia* 'Adolphe Audusson' close by. In the sunniest spot an old fig has been replaced. Ivy clings to the north-facing chapel wall and *Viburnum plicatum* and *Chaemomeles speciosa* 'Moerloosei' grow well.

The roses in the more open flower beds were all chosen for their wind resistance and to smother the ground quickly. They are all suitable for growing in restricted beds or even in containers. More robust and taller than miniatures, they grow to 60 cm (2 ft): at this height, they withstand the gusts of wind that so often destabilize rose bushes. Most are of recent introduction, but an old variety dating from 1910, 'Yvonne Rabier', is on the right scale. It is of Polyantha type; vigorous, and with scented flowers, it will perform all summer if regularly dead-headed.

The new rose planting echoes the original Dillistone colours. The modern red and pink roses in the Chapel Garden are now introduced in catalogues as Patio types. 'Robin Redbreast' has dark red flowers with a yellowish white eye and bears its blooms in dense clusters, and 'Petit Four' has clear pink semi-double flowers carried all through the season from June onwards. In the more open bed, clumps of 'Petit Four' and 'Robin Redbreast' alternate with low-growing lavender, *Lavandula angustifolia*

'Hidcote', and box bushes framing steps and stonework. On the southern side more lavender bushes separate large groups of pink 'Petit Four', which surround clumps of the old double white rose 'Yvonne Rabier', mentioned above.

The National Trust is fortunate in owning houses which vary in size from the massive Elizabethan to the more modest elegant eighteenth-century, and even to quite humble cottages. Plants which grow upon the walls or in beds against the walls should match the scale of the building. The twining honeysuckle, jasmine and rambling roses appropriate to a cottage porch will look ridiculous on 18 m (60 ft) high stone and brick walls. Similarly bushes grown against these imposing walls, or in the beds at their bases, must match the scale. Strong evergreen shapes against the lower walls act as living and growing buttresses, and anchor a building securely to its site. Just as a house on a slope needs a flat terrace on which it can visually rest, so a great house benefits from dense-growing architectural plants which seem to prop it up. At PENRHYN CASTLE Virginia creeper grows on the west side, but elsewhere the masonry is kept clear of planting. At GAWTHORPE HALL a narrow border at the base of the house walls is filled with evergreen shrubs which will create a solid base as they grow together. They include mahonias, the dense-leaved small cherry laurel (*Prunus laurocerasus* 'Otto Luyken'), evergreen berberis, *Euonymus fortunei* 'Coloratus', and low-growing periwinkle (*Vinca minor*). Rounded leathery leaves of bergenia and dark-foliaged *Euphorbia amygdaloides robbiae* spill over the edges of the beds.

Mounded yew topiary shapes match the architecture at CHIRK CASTLE and provide protective wings to stabilize the building. Behind these, climbers reach up the wall to flower in profusion in the light. *Hydrangea anomala petiolaris* becomes a dense host plant to intertwining honeysuckle which would look too fragile on its own. At both ICKWORTH and THE VYNE, elegant old plants of the evergreen *Phillyrea latifolia* fill in space near the walls of the houses. Unfortunately very slow-growing, which is probably the reason for its scarcity, this is one of the best of small evergreen trees, making either a spreading canopy or responding to clipping into tight shapes.

(Previous pages) At Gunby Hall in Lincolnshire mellow brick walls protect plants from east winds.

At POWIS CASTLE the ancient yews extend the architecture, towering above the terraces on which many unusual plants thrive. Powis does not have a particularly favourable climate, but the moisture-retentive upper south-easterly facing terraces, almost cut out of the pink limestone rock, provide microclimatic pockets where tender plants will grow in the wide beds and against the heat-retaining brick walls. Banksian roses decorate the roof of the aviary.

Mr Jimmy Hancock, the Head Gardener, finds that many tender plants which he grows from cuttings each autumn and keeps in cool greenhouses, using electric fan heaters to remove excessive moisture, all winter can be put out early in the season. On the lower terraces wide borders, edged with box, have unexpectedly moist soil suitable for lush herbaceous perennials, but the exposure to full sun can scorch foliage in summer. In all such terrace planting there is constant revision of border plans as different factors of frost, drainage, exposure and rainfall play their part in affecting the general aspect. Walls provide shelter and reflected heat to ripen wood, yet create rain-shadows close to the base of the wall; terraces provide free drainage for damp and frost, making perfect sites for many tender plants, yet some plants find the southern aspect too hot and welcome an overhead canopy of branches. A gardener like Mr Hancock gets to know the vagaries of his site.

In the lower garden, *Ceanothus* 'Puget Blue' flowers well surrounded by massed planting of Bowles' Mauve wallflower (*Erysimum* 'Bowles' Mauve'). With its grey-green leaves, this bears its mauve flowers all summer if dead-heads are removed and will flower throughout mild winter spells.

In a narrow bed under the south wall of his own house which fronts on a corner of the lower garden, Mr Hancock grows *Billardiera longiflora* (the large purple berries are striking from September onwards), as well as *Fremontodendron californicum*, *Carpenteria californica*, the hardy form of the silvery-leaved *Artemisia arborescens* and *Cistus* × *aguilarii*. The florist's broom *Genista maderensis* survives mild winters here. Lower-growing plants include yellow *Othonna cheirifolia* (syn. *Othonnopsis cheiri-folia*), the silvery-leaved *Convolvulus cneorum*, and *C. sabatius* (syn. *C. mauritanicus*), with its trailing pale blue flowers. Mr Hancock also has a new form of this plant with much darker Oxford-blue saucers. Another Californian plant, *Zauschneria californica cona* (syn. *Epilobium canum*) with scarlet tubular flowers and grey leaves, thrives here, but some less hardy salvias cannot survive the frosts. The dark red shrubby *Salvia blepharophylla* will stand up to −8°C of frost but it is sensible to have cuttings taken in the autumn.

Trees and shrubs which grow large should not be planted too close to a house or garden wall. Poplars, which are deep-rooted but sucker easily, have a bad reputation for damaging foundations. The Trust has often inherited a property where fine old magnolias or other wall shrubs threaten wall stability, even where the fundations are substantial, and has had to sacrifice mature plants. Modern buildings and smaller houses are at even greater risk. In general this proves most destructive if the soil is a heavy shrinkable clay, from which roots take moisture and cause movement of the substructure.

Unless the plants being placed at the base of the wall prefer poor soil, it may be worth enriching the topsoil, or even replacing it to provide suitable conditions for plants going into a permanent site. Generally it is worth positioning plants at least 45 cm (18 in) away from the wall, rather than immediately against it, and then tying them back to supports fixed to the wall. However, it is possible to take advantage of even a narrow bed separating a wall from the gravel or hardcore surface of a path, since roots will spread beneath this and even benefit from the protection it gives from hot sun.

Climbing plants, except for those with adhesive root pads and those like ivy with aerial roots at the end of each shoot, need some sort of frame or support on a wall. Most having twining tendrils or twining stems which hook on to or twine around wires, trellis, or another plant which becomes its host. Many clematis will grow successfully through the branches and foliage of another climber or shrub. The silver-leaved *Senecio viravira* (syn. *S. leucostachys*) will in a season clamber up through a 2.4 m (8 ft) trellis or into an established climber, but the delicate foliage dies back in winter. The rarer *S. scandens* which flowers in late summer can climb through a spring-flowering ceanothus without harming it. Annuals such as *Cobaea scandens* also climb high in a season if given some initial support. Climbing roses have specially recurved hooks which anchor them to supports or frames.

For most climbers some sort of galvanized wire support (a

gauge of 1.6 mm is recommended), is permanently fixed on the wall and fastened to galvanized vine-eyes driven into the mortar. The wire comes in reels and can be stretched horizontally and vertically over the wall surface. The horizontal wires will usually be about 30 cm (12 in) apart and the vertical wires more widely spaced. The metal hooks or vine-eyes are inserted into a new wall while it is being built, but the Trust often has to repair old walls and drilled holes are needed to fasten these supports firmly and securely into the masonry.

At BODNANT under the south-facing high wall, where greenhouses used to stand, tender climbing and wall shrubs are used to make a backdrop to a wide border. Although near the coast of North Wales, the climate is not as favourable as in many west coast or Cornish gardens, but nevertheless Mr Martin Puddle, the Head Gardener, knows the best spots which will allow the more tender plants to flourish. The wall bed is narrow, a path running along at the back of the border for easy access to shrubs and climbers. *Clematis armandii*, *C. tangutica* and the scarlet trumpet honeysuckle (*Lonicera* × *brownii* 'Fuchsioides') twine on the wall. below them, bushes of shrubby azara, *Piptanthus nepalensis*, *Cytisus battandieri* and *Abutilon* × *suntense* flower in early summer, while the border is full of drifts of scarlet poppy (*Papaver orientale*). Earlier, after a mild winter, the silver wattle (*Acacia dealbata*), the mimosa of florists, is covered with pale yellow fragrant flowers. Callistemons also take advantage of the warm wall where their wood ripens in full sun, to ensure flowering the following season.

At Bodnant the maximum advantage is taken of any factors which contribute to creating microclimatic sites. The steep fall of the ground, overhanging plants and pergolas, and the projecting masonry buttresses which support high walls all contribute. On a lower terrace where white wisteria hangs over the balustrade, *Photinia glomerata*, with mature leaves to 12.5 cm (5 in) long and bright red translucent young foliage, avoids frosts in its position tight against the wall. Schisandras, *Camellia reticulata*, crinodendrons, *Drimys winteri*, lespedeza and *Carpenteria californica* also thrive with some overhead protection from climbers on the pergola. In many smaller gardens some of these characteristics or features exist to be exploited to improve the microclimatic conditions.

Projecting wings give the great south-facing forecourt at

LANHYDROCK three high walls, against which evergreen shrubs are suitably bulky. Camellias are carefully trained back on to wires stretched against the wall. Pruning has to be done carefully to ensure flowering shoots, but when, after flowering is over in late spring, the plants spread jungle-like over the windows, ruthless cutting is in order. In these narrow 90 cm (3 ft) beds under the high walls the soil gets very dry. In periods of drought some of these evergreen shrubs which carry a heavy load of leaves can be reduced in size to prevent excessive transpiration. In the east-facing shady border skimmias are massed, contributing their bright berries by the middle of summer. *Pileostegia viburnoides*, an evergreen climber with self-clinging pads, will reach 6 m (20 ft) in a favourable climate, as here. The flowers are terminal creamy panicles and are useful in late summer when few other climbers give of their best. *Daphne odora* 'Aureomarginata' has scented flowers in spring while glossy-leaved sarcococca species start to flower in the middle of winter. Known as Christmas box, their flowers fill the air with fragrance. In the more sunny narrow bed against the stone walls of the house there is a large *Magnolia grandiflora*, also pruned back rather than permitted to make a 'bushy' shape. Besides encouraging flowering, pruning exposes more wood to the sun, and it hardens off to give frost protection. Potentillas in shade and hebes in sun give summer colour.

At TRERICE, not far away from the Atlantic north coast of Cornwall, a small sixteenth-century manor house retains its early walled and terraced enclosures. The alkaline soil conditions are comparatively rare in Cornwall, and lower rainfall – only 90 cm (36 in) instead of the average of at least 112 cm (45 in) in the gardens on the south Cornish coasts, makes this one of the few Cornish gardens where the style is not that of informal woodland. Rhododendrons, camellias and other acid-loving exotics do not thrive, but the mild climate and raised terraces encourage more Mediterranean-type planting.

In the sheltered and sunny wall borders, silvery-leaved *Convolvulus cneorum* and cistus are massed above creeping spurge (*Euphorbia myrsinites*), with glaucous leaves and sulphur-yellow flowers. Prostrate rosemaries, usually more tender than the type and vulnerable in more inland gardens, trail down terrace walls. Fuchsias are interplanted with *Prostranthera cuneata*, *Euphorbia* × *martinii*, *E. amygaloides* 'Rubra', *Geranium tuberosum* and *Ajuga reptans* 'Atropurpurea' in a narrow bed alongside a broad raised walk or bowling green. Pyramid-shaped *Drimys lanceolata* bushes are repeated in a regular pattern beside a wall. Abutilons, figs, *Abelia floribunda* and the mauve-flowered potato, *Solanum crispum* 'Glasnevin', cover stone walls in sun with flower and foliage, each separate walled or terraced enclosure planned as a definite colour scheme. A modern fern-leaved rose 'Helen Knight' has been trained on one side of the projecting porch. Mr Derek Chapman, the Gardener-in-charge, uses good ground-cover plants to suppress weeds. Forms of comfrey such as *Symphytum grandiflorum* and the less vigorous lamiums such as *Lamium* 'Beacon Silver' fill in gaps between clumps of day-lilies and the prostrate-growing evergreen shrub *Viburnum davidii*. In a newly constructed east-facing walled courtyard planting is very simple; a 'Mermaid' rose, *Trachelospermum jasminoides*, ceanothus, honeysuckle and chaenomeles are planted against the low walls. Across the yard, clambering against a farm building in full sun, the rare evergreen climber from South America, *Araujia sericofera*, thrives. Known as the cruel plant, its flowers trap the long probosces of night-flying moths in its native land. The creamy flowers held in short racemes are followed by grooved yellowish-green pods, sometimes 12.5 cm (5 in) long.

At NYMANS climbing plants grow against the ruins of the old house, and shrubs are planted at the base of the walls. *Clematis armandii* flowers early, followed by neighbouring yellow-flowered *Piptanthus nepalensis* and *Abutilon vitifolium* 'Veronica Tennant', with papery white mallow flowers. *Genista cinerea* is a mass of golden yellow in June, beside bushes of crimson rose 'Fellenberg'. By July a cultivar of *Lonicera etrusca*, 'Michael Rosse', is outstanding, its creamy-yellow flowers faintly tinged with pink. Other shrubs which benefit from the shelter of the high walls are lower-growing corokias and the spreading *Ceratostigma willmottianum*, which is covered with bright blue flowers in late summer.

In a corner made by low walls near by, *Clematis* 'Etoile Rose', with nodding silvery-pink flowers, and *Lonicera* × *brownii* 'Fuchsioides' make a group with a bush of the thornless rose 'Zéphirine Drouhin'.

At BENINGBROUGH HALL Siberian crab-apples are planted outside the north walls of the old kitchen garden. Nearer the house, beds under the south-facing walls of soft pink brick provide a favoured situation for sun-loving perennials. Rainfall on the east of the Pennines is low and the soil is alklaline. *Limonium lati-folium*, libertia, dorycnium, *Linum perenne*, sea kale, southern-wood, *Achillea* 'Moonshine', an old rose 'Climbing Mrs Herbert Stevens', *Geranium renardii*, the shrubby silver-leaved *Artemisia* 'Powis Castle', *Hemerocallis* 'Marion Vaughn', and *Anthemis tinctoria* 'E. C. Buxton', all with pale flowers, enjoy the warm site, and the small shrub *Abelia chinensis*, with rose-tinted flowers in late summer, has a sheltered corner.

At BLICKLING HALL, at the bottom of the dry moat and well sheltered from cold winds, plants are grown against the east wall of the early-seventeenth-century house. The soil in the garden is lime-free, but under the brick walls it is likely to be more alkaline. The tender Cooper's Burma rose, a cultivar of the Cherokee rose (*Rosa laevigata*) with white single flowers thrives here, and its success perhaps reflects the dry climate with plenty of hot sun in summer, which ripens the wood. Near by *Trachelospermum jasminoides* 'Variegatum', with strongly scented summer flowers, and the large-leaved *Buddleja farreri* are tender in many gardens, but here they seem safe out of the wind. Along the wall other climbers include *Vitis* 'Brant', which fruits freely, the yellow-flowered honeysuckle, *Lonicera* × *tellmanniana*, beautiful but unfortunately with no scent, *Clematis* 'Ville de Lyon' and some climbing roses: 'Le Rêve' and 'Paul's Perpetual White'. Other shrubs include *Fuchsia magellanica* 'Versicolor', *Ceanothus* 'Gloire de Versailles' and *Caryopteris* × *clandonensis*, all of which are hard-pruned in early spring. *Hydrangea aspera* Villosa Group, the evergreen *Abelia* × *grandiflora* and its golden-leaved cultivar, and *Ceratostigma willmottianum* flower at the end of the summer. The tender sub-shrub *Salvia microphylla* (syn. *S. grahamii*), although sometimes cut to the ground in winter, carries its rich red flowers for a long period from June until the first frost.

At LYTES CARY in Somerset the narrow border at the base of the Elizabethan house is filled to overflowing with plants which could have been grown in Sir Henry Lyte's time: the pale pink form of *Lathyrus latifolius*, forms of *Clematis viticella*, southern-wood (*Artemisia abrotanum*), Jerusalem sage (*Phlomis fruticosa*), catmint and myrtle (*Myrtus communis*) although the Mediterranean evergreen is often cut sharply back in winter. Above this border a yellow Banksian rose of later introduction from China flowers in spring and then needs pruning back immediately afterwards.

At TINTINHULL the completely shaded north wall of the house supports vigorous plants of the early-flowering double pink rose 'Madame Grégoire Staechelin'. Although flowering only once, in June, this rose is outstanding and throws out long healthy shoots each year. Its pruning is discussed in the chapter on rose gardens. In the bed at the base of the wall a large plant of the free-flowering *Mahonia pinnata* and yellow and white single and double cultivars of *Rosa pimpinellifolia* are established in strong suckering groups, while other mahonias make evergreen clumps to frame a doorway which leads to the sunny west-facing court in front of the eighteenth-century facade of the house. By midsummer, and continuing until October, the flame nasturtium (*Tropaeolum speciosum*) bears its startling scarlet flowers among fresh green leaves, and twines over the prickly rose stems and up the wall. By the yard doorway, in deepest shade, the fern *Adiantum pedatum* carries its fronds of delicate beauty on black wire-like stems.

At CHARLECOTE PARK a north wall of the house is simply planted. The semi-herbaceous late-summer-flowering clematis, *Clematis × jouiniana*, with china-blue flowers, is annually trained up the walls to make a fan shape. At its feet glossy-leaved bergenias shine through all the seasons, especially if their unsightly dying leaves are removed, and flower in early spring. This pattern is repeated along the wall three times. Maintenance in this bed consists of cutting down the dead clematis foliage each spring, training new growth on to fan-shaped wires, and of keeping the bergenias tidy all year round.

At SIZERGH CASTLE a high stone wall has been faced with brick, which retains more heat. The grey leaved shrub *Brachyglottis* 'Sunshine' has been tied back and hangs like a curtain on the warm wall. Also in the wall border are some normally tender shrubs *Abutilon × suntense*, *Escallonia* 'Iveyi', ceanothus *Genista aetnensis*, the grey cultivar of *Buddleja alternifolia*, *Itea ilicifolia* and the difficult *Pileostegia viburnoides* all do well in this northern garden, the flower bed on a raised terrace giving the plants excellent drainage. Similarly, at WALLINGTON a double walled terrace runs along a wall of the old kitchen garden, giving extra drainage for tender wall plants in the bed above.

At SISSINGHURST CASTLE walls, hedges and fences divide the garden into compartments. Correct pruning at the right time of the year for wall shrubs and climbers is vital. Standards at

Sissinghurst are impeccable. **Miss Sibylle Kreutzberger**, a former Head Gardener there, sums up the essentials:

❧ The pruning of shrubs and climbers trained on walls or fences is often a cause of concern and bewilderment to many people faced with a plant that has got too big, too old, or has fallen flat on its face. 'What can I do about it?' we are frequently asked. The question is – to prune or not to prune? Here, then, is a brief summary of what is done at Sissinghurst.

The first thing is to recognize whether a shrub or climber flowers on old or new wood; that is, wood made by the previous season's growth or wood made in the current season. This is almost more important than knowing and identifying the plant; once you know on which wood it flowers you are halfway to deciding how to act. For ease of recognition I shall divide them into the following categories:

a Those shrubs and climbers flowering before mid-June can only flower on growth made the previous season. If, therefore, these are cut in winter or spring the flowering will be reduced. The right time to thin or cut back these shrubs is immediately after flowering. This allows plants the maximum time possible for making new wood in preparation for flowering the following season.

Examples of shrubs and climbers in this category would be *Osmanthus delavayi*, *Buddleja alternifolia*, early-flowering clematis and true Rambler roses. Some of these shrubs and climbers can be more easily managed by creating a spur system rather than allowing a free-for-all. If they are pruned immediately after spring-flowering, growth is very vigorous. Chaenomeles, schisandra and wisteria are plants which benefit from the new shoots being shortened to 15 cm (6 in) in July and again in December–January, cutting back to two or three buds.

b Those shrubs and climbers flowering between midsummer and autumn, the majority of which will be flowering on the current year's wood. Any pruning is best done in winter or early spring to encourage new vigorous growth. Cut back flowered wood to the new shoots and tie in replacement shoots, shortening them by a third. Prune the laterals to two or three buds in early spring. In July vigorous new non-flowering growth can be shortened.

Examples would be deciduous ceanothus, most other buddleja species, *Campsis radicans*, *Solanum jasminoides* and *Vitis vinifera*. The latter should be pruned in mid-winter before the sap rises.

c Those climbers which are more or less herbaceous, i.e. dying down to a perennial rootstock each winter or being treated in the same way (this will include tender woody plants which will shoot from the base each spring). Examples of shrubs and climbers which are cut down to a few buds from their base each spring would be many clematis, tropaeolum species, *Humulus lupulus*, *Aconitum hemsleyanum*, eccremocarpus and tender perennials such as cobaea and maurandya.

d Those wall plants and climbers which require only intermittent pruning to keep them within bounds and to promote the continued production of new wood. This makes it possible to cut out an old leg from time to time, thereby invigorating and prolonging the life the plant. This is particularly necessary for shrubs grown for their foliage effect. Examples in this category are *Carpenteria californica*, *Fremontodendron californicum*, coronilla, evergreen ceanothus. Ceanothus should ideally have their branches layed in to form a fan-shape. Weak and straggly branches can be removed from time to time, cutting back to a vigorous young shoot lower down, which is then used to 'lay' in. These shoots should be tied in very loosely as they can easily strangle. The climbing hydrangea (*Hydrangea anomala petiolaris*) generally needs little pruning but, if flowering branches get too far from the wall, it is possible to cut a proportion of these back to encourage the production of new wood close to the wall surface. This would also apply to schizophragma species.

The care and maintenance of 'climbers' embraces more than just pruning. Feeding, mulching, adequate tying-in and possible watering and spraying (with fungicides and insecticides) all contribute to their successful performance. Here are a few guidelines:

1 Choose a good well-branched plant when you buy. If necessary, pinch out the tips of the stronger shoots to encourage several new shoots of equal strength, rather than a leader with side shoots.

2 Prepare the planting hole generously, and not too close to the wall or fence: this is a dry spot. Water the pot or shrub before planting and again afterwards.

3 Provide adequate support in the way of wires, mesh or stout nails so that the plant can be trained in from the start.

4 In the case of tender shrubs, particularly evergreens, give protection during the first winter or two with a mulch over the roots.

CLEMATIS

Few climbers flower more profusely or give greater pleasure than well grown clematis.

Planting Prepare a good-sized hole and incorporate as much rotted manure, compost or leaf-mould as possible. Spread out the roots, and plant about 5 cm (2 in) deeper than the original soil level of the pot. Firm, water and mulch if you can. Most clematis are not fussy about aspect, and they like their roots cool and shady; the mulch will ensure this.

Pruning This is really much less complicated than it sounds, and you do not have to know the name of the clematis to get it right. If in any doubt of what to do leave it for a season and notice when it flowers, and *where* on the plant the flowers come.

1 As a rough guide, those flowering in April, May and early June need no regular pruning. If they get too large, contain too much dead wood or are straggly and out-growing their site, cut them back into the old wood. This can be done, cutting right back to the ground, if necessary, immediately after flowering is over. *Clematis montana, C. montana sericea* (syn *C. chrysocoma sericea*) *C. macropetala, C. alpina* and *C. armandii* all fall into this category and should be treated accordingly.

2 Large-flowered hybrids flowering on the old wood in May and June. These include the Patens Group, which flower early on short shoots from the previous year's wood. These require no regular pruning but spent flower-heads can be cut back to an active bud and dead wood removed. Every few years cut them right down after flowering, for complete rejuvenation.

3 Large-flowered hybrids which flower in June to October on old and young wood are treated in the same way. Some young shoots are thinned out in spring to encourage basal growth. These include the Lanuginosa Group.

4 Clematis which flower in July to October on the current season's wood. These include Jackmanii, Viticella and Texensis hybrids, *CC. tangutica, tibetana vernayi,* (*C. orientalis* misapplied) , *flammula* and *rehderiana.* Cut back to 45 cm (18 in) or less from the base each spring. Cut out a proportion of shoots entirely, in order to promote a multi-stemmed plant.

Young clematis of all types should be pruned hard in the first year or two to encourage branching. Then if wilt does strike, the plant will probably survive. If left unpruned these clematis will flower quite well, but the flowering starts high up and the base will become increasingly bare.

Clematis macropetala *flowers profusely at Sissinghurst in the Rose Garden.*

Training Clematis hate to swing about. Tie them in, spacing out the shoots before they get entangled, and do this several times during the growing season so that they are well displayed. A saddle of sheep- or pig-netting astride the wall will help to anchor the clematis when it reaches the top. Stem ties are good for fixing them and much quicker to use and safer than string. Always tie loosely.

At Sissinghurst we use a variety of training systems:

1 Direct on walls covered with wire-mesh, Netlon or pig-netting.
2 On tripods made of three stout poles, set firmly astride the plant, and tied together at the top some 1.8–2.1 m (6–7 ft) from the ground. Shoots are spaced out as they grow, so that the tripod is well furnished by flowering time.
3 On or through small trees or shrubs, choosing as hosts these which flower on the current season's wood.
4 The less vigorous clematis can be grown in large pots and will train downwards.

Feeding, mulching and watering Plants on walls get very little moisture. Clematis hate to be dry, and poor soil and dry roots are often the cause of failure. Mulching with compost, manure or bark will keep the soil moist, as well as shading the roots and cutting down the need for watering in dry periods. They are fed each year with a general fertilizer,

Pests and diseases There are three main problems encountered when growing clematis: earwigs, mildew and wilt. Earwigs are controlled by application of a systemic insecticide; the earwigs usually make holes in the flowers in late summer. Fungicides are used against mildew. Wilt is the most serious and difficult to control. It is caused by a fungus and may suddenly attack a single shoot or the entire plant. It seems to occur most often when tying in has not been done regularly, and shoots have been blown about and bent, perhaps restricting the flow of sap. Sissinghurst doesn't suffer much from wilt. Enough moisture, good growing conditions and the minimum of handling, except for careful tying in, seem to help the plants resist its occurrence. The application of a suitable fungicide may give some protection. If wilt does occur, cut out the affected part and hope for the best. Mice can sometimes be a problem, eating the young shoots as they emerge. ❧

ORCHARDS AND KITCHEN GARDENS

The introduction to this chapter touched on the fate of some of the old walled kitchen gardens: how the passage of time and contemporary needs have changed their use. Much as the Trust would like to keep kitchen gardens and orchards in their traditional productive role, in very few cases is it economically possible to do so. Instead these areas now provide other services rather than provisioning the inhabitants of the house. Where 'food-growing' garden areas still exist, walled or not, the Trust is often concerned with replacing old plants, especially old fruit varieties now seldom available in commercial nurseries. By this policy the Trust ensures that historic names are not lost for ever.

Occasionally, the plants have distinct local associations. For instance, at WIGHTWICK MANOR on the outskirts of Wolverhampton there are old specimens of a pear called 'Tettenhall Dick' named after the nearby village of Tettenhall. These were planted before the garden was designed by Alfred Parsons at the turn of the century. Beyond, a nuttery dates the garden to the

Edwardian era. More recently the Trust has added a weeping mulberry (*Morus alba* 'Pendula') to cascade on to the front lawn beside a Judas tree (*Cercis siliquastrum*) and a neighbouring medlar (*Mespilus germanica*).

Medlar and mulberry are also among the period plants chosen for the theme of the recreated gardens at MOSELEY OLD HALL, where planting is restricted to those plants already known and grown towards the end of the seventeenth century. A wooden framed walk leads to a corner arbour of hornbeam and to a nut walk; turning back towards the brick house the stone-flagged pathway is lined with pairs of quince (*Cydonia oblonga*), mulberry (*Morus nigra*) and medlar, which, like the orchard beyond, provide both spring blossom and later fruit.

In the enclosure in which the new herb garden and the flowers for cutting are grown at HARDWICK HALL, a very old walnut overhangs an original nuttery. Recently this has been expanded; young walnut trees have been planted and new nuts include filberts and 'Pearson's Prolific' (syn. 'Nottingham Cob'). Beyond the herbs a new mulberry (*Morus nigra*) walk runs down to the Banqueting House by the wild border at the bottom of the garden.

To the east of the herb garden and the yew/hornbeam roundel an orchard containing many well-known and tried varieties of old fruit trees was replanted with specimen pears which include 'Packham's Triumph', 'Marie Louise' and 'Pitmaston Duchess', all grown as standard trees. The damsons 'Merryweather' and 'Farleigh Damson' are also making good progress as standards, while original specimens of 'Ouillin's Golden Gage' are also found. New trees of the two latter gages have been added. The apple 'Rev. W. Wilks', a seedling introduced to commerce by Veitch's Chelsea nursery and dating back to the turn of the century, grows in the rough grass beyond the east-facing shrub rose border. This apple for dessert or culinary use has large slightly conical fruit, white or very pale primrose with a few streaks of clear red. Beehives safely situated at the far end of the orchard make the scene pleasantly domestic.

Other old fruit trees in the orchards at Hardwick include 'Norfolk Beefing' and newly grafted young plants, and three 'Duke of Devonshire' apples (Hardwick was one of the homes of the Dukes of Devonshire).

In the ornamental orchard many bulbs and wild flowers grow,

and the grass is left long as a meadow. In this rough grass, in areas defined by mown paths which meet at the centre, ornamental crabs such as *Malus hupehensis* and 'Jargonelle' pears are planted.

It has often been customary to grow flowers to cut for the house in the vicinity of the kitchen garden. This is where many old perennials survived during the years when they were banned from parkland and parterres, before they were once again invited to reappear before society in the newly fashionable herbaceous border.

Flowers for arrangements in the public rooms in National Trust houses are chosen according to themes agreed with the Historic Buildings Representative and the Gardens Adviser. At Hardwick, Mr Allan grows flowers for cutting in two long borders flanking the herb garden. Colours are planned carefully so that the best use is made of the available growing space, and plants grown include: 'Iceberg' roses, dahlias, Madame Butterfly antirrhinums, *Limonium sinuatum* (syn. *Statice sinuata*), *Eremurus stenophyllus* (syn. *E. bungei*), teasels, *Lilium regale*, *Agapanthus*, tulips, daffodils (in particular a stock of virus-free 'St Keverne'), *Dianthus* 'Houndspool Ruby', *Rudbeckia* 'Marmalade', *Centaurea cyanus* 'Blue Diadem', pyrethrums, *Iris orientalis* (syn. *I. ochroleuca*), *Lychnis chalcedonica*, *Alstroemeria aurea* (syn. *A. aurantiaca*), campanulas, lupins, the National Collection of *Scabiosa caucasica*, both blue and white, sweet Williams, delphiniums, gypsophila, *Cleome spinosa*, *Helenium hoopesii* (broad grey-green leaves, yellow daisies), *Leucanthemum* × *superbum* 'Everest', *Veronicastrum virginicum album*, *Iris sibirica*, *Artemisia lactiflora* and lily of the valley 'Hardwick Hall' with cream edging to leaf. Beyond the hedge of sweet briar roses there are more sweet Williams, chrysanthemums, gladiolus, sweet rocket, larkspur, and *Lavatera* 'Silver Cup'.

At the end of the nineteenth century much of the flat area below the great hanging terraces to the east of POWIS CASTLE was still occupied by glasshouses which supplied hothouse plants and grapes. By the first years of this century all this was swept away, after a storm brought down the giant elms that had stood here, and by so doing exposed the view for the first time; a new formal garden was made with dividing yew and holly hedges, leaving a double avenue of pyramid apples and pears and a cross-walk of grapevines grown over ornamental hoops, which could

At Beningbrough Hall old espalier pears lining the central path through the walled kitchen garden have been trained to make curving arches.

be glimpsed from points along the terraced walks. Since the Trust acquired the property, this area, while maintaining its symmetry, has been considerably developed.

The fruit trees, now more than 80 years old, are still carefully pruned to shape, those neglected over the war years retrimmed, and new trees planted to complete the pattern. Few, in fact, of these old types fruit freely, but their mature and often gnarled branches give the appearance of age, and interestingly more modern varieties such as 'Bramley's Seedling' do not respond willingly to this type of pruning. Among the original trees is 'Tower of Glamis', which originated in Scotland before 1800.

Around the base of each tree large circles 3 m (10 ft) across have been cut in the grass and planted with a strong ornamental ground cover, arranged in symmetrical pairs: the non-flowering grey-leaved *Stachys byzantina* (syn. *S. olympica*) 'Silver Carpet', mauve-flowered *Lamium maculatum*, golden marjoram (*Origanum vulgare* 'Aureum'), and blue-flowered bugle (*Ajuga reptans*).

The soil in this lower garden is rich and moist and original plantings of Jackman's rue (*Ruta graveolens* 'Jackman's Blue') and cotton lavenders (*Santolina*) were lost each winter, but the Head Gardener, Mr Jimmy Hancock, continues to experiment with other greys and silvers in another formal walk where the June–July-flowering hybrid honeysuckle *Lonicera* × *americana* twines up central poles, around which are planted cultivars of *Carex* or *Ophiopogon planiscapus* 'Nigrescens'. In other squares surrounding the honeysuckle he plants a little feathery silver-leaved anthemis with yellow daisy-flowers (*Anthemis marschalliana*), *Viola* 'Irish Molly', which has yellowy-brown flowers, and *V.* 'Limelight', with lemony-yellow blooms, both of which are only temporary plantings. In other beds he uses the black-leaved and variegated cultivars of ophiopogon (such as *Ophiopogon planiscapus* 'Nigrescens'). Each plant is massed separately in 3 m (10 ft) squares, over a period forming a weed-suppressing carpet.

The hooped vines, now growing on a newly erected vine-tunnel arbour, are planted 2.5 m (8 ft) apart, with the highest part of the hoop at about 2.25 m (7 ft). Cool and shady in summer, this is an important feature, breaking up the large expanse of flat lawn between the hedges and fruit avenues. The north-east end of the arbour leads to a painted seat set between wings of box, cut to a comfortable 1.5 m (5 ft) in height, and at the opposite south-west point the arbour carries the eye up steep yew-lined steps to the wilderness beyond. Most of the vines are the fruiting *Vitis vinifera* but at either end plants of the large-leaved *V. coignetiae* tend to overwhelm the ordinary grapes (which in fact seldom set fruit) and provide spectacular early-autumn red and orange tints. Round the base of each vine a 50 cm (20 in) square planting of the vivid young leaves of golden marjoram (*Origanum vulgare* 'Aureum') contributes patches of colour in summer and has proved to be a very good ground cover for moist soil over the last twenty years.

At FELBRIGG HALL the old kitchen garden has been completely replanted since the Trust acquired it in 1971. Along one south-facing wall, borders are interrupted by a handsome dovecote. In the western section herbs are grown in front of a large fig, which fruits regularly, while to the east the planting is more general to include shrub roses and grapevines. The latter, symmetrically planted in groups along the centre of the border, are trained decoratively on architectural frames. **Mr Ted Bullock**, the Head Gardener at Felbrigg, writes about the 'wigwams' which have been constructed as frames for the vines:

🦋 These timber supports, called 'quadripods' were tanalized and have recently replaced others which were in place for seventeen years. The posts were originally purchased from a local timber merchant as 2.7 m (9 ft) lengths, 38 × 38 mm (1½ in) sawn pressure-tanalized deal.

The vines grown on the quadripods are 'Müller-Thurgau', 'Brant', 'Seyval Blanc', 'Morio Muscat', and 'Wrotham Pinot' (syn. 'Miller's Burgundy'). They are trained on the four stakes each of which is 1.95 m (6 ft 6 in) high. They meet so that the diameter of the space at their bases is about 1.5 m (5 ft) across. The vines are wound round the stakes as they grow. Pruning is done in January. This involves cutting back laterals to two buds on the knuckles or 'stubs'. If the sublateral shoots are not pinched out during the summer, the vines become a tangled mass of growth. The vines are mulched with well-rotted compost in the autumn and the compound fertilizer, Vitax Q4, is applied in the spring. Mildew is often a problem, especially in humid conditions, and PBI 'Supercarb' (carbendazim) is used to control the disease.

The varieties at Felbrigg are all well known by growers and good nurseries, such as Scotts of Merriott and Reads of Loddon, Norfolk, should be able to supply them. The name of the vineyard I arranged to visit was R. S. Don at North Elmham in Norfolk. 🦋

The recent history of the apple trees in the walled garden at Felbrigg – both the upkeep of the existing plants and the mixed success of some of the newer plantings – offers food for thought. Ted Bullock comments on what has been done recently and reflects on some of the difficulties that have been experienced here:

🦋 Our original planting in February 1975 of 'Wellspur Delicious' grafted on semi-dwarfing stock MM106, to be trained as pyramids, was not successful. Over the years the trees did not produce sufficient growth to train into the shape required, although there was always an abundance of fruit spurs produced, followed by a heavy crop of apples. I would not advise, therefore, that this variety should be avoided in other gardens – I believe it would be a mistake to do so. The incorrect stock for our soil type may have been chosen, or perhaps there was a 'replant' problem. These young trees were planted on the site of an old apple orchard. Specific Apple Replant Disease, known as SARD, may therefore have been the major cause of problems. A great deal of research has taken place on SARD in the last few years. Interestingly the same 'Wellspur Delicious' bushes also proved a failure at GUNBY HALL in Lincolnshire, where they had also been placed in an old orchard.

A new planting was made in winter 1983. First the soil was thoroughly sterilized. These new trees, 'Norfolk Royal Russet' grafted on MM106, have responded well so far. The growth is most encouraging and this is now being trained so that the shapes of dwarf pyramids will be achieved.

Using methods rather similar to that of growing spindle-bush apple trees, practised by commercial growers, we have been training our trees, using twine and pegs. This is finicky but worth the effort. In August three or four of the new shoots on each two-year old plant are selected for tying down; the shoots chosen are well spaced about the main stem of the tree and are bent down to the horizontal, using twine or string. A loop – not a tie or a knot – is made about halfway along the shoot and tied to a tent peg in the soil, driven in at an angle to resist the upward pull of the shoots. This tying down does enable one to obtain the desired position of the shoots and encourages the growth of fruit buds.

A number of old neglected orchard trees in the same area were rejuvenated over a period of two or three years by the removal of large branches, which were riddled with canker. These trees were finally cut back to about half their original height.

Scab and mildew are a constant problem in old enclosed orchards and the trees are sprayed whenever possible to control these diseases. Since 1980 we have been planting older varieties of apples (and some pears) in the walled garden and these are listed below.

All our fruit trees, especially the wall-trained plums, peaches, apricots, cherries, apples and pears are pruned annually, with special attention to summer pruning – the vital finger-and-thumb pruning, not the often excessive use of secateurs and

*The walled kitchen garden at Felbrigg Hall supports a
range of vegetables as well as thorn and apple trees.*

loppers. Sadly larger orchard trees have to fend for themselves
as best they can. The lack of time and staff means that we
cannot give the regular spraying programme which is desirable.
Our young trees are given more attention, being sprayed against
disease and given Vitax Q4 fertilizer, which is most beneficial
for their growth. ❧

At Felbrigg Hall a part of the kitchen walled garden has been
planted with specimens of thorn tree (*Crataegus*). Ted Bullock
describes his experience:

❧ We obtained twenty species of thorn from Hilliers'
Nurseries in January 1974 for planting in the walled garden.
These were obtained as standard trees, some with rather large
heads and tall spindly stems, which later caused a problem.
Strong winds from the east are prevalent at Felbrigg in spring
and it was found that each tree needed to be supported with guy
wires, four per specimen, attached to posts driven into the
ground at an angle. Although effective, the wires made mowing
and upkeep impossible.

Replacements have since been obtained as half-standards with 1.2 m (4 ft) stems as a maximum height. A small stout stake 1 m (3 ft) driven in about halfway is usually adequate support for a tree of this size.

Little pruning is necessary on these thorns, apart from removing crossing or rubbing branches, and any lower branches which obstruct machinery used for cutting the grass surrounding them. Suckers which arise from the rootstock are removed as early as possible while the growth is still soft.

When preparing planting positions a large circle or square of turf, at least 60 cm (2 ft) across, was lifted and the planting soil well prepared. The area surrounding the trunk of each tree should be kept clean and weed-free for at least four years; after that the turf may be allowed to close in. We did consider the use of tree spats to keep encroaching grass away, but because these looked unsightly we now use a mulch of mushroom compost 10 cm (4 in) thick to suppress weed growth. After four years with grass allowed to grow up to the trunk we give an annual dressing of nitro-chalk in the spring. ❧

APPLES AT FELBRIGG

'Hubbard's Pearmain', 'Norfolk Beefing', 'Old English Pearmain', 'Striped Beefing' and 'Winter Majetin' – were grafted at Felbrigg from budwood obtained from Wisley gardens in 1982. The rest were planted in 1980, and comprise: 'Ashmead's Kernel', 'Braddick Nonpareil', 'Court Pendu Plat', 'D'Arcy Spice', 'Emneth Early', 'Golden Reinette', 'Nonpareil', 'French Crab', 'Pitmaston Pine Apple', 'Wagener' and 'Wyken Pippin'.

THORNS AT FELBRIGG

Ted Bullock notes the particular interest of different species. The collection has been increased over the years. Perhaps the most beautiful of the thorns at Felbrigg is *Crataegus laevigata* 'Gireoudii', which is a spectacular sight in early summer, clothed with young pink and white foliage.

× *Crataemespilus grandiflora* (a bi-generic hybrid from *Crataegus* × *Mespilus*) of natural origin from France. Thought to be from *Crataegus laevigata* (syn. *C. oxyacantha*), the midland hawthorn, and the medlar *Mespilus germanica*, this sterile hybrid has a broad head and large yellowish-brown fruits, and good autumn colour.

+ *Crataegomespilus dardarii* 'Jules d'Asnières', a graft hybrid.

Crataegus dsungarica (a spiny tree with purplish-black fruits), *CC. altaica, arkansana, amoldiana, azarolus* (the azarole – very choice tree, white flowers and edible orange fruits), *coccinioides, crus-galli* (the Cockspur thorn), × *durobrivensis, holmesiana* (oblong red fruits), *laciniata, succulenta, macracantha* (largest spined of all crataegus), *maximowiczii, mexicana, monogyna* 'Stricta' (with almost fastigiate growth), *nitida* (quite distinct spreading habit), *laciniata* (syn. *C. orientalis*) (fruits large orange-red), *laevigata, phaenopyrum* (known as the Washington thorn), *pinnatifida, persimilis* 'Prunifolia' (lovely tree – rounded head), *punctata, pubescens, stipulacea* (syn. *mexicano*), *submollis* and *calpodendron* (syn. *tomentosa*).

The three species, *CC. crus-galli, monogyna* and *laevigata* are all used as stock on which the other trees have been grafted, although it is not certain which for individual trees. The Royal Horticultural Society's *Dictionary of Gardening* suggests that most species, and particularly the American ones, will be grafted on *Crataegus monogyna*.

At LYTES CARY in Somerset a large square orchard has grass kept to about 10 cm (4 in) under fruit trees, with tightly mown grass paths on cross-diagonals surrounding a sundial. At the four corners of the orchard an arbour or archway of weeping ash has been constructed on four 2 m (6 ft) posts with cross bars to which the young ash shoots are tied. In flower beds round the base of each ash shrubs such as the guelder rose (*Viburnum opulus*) and lilacs have been planted. In the open area medlars (*Mespilus germanica*) and the crab *Malus* 'John Downie' are notable. To the south and marking the garden boundary a row of willows, to match the local osier (*Salix viminalis*) still grown for commercial use in Somerset fields, carries the eye into the landscape and gives wind protection.

Near the house, in the first lawn enclosure, two old apple trees reduce formality, and remind one that the house will have been surrounded by orchards in the seventeenth century. Two more recently planted mulberries are beginning to take hold. In the second rectangular compartment, hedged round with yew, single specimens of the strawberry tree (*Arbutus unedo*) have been planted in the four corners of the lawn.

At TINTINHULL HOUSE, also in Somerset, a rectangular kitchen garden is at a lower level than the rest of the garden.

Here a cross path leading to a typical Somerset cider orchard is lined with giant catmint (*Nepeta* 'Six Hills Giant'). From the Fountain Garden to the south, where silvery-foliaged and white-flowered plants are grown formally, the eye is carried between a pair of crabs (*Malus* 'John Downie') and two pears (*Pyrus calleryana* 'Chanticleer'), along the central gravel path to a gate and orchard beyond. An avenue of standard apples carries the view further. Many of the fruit trees are old and two large trees of 'Morgan's Sweet' have grown to 12 m (40 ft); in 1980 the Trust replaced and filled in some gaps with specimens of 'Tydeman's Early Worcester' and 'Ellison's Orange'. The soil round the young trees is kept clean with the systemic herbicide glyphosate. The orchard is not intended for commercial fruit; rather it acts as a link between the house and formal 'compartmental' gardens in the foreground, and the Somerset farmland beyond.

Crossing the main path in the kitchen garden, a paved way runs between espalier pear trees, with a foreground planting of pink roses and blue-flowered *Caryopteris × clandonensis*. The pears are traditional at Tintinhull but new plants had to be obtained in 1981. Fortunately three-tiered specimens of 'Doyenné du Comice', 'Pitmaston Duchess', and 'Williams' Bon Chrétien' were available from a Devon nursery.

Espalier fruit where usually two or three tiers of branches stretch horizontally along tight wires, are grown formally against walls or, as often in the past, mark out free-standing divisions in walled fruit and vegetable gardens. Plants are placed 3–4 m (10–13 ft) apart and correct and regular pruning is essential. The plants are usually first trained by the nursery from which they are obtained; the espalier needing several years of exact selection

FIGURE 1 AN ESPALIER

At Tintinhull House a path down the centre of the vegetable garden is lined with catmint. Beyond the garden lies a typical Somerset cider orchard.

and tying in of the best placed shoots to make the desired framework, and the elimination and pinching back of the remainder. Fruiting spurs will then develop along the horizontal stems (see Figure 1). After the shape has been established and the plants are in their permanent growing site with branches trained along stiff wires, regular pruning for producing fruit is then carried out. While free-growing bushes or trees are generally pruned only in winter, the espalier is summer-pruned to maintain the shape, and to remove extra live foliage which reduces the vigour of the plant. In mid-August, once the base of new shoots begins to ripen, they can each be cut back to 10–13 cm (4–5 in) above the place where the new growth began. In winter, further cutting back is necessary, thinning out fruiting spurs to discourage over-cropping.

Vegetables are grown in straight rows in traditional fashion at Tintinhull, but round the outer edge of the rectangular garden shrub roses and other plants add interest: they include ordinary fennel (*Foeniculum vulgare*) for cooking, lovage, the biennial

Angelica archangelica with ornamental leaves and attractive sulphur-yellow flower umbels, and the red-stemmed Swiss chard. The giant fennel from southern Europe, *Ferula communis* and *F. tingitana*, have still to produce their 2.25 m (7 ft) stems bearing yellow cow-parsley-like flowers, but the feathery mounds of foliage are ornamental in themselves. Statuesque artichokes, (*Cynara cardunculus* Scolymus Group) with silvery leaves, mark the corners of the rose beds by the pear espalier walk. Plants such as the biennial woad (*Isatis tinctoria*), a now rare British native, the double-flowered soapwort or bouncing Bet (*Saponaria officinalis* 'Rosea Plena'), sweet Cicely (*Myrrhis odorata*) and Bowles' grey-leaved mint keep the utilitarian theme in mind. Sweet peas are trained over tripods and dahlias, with pale pink flowers especially chosen for the drawing-room, which is open to visitors, are thinned to 4–6 plant stems which are then tied to sticks that were put in when the tubers were planted. The ground is well dug, and plenty of farmyard manure incorporated before the plants are put in at the end of May.

At UPTON HOUSE a south-sloping kitchen garden makes the optimum use of the sun's rays. The soil heats up earlier in the year, producing crops several weeks ahead of a garden which is flat, and, of course, the growing season is also prolonged at the end of the summer. At TRENGWAINTON, too, beds sloping west, raised against walls at an angle of 45 degrees were especially constructed in 1820 for early vegetable cropping. There is only 30–38 cm (12–15 in) of soil lying over drainage rubble, and into it well-rotted manure is dug during the winter months. the gardeners work down the slope. **Mr Peter Horder**, the Head Gardener, writes that:

✿ They use a long-handled Cornish fork and shovel to ease the strain on the back. The soil is turned uphill and any soil replacement is at the bottom as required. These sloping beds in the lower walled garden are still cultivated annually with vegetable crops as originally intended and provide great interest to visitors. The crops include: shallots, onions, spring onions, lettuce, radish, dwarf peas and beans and marrows. Some watering is necessary from time to time and generally we find that in dry seasons plants bolt more quickly on the slope than on a flat site. However, the exposure to the sun's rays does ensure that crops mature significantly earlier. ✿

——— I V ———

INFORMAL

PLANTING

———

W here no wall or hedge gives a clear demarcation, and where woodland or open countryside can be seen, the outer fringes of the garden – whether woodland, shrubbery or meadow – should appear to be informally planted, the garden blending gradually into the landscape beyond. In fact this sort of 'natural' gardening needs planning and programming as carefully as the more formally defined themes nearer the house. But because clear-cut patterns and geometrical rules cannot be followed in this apparent imitation of nature, the gardener has to rely more on observation and experience of plant behaviour and requirements, as well as developing a sound sense of scale.

Whether the area in question is the transitional zone between the garden and the surrounding countryside or simply an area within the garden where rules are apparently relaxed and an element of 'wilderness' is allowed to prevail to create some sense of mystery, the principle is that planting should not look artificial or contrived. Exotics, which always look more appropriate when seen against the man-made structure of the house, should seem at home in their new environment placed side by side with British natives. Single plants should not call attention to themselves, but should rather harmonize with their neighbours. In spite of Robinson's strictures, plants are often distributed on a rather *ad hoc* basis, shrubberies added to with surplus bushes, coloured foliage turning trees into 'eye catchers' where the prevailing effects should be quiet and green. Misplaced rockeries and pools that do not lie in the lowest hollows are similar lapses. At ground level plants need to make curving, interweaving shapes, bulbs to grow in drifts as they would naturalize in their own habitat, and even wild-flower meadows to be entirely successful should be confined to local flora.

This apparently more casual atmosphere is not necessarily more labour-saving than are expressly formal designs.

Hidcote is well known for its garden compartments; in woodland beyond the more formal areas, planting patterns are more relaxed.

WOODLAND

Many woodland gardens began as a collection of plants; there was little deliberate interpretation of a 'style'. As plants arrived from overseas in rapidly increasing numbers, gardeners, without conscious thought about the aesthetics or 'rules' for their arrangement, evolved their own methods of cultivation. The primary concern had to be the well-being of the plant, and the quality and condition of the individual specimen was at first far more important than any contribution it could make to an overall garden design. What at first tended to be a plantsman's collection, arranged as an exotic wilderness entirely for the benefit of the individual plant, later developed into a much more definite and self-conscious desire to create woodland scenes which unfolded for the spectator as a series of static pictures.

As a form of garden craft the planted woodland lies closer to natural laws than any other, any attempt to use geometrical or even symmetrical planting schemes immediately destroying its whole spirit. Each plant chosen for the site should not only suit the conditions and general aspect from a practical point of view but should definitely seem to become part of an idealized 'paradise'. Perhaps like the 'wild' gardening recommended by William Robinson during the last quarter of the nineteenth century, it is the most difficult stylistic form of gardening. There is a constant need to balance almost ecological qualities with a coherent overall design, which firmly establishes that it is a garden and not a wilderness. The planting and layout should resemble nature, but should be firmly under man's control. In more domestic garden styles plants (even trees) are manipulated and contained; the essence of woodland planting is their apparent freedom.

As trees and shrubs came in, especially from North America, in the middle of the eighteenth century, several landowners found it possible to incorporate collections of these exotics inside their parkland. At BENINGBROUGH HALL and FELBRIGG HALL American gardens were established where trees such as *Quercus rubra*, the black walnut (*Juglans nigra*) acers, catalpa and tulip trees (*Liriodendron tulipifera*) and acid-loving shrubs such as kalmia, deciduous rhododendrons, vacciniums and magnolias were planted in groves. Interestingly, Holford's first planting in the arboretum at Westonbirt (1829) was in seventeenth-century style, with great blocks of trees divided by alleys in quite formal and related patterns. As the trees developed, each specimen needed space to realize its full potential, and gradually their shapes and habits took over the design. Paths and rides were diverted and curved to reveal a tree or group where tree and shrub association was particularly successful and natural open planting of low-growing foliage and flowering trees such as maples succeeded thick planting of dark conifers. Today the mature arboretum, owing much to the Victorian passion for collecting, shows woodland gardening as an art form, grassy sunlit glades alternating with shady groves, and many shrubs thriving under the natural canopies made by overhanging branches.

By the end of the nineteenth century woodland gardening became closely linked and almost synonymous with great plantings of rhododendrons introduced in quantity from the Himalayas. Sir Joseph Hooker (1817–1911), at first working in Glasgow but later director at Kew, in succession to his father, also took part in major plant-hunting expeditions. From Sikkim *Rhododendron arboreum* and many of its hybrids were planted in Trust gardens such as BODNANT, KILLERTON, LANHYDROCK, NYMANS, PLAS NEWYDD, TRENGWAINTON and WAKEHURST PLACE.

KILLERTON, in fact, was already developing in the 1770s, when Sir Thomas Acland with the help of his Agent John Veitch, who later founded the great nursery of that name, laid out the park and planted some of the trees which later provided shelter and shade for further exotic introductions. Veitch's nursery, later transferred to Exeter a few miles away and with a branch in London, sent out plant-hunters all over the world, and became a source of plants for the whole country. Conifers and trees from America and the Far East grew from the seed collected, and the south slopes at Killerton provided the ideal situation for the groves of *Rhododendron arboreum*. Today many of these grow into huge bushes, the true species usually tall and growing to reveal erect trunks. At BODNANT the second Lord Aberconway, whose grandfather had started by planting newly introduced conifers and other trees in the glen, developed the whole garden into a great terraced landscape, partly formal in concept, but retaining the steep-sided gullies ideal for rhododendron cultivation. After 1905 many new hybrids were introduced here, where the acid soil, humid atmosphere and high rainfall, combined with the dappled shade of overhead tree canopies, provided suitable conditions. Bodnant, in fact, does not have very mild winters, but the site and the tree planting in the glen help to create favourable pockets of microclimate for tender plants. The average lowest temperature each winter at Bodnant is −10°C (14°F) and in 1981–82 temperatures fell to −14°C (7°F) combining with a Force 8 gale to produce a considerable chill factor. Thousands of rhododendrons died (Mr Martin Puddle, the Head Gardener, says it could be as many as 10,000), including 80 per cent of the large-leaved varieties.

As the woodland garden developed beyond the idea of being just a collection of trees, it was realized that favoured coastal strips in the west and south-west, with a high rainfall, had microclimates where the more tender plants would thrive. Shelter belts to provide protection against salt-laden winds were planted. The acid but often poor soil could be improved and extra topsoil imported. For the shelter belts it was found that the Monterey pine (*Pinus radiata*) and Monterey cypress (*Cupressus macrocarpa*) grew quickly and survived the worst gales. Some of these coastal gardens, among which GLENDURGAN, OVERBECKS, TRELISSICK and TRENGWAINTON belong today to the Trust, are notable for their rare 'plantsmen's' collections (see Appendix 1).

The grand-style rhododendron gardens still exist today. Among National Trust properties perhaps PLAS NEWYDD now has the most favourable conditions. Inevitably, rhododendrons tend to become the specialist's obsession, and their culture, breeding and nomenclature highly skilled and technical. For these reasons this book will not describe the garden landscapes which are entirely dominated by the genus. Instead rhododendrons will be mentioned when, as so often, they are part of a rather broader scheme. Although they require many of the same climatic and soil conditions as do a great number of exotics which can be cultivated in our temperate climate, yet they do not permit the three layers of plant growth which seem to be such a satisfying feature of woodland gardening: their dense evergreen canopy does not allow other plants to thrive beneath them.

In 1881 William Robinson published *The Wild Garden*. In this book, written when the Victorian bedding craze was at its height, he advised growing hardy plants, both native and exotic, in conditions where they would thrive. What seems common sense to us was revolutionary to the Victorians.

The site for each plant would provide as nearly as possible the conditions of a plant's native habitat. In the outer garden fringes, in woodland and by streams, native and hardy plants from northern and temperate areas of the world might be naturalized together. To quote Robinson in the use of the hardy exotics: 'What it does mean is best explained by the winter aconite flowering under a grove of native trees in February; by the Snowflake growing abundantly in meadows by the Thames side . . . and by the Apennine anemone staining an English wood blue before the blooming of our blue bells.' Lilies, bluebells, foxgloves, irises, windflowers, columbines, rock-roses, violets, cranesbills, countless pea-flowers, mountain avens, brambles, cinquefoils, evening primroses, clematis, honeysuckle, Michaelmas daisy, wood-hyacinths, daffodils, bindweeds, forget-me-nots, omphalodes, primroses, day-lilies, asphodels and St Bruno's lily were some that he recommended. In his natural woodland native wood anemones (*Anemone nemorosa*), lily-of-the-valley (*Convallaria majalis*), Lent lily (*Narcissus pseudonarcissus*), snowdrops (*Galanthus nivalis*), Solomon's seal (species and hybrids of polygonatum), woodruff (*Galium odoratum*) and sweet violet (*Viola odorata*) would spread happily in drifts between hardy exotic woodlanders, which proved equally adaptable in suitable conditions. Small cyclamen species from Europe would contribute flowers and leaves through most of the months, and members of the Boraginaceae such as the blue-flowered *Brunnera macrophylla*, omphalodes, and coarse-leaved *Trachystemon orientale* would flourish beside the native forget-me-not (*Myosotis alpestris*).

At the time Robinson was writing many of the woodland gardens administered by the Trust today were being planted. A whole new garden 'style' was being established, a style which allowed for Robinsonian principles to be adopted. These hardy plants made the ideal 'cover' below tiers of deciduous shrub and tree canopies, and filled pockets of bare earth between rhododendron and other evergreen exotics. Since Robinson's time many new plants have been introduced from abroad and new cultivars of those he knew have much extended the choice.

The smaller perennials, bulbs (or even shrubs) that thrive at ground level below the skirts of taller, mainly deciduous, trees and shrubs make woodland planting seem natural. These plants can be native: snowdrops, wood anemones, primroses, bluebells, foxgloves and ferns, besides other woodlanders which we may consider weeds, such as rose bay willow herb, and dog's mercury, thrive at the lower edge of a wood, germinating and spreading rapidly from dispersed seed. The use of native vegetation clearly encourages the illusion that planting is natural, and emphasizes the woodland and 'wild' character of a site, but there are plenty of introduced small hardy plants which play their part.

Golden aconites (*Eranthis hyemalis*) spread under the bole of some large deciduous forest tree, and marbled-leaved cyclamen, among which *Cyclamen coum*, *C. repandum* or *C. hederifolium* are in leaf or flower most months of the year. Little anemones from Europe (including *Anemone blanda* and *A. apennina*), erythroniums, blue-eyed Mary (*Omphalodes verna*) from southern Europe and *O. cappadocica* from Turkey thrive in cool shade. In moist shade astilbes and hostas contribute both interesting foliage and flowers, and symphytum species and cultivars will carpet the ground to suppress weeds. One of the most invasive small shrubs, *Gaultheria shallon* with leathery evergreen leaves and pinkish-white flowers, flourishes where an overhead canopy is quite dense, and will colonize in moist lime-free soil. At CRAGSIDE it has become dominant over vast areas of the pleasure grounds. Many of these plants if given a cool root run are not fussy about soil type; in woods fallen leaves are a natural humus-making mulch which they find hospitable. In the alkaline soil at HIDCOTE both *Symphytum* 'Hidcote Pink' and *S.* 'Hidcote Blue' have effectively colonized shady beds by the stream. At POLESDEN LACEY aconites, crocus and scillas underplant winter- and spring-flowering shrubs, to make an attractive area in a garden which remains open to visitors the whole year.

Many newly introduced trees and shrubs, including the rhododendron, were found to need not so much protection from extreme cold but shelter from dehydrating sunshine and cold winds. These plants, in order to develop their potential, required an aspect as nearly as possible like that of their native habitat. The woodland garden evolved to provide these 'natural' sites, where plants in beautiful associations with each other could thrive. Often the most suitable gardens were those where existing woodland already made adequate shelter belts round the most exposed part of a property, and where in reasonably mature groves, clearings could be made, with access paths following easy natural contours. Overhead branches of deciduous trees provided just the right amount of frost protection and summer shading. It was far more difficult to start in an open virgin site, where even establishing perimeter shelter belts could take years, and newly planted specimen trees needed firm staking as well as a summer mulch to prevent the soil drying out.

In a smaller garden the existence of a single large tree may be enough to create some of the same effects as extended woodland, at least providing some overhead shelter, although if shallow-rooting it may not be possible to plant near the bole. The roots of birch are very near the surface, taking all the moisture, while beech trees have such a dense overhead canopy and root system that few plants will thrive near or under them. Deciduous oaks are more benign but slow-growing, taking at least 30 years to influence the character of the planting site, while evergreen oaks, especially *Quercus ilex*, have such dense foliage that no rain showers can penetrate. At TINTINHULL HOUSE two large *Quercus ilex* shade camellias and azaleas growing in neutral soil, but even in winter the ground never becomes sufficiently saturated for the plants to do well. Unfortunately local tap-water is alkaline. Even a few large spreading shrubs provide the shade at ground level which allows this type of planting. Just as in other forms of gardening the whole scale is not so important as adjusting relative size of planting areas.

A wood or shrubbery does not necessitate a vast acreage, and many Trust gardens, perhaps better known for sunny borders or formal parterres, reflect the Victorian love of shrubberies, and have developed these in the Robinsonian sense with attractive lower layers of smaller herbaceous perennials and bulbs.

In the woodland at SHUGBOROUGH winding walks surround beds on the edges of which suitable low-upkeep perennials such as *Geranium endressii*, which flowers all through the summer, spring-flowering *Brunnera macrophylla*, the lady's mantle (*Alchemilla mollis*) and drifts of hostas cover the ground and much reduce hand-weeding. Between the shrub beds and around specimen cedars and beech, daffodils are naturalized to make a yellow carpet in spring, while in denser shade bluebells thrive to flower in May.

In many ways it may be the pattern of gardening which is most adaptable to a much more restricted space. In the 1930s at the annual Chelsea Flower Show, Percy Cane first introduced the idea of a woodland glade incorporated into a suburban setting. Quite obviously man-made, with well-trimmed grass verges, selected plant areas were broken up with groups of birch and dogwood under which smaller plants rather than grass made a carpet. Planting appeared as informal as possible, but its success depended on keeping the scale in balance, and a willingness to replant and replace when essential framework plants grew too large. Winding grass paths linked each area and with the tree canopies above gave the garden a unity of design which seemed restful and satisfying. Each garden would appear to have been carved out of existing woodland, with as many natural features and contours as possible.

A great woodland garden such as KNIGHTSHAYES COURT can today be a model for such quite small-scale planting. A modern Scandinavian garden is of this type, an area surrounded by enfolding woodland, with almost nothing except a sculpture or garden seat to emphasize its reclamation from the wild. Woodland streams with 'natural' waterfalls might run through such a property or be artificially constructed, extending the range of suitable plants. Obviously in a small garden it is not possible to imitate the natural habitat of Himalayan plants; in this sort of gardening the use of plants of appropriate scale and type is all-important.

For many amateurs the best lessons are learned from visiting large Trust gardens and then adapting a small part of one to the home site. Bedding out and traditional herbaceous borders call for a high degree of technical expertise, but there are limits to each plan and pattern. Successful woodland gardening, because there are no rules of design, depends on sympathetic interpretation of each site's possibilities and an awareness of appropriate plant association which can most easily be gained by observation in good gardens, which set a standard not only of how to plant but how best to maintain the planting over a period of years. While most perennial plants achieve their full potential in a few seasons at the most, trees and shrubs, which dictate neighbouring planting, and ultimately affect the site's characteristics, take many years to reach their maturity.

The fortunate owner acquires land which already is partly wooded. If this has been neglected, indigenous brambles, dog's mercury, bluebells, elder and sycamore seedlings may well have invaded. Many native British trees do not like shade and their

*The garden in the wood at Knightshayes Court. The essence of
woodland gardens lies in making plants appear to grow as naturally
as they would in their native habitats.*

seedlings do not germinate for natural regeneration where man
has interfered, but seedlings of sycamore (*Acer pseudoplatanus*,
probably introduced by the Romans) and the common elder
(*Sambucus nigra*) will germinate in almost any conditions. The
first task is to clear old wood and undesirable undergrowth,
using machinery and modern chemicals if necessary. Then,
before planting, thin back lower tree branches to let in light and
air.

If the area is large enough, plan at the outset to have open
glades planted with grass to contrast with thicker planting, but it
is useless to attempt to make grass grow under shade trees. It is
important to remember that taking out a mature tree permanently changes the site's character, and any replacement needs a
lifetime to grow. As at Knightshayes, it is important to ensure
adequate replacements of mature trees many years before they
are likely to fail. By so doing the essential woodland characteristics are maintained. If all the forest trees had to be felled at one
time the next layer of canopy would be totally exposed to wind
and sun.

The 'garden in the wood' at Knightshayes has been made

since the Second World War by Sir John and Lady Heathcoat Amory. Now administered and owned by the National Trust, to whom Sir John left the house and gardens, the plantings of magnolias and other exotics which took place within the last thirty or forty years have matured. At the same time the garden continues to grow in botanical richness, as new plants are introduced from modern plant-hunting expeditions. No garden stands still, fixed in time in a particular historical context, least of all Knightshayes, which expresses the vision of the Heathcoat Amorys and will continue to change and to be enriched as plants of quality become available. Gardening on this scale, as much as in a more modest-sized garden, requires a constant awareness of the growth potential of each tree or shrub, and the disciplined organization to ensure that each specimen can be allowed space to develop naturally. At times trees and smaller plants have to be removed to give space to neighbouring plant growth; the Head Gardener, Mr Michael Hickson, in common with the Trust as a whole, thinks and plans not only for a year ahead but for a far-distant future.

Knightshayes remains, perhaps, the best example of post-war woodland planting in any Trust garden. On a south-sloping site, in acid soil, large trees mostly planted in the nineteenth century) were judiciously thinned (never easy, because of letting in wind) and successive layers of smaller deciduous trees and conifers, shrubs, carpeting plants and bulbs have been used to create one of the most beautiful and botanically interesting gardens in Britain. Wide grass paths follow open glades, and curl round the natural contours, while steeper ancillary ways follow steps cut between thick planting. Any quite small woodland garden could follow a similar pattern, although few sites offer such favourable aspect and soil conditions as this in East Devon. The planting at Knightshayes demonstrates how many good plants tolerate and welcome light shade; and how effectively overhead canopies prevent the worst frost damage. Young shrubs suffer particular damage from untimely frosts in late spring and early autumn. In spring the young shoots are vulnerable, and in autumn, especially after a good growing summer, lax vegetative growth has not had a chance to ripen and harden. Our island climate isolates Britain from the low winter temperatures and hot summers of mid-Europe, but its unpredictable quality is confusing to plants which are used to the extremes of a long period of cold, followed by a growing season of predictable elngth. So many gardeners want a garden site in an open situation where planting has to be limited to sun-lovers. In the Knightshayes wood vast roses, species clematis and honeysuckle clamber through shrubs and trees to reach the light, their roots in cool shade, in conditions approximating to their native habitats. The south-sloping site allowing free frost drainage and the rich lime-free soil together provide enviable conditions.

In one of the glades at Knightshayes an island bed, almost elliptical in outline, is planted with groups of shrubs, perennials, bulbs and grasses. To the south-west a tall golden Atlas cedar (*Cedrus libani atlantica* 'Aurea') casts shade and a more fastigiate *Ginkgo biloba* grows on the south-eastern edge of the bed. Along the south a thicket of *Philadelphus coronarius* dates from earlier in this century when it marked the line of a path leading through the wood to the village church. The white flowers still fill the wood with fragrance in late June.

Pterostyrax hispida makes a light foliage canopy and contributes racemes of scented white flowers in early summer, flowers which hang on as attractive fruits during winter. Its leaves colour well in autumn. Michael Hickson considers this one of the best small ornamental trees, happy to grow in most soils (except perhaps in very shallow chalk) and conditions, and particularly suitable for a small garden. An E. H. Wilson introduction, *Sorbus megalocarpa* with brownish-purple twigs, makes a loose spreading bush above clumps of hostas, and two birch seedlings have grown to substantial proportions.

Hedera helix 'Conglomerata' grows to a dense hummock edging the path near by, and does well in the dry soil, where Spanish bluebells (*Hyacinthoides hispanica* 'Chevithorne') have naturalized. Along the front groups of purple-leaved and golden variegated sage (*Salvia officinalis* 'Purpurascens' and *S.o.* 'Icterina') give bulk, but need renewing from cuttings quite frequently, as they become woody and unshapely. Bushes of *Hypericum* 'Rowallane', a garden hybrid, thrive in this sheltered site, and produce their wide yellow saucers in late summer. This shrub is not reliably hardy in many gardens, often getting cut back in a severe winter. The rare *H. bellum* is also in the bed; smaller and denser in habit, its more cupped flowers are a deep yellow. At the back some new philadelphus plants, grown from seed introduced from Asia in the last few years, have been planted in groups.

Groups of hostas include *Hosta sieboldiana*, with perhaps the largest and most imposing leaves of the genus, grey to glaucous in colour, but with short stumpy flower-heads of pale lilac. *H. fortunei hyacinthina* is very similar, its grey-green leaves, edged with a paler grey line, and its flowers held on taller stems. There are also drifts of the green-leaved *H. fortunei*. These hostas can be left undisturbed for five or seven years. Growing tightly together, they prevent germination of annual weeds. At the back tall euphorbias, a cultivar from Margery Fish called *Euphorbia characias wulfenii* 'Lambrook Gold', has yellowish-green flower-bracts carried above narrow grey-green leaves. Although very ready to seed prolifically, seed which often produces interesting variants, cuttings need to be taken regularly to perpetuate this particularly good strain. Running through the bed are pockets of self-seeding *Euphorbia dulcis*; growing to only 30 cm (12 in), this has leaves which colour vividly in late summer. The rampant spreading feathery *E. cyparissias* is controlled to make carpets under the spreading shrubs.

In 1976, the year of the drought, many meconopsis died away completely, but a new stock is being built up. Monocarpic and self-hybridizing in the wild and in gardens, the seed is precious and is unfortunately tempting to visitors. Here mostly forms of *Meconopsis betonicifolia*, M*M. grandis* and *regia* (the latter hybridized with *M. napaulensis*) are grown. They normally take two to three years to flower: seeds taken in summer are grown as seedlings to be planted out the following spring. These young seedlings are always planted in rich moisture-retaining compost. Foxgloves, originally from Sutton's Excelsior white strain are grown, this type of digitalis differing from the ordinary native *Digitalis purpurea* by flowering all round the stem, instead of only on the side facing the light, and the tubular florets are held horizontally to reveal the markings.

Three different grasses complete the planting scheme. The Lyme grass *Leymus arenarius* (syn. *Elymus arenarius*) is graceful, if invasive, with arching blue-grey broad leaves with wheat-like flower-spikes in summer. The bright gold *Carex elata* 'Knightshayes' and Bowles' golden grass (*Milium effusum* 'Aureum') make eye-catching clumps throughout the bed, the latter being allowed to seed at will, to increase the casual atmosphere.

Cost of upkeep and general maintenance is low considering

the area involved, but skilled hand-weeding is necessary, while the use of a hoe is forbidden, so that 'natural' seeding of the more desirable species is encouraged. The edges next to the grass path are cut with a strimmer using a nylon cord rather than tough saw-edged blades. In this nutrient-rich soil feeding and mulches seem not to be necessary.

Lower down in the wood at Knightshayes conditions for small woodland and alpine plants are improved by raising the beds with peat blocks which will give an easy acid root run. To be successful these must never be allowed to dry out, and need a shady situation and high rainfall or high atmospheric humidity.

Woodland gardening can be a whole ecological world, closely related to 'meadow' gardening where native wild flowers are encouraged to spread and seed, and planting can be only of indigenous trees and shrubs. Great garden writers such as Gertrude Jekyll stress the importance of letting the outer rougher garden fade imperceptibly into countryside beyond the garden boundary, by merging foreign trees and shrubs with native plantings. In her own Surrey garden she prevented any abrupt transition between garden and landscape beyond by free planting of juniper, holly and birch, where the more formal garden ended. Most foreign woodland plants, particularly those from Asia, need the deep acid soil which allows them to take up traces of iron in the soil, and fortunately many thickly wooded areas in Britain have at least a top acid layer, which makes growing them possible. Lime-loving plants usually grow quite happily in these conditions and soil can easily be 'improved' for them. It is possible to bring in acid soil and make special beds for shallow-rooted acid-dependent plants, but this is seldom possible on a large scale. Nor indeed is it entirely desirable. In a region where the soil is clearly calcareous with corresponding native shrubs and flowers, it is rarely satisfactory to come across a garden, or a bed in a garden, where the planting is 'unnatural'. At BARRINGTON COURT azaleas grown in specially prepared soil fill central beds in the lily garden. Slightly raised to minimize leaching of alkaline garden soil, the beds are surrounded by a brick kerb. The massed planting, of deciduous early flowering scented *Rhododendron luteum*, works well, its flower colouring of orange-yellow and scarlet autumn foliage matching the predominantly 'hot' colouring used in this garden compartment. In a sheltered woodland corner at Barrington a similar scheme would look absurd against trees and shrubs suited to the alkaline conditions.

DUNSTER CASTLE on the northern coast of Somerset has a specially favoured climate, and recently many evergreen shrubs which would be considered marginally hardy in most gardens have been planted in the steeply sloping woodland and in beds surrounding the keep above. Three gardeners, under Mr Michael Marshall, look after 17 acres designed for relatively low upkeep. Shrubs such as *Choisya ternata*, *Brachyglottis* 'Sunshine' and various hypericums (including *Hypericum calycinum* which is trimmed each spring with a weed-eater) are massed to give a splendid effect of contrasting textures in green and grey in the upper wood. The apple-green leaves of *Griselinia littoralis*, which will grow tall in this favoured garden, catch the light at the bottom of the slope. Rising on the rock, the castle is massive, and ephemeral flowers and 'colour' seem almost an irrelevance. Trust policy in the last few years continues a programme of gradual clearance of common cherry laurel (*Prunus laurocerasus*) to make space for what will be a unique woodland of strawberry trees (*Arbutus unedo*). The slopes are too steep for roots to be extracted without danger of banks collapsing, so each laurel stump is painted with glyphosate and triclopyr as it is cut back. So far 300 new arbutus have already been planted in the hanging woods. Many other good evergreens such as azara, *Bupleurum fruticosum* and *Prunus laurocerasus* 'Zabeliana', are also in large groups, under which, in separate areas, ground-cover plants are beginning to grow densely together, covering the bare earth. Among these *Rubus tricolor*, with burnished trailing stems and glossy heart-shaped leaves, spreads quickly where the ground is almost bare rock. this tough colonizer was put in almost without roots, each hole made with a crowbar. In another place the upright-growing bushes of an uncommon privet, *Ligustrum quihoui*, which has panicles of white flowers in summer are grown. In fact, although flower colour is not the primary consideration, groups of philadelphus, libertia and, lower down the slope, in the damp Mill Garden, small brightly flowering azaleas, do contribute extra interest. The brown peeling stems of neillias and stephanandra arch above the invasive dead-nettle, *Lamium galeobdolon* (syn. *Lamiastrum galeobdolon*), which here has adequate space, but is seldom recommended for a small garden. Many other tender plants are grouped in the wood, and are grown as specimens near the castle walls.

Many gardens which become woodland in character as trees grow through the years initially had a period style. A seventeenth-century 'wilderness' might have been planned with shady walks which radiated from a lawn or central focus; over the centuries while the original design was neglected, the site might become a 'natural' wood. Sometimes even a formal garden can, over the years, develop a new character of its own. Trees and shrubs, especially evergreens, mature and create woodland where none was intended. In Italy, too, many of the great Renaissance villas, once in open sites surrounded by green alleys of cypress, clipped ilex and box have by the twentieth century developed a haunting woodland character, as trees have grown mature and spreading canopies filter the strong Italian sunlight.

Something of a similar atmosphere is evoked at ICKWORTH. The classically proportioned rotunda with its curving wings is today framed by great cedars planted in the early nineteenth century, just after the house was built, and evergreen trees and shrubs, originally chosen for their Mediterranean flavour, have turned open lawns to the south into shady walks. Instead of the tender aromatic myrtles and cistus of Italian woods, hollies, phillyreas and box are hardy in the cold but dry East Anglian climate. What was once a formal layout is now more sylvan, just as in Italy time and plant growth has often disguised and softened the clear-cut edges of an original design.

To the early planting of cedars of Lebanon (*Cedrus libani*) which described a sweeping curve to the north of the house, Atlas cedars (*C.l. atlantica*) were later added, and in the 1880s a collection of wellingtonias (*Sequoiadendron giganteum*) were planted and still thrive. To the south of the house more evergreen trees and appropriate shrubs were massed to give a distinguished setting to the classical rotunda and curving wings of the house. *Quercus ilex*, phillyreas, ligustrum, ilex and box weave a pattern of textured green, some planted informally in groups, others lining paths or edging green alleys. Against the house walls a specimen Lawson cypress (*Chamaecyparis lawsoniana*) and *Phillyrea latifolia* have grown large, but planting today continues in the same theme. *Ilex latifolia, Osmanthus decorus* (until recently still *Phillyrea decora*), *Ligustrum japonicum* 'Macrophyllum' and *L. quihoui* and Portugal laurel (*Prunus lusitanica*) are underplanted with large-leaved ivy, both *Hedera colchica* and its arborescent form, the Alexandrian laurel (*Danaë racemosa*) from southern Europe which thrives in dry shade, and with hellebores and ferns.

When the Trust took over the garden in 1956 it found that many of the originally planted evergreen trees needed severe pruning and this has now been carried out, at the same time as continuing to plant in the same theme.

Mr Jan Michalak, the Head Gardener, has played a part in the restoration of the garden. He comments that in the first years the dense planting to the south of the house needed to be partly cleared and large areas were put down to lawn. Eventually the big *Quercus ilex* had to be severely cut back, and it took eight years or so for these trees to make enough regrowth to once more assume their graceful proportions. At the same time shrubberies have been replanted to make dense masses of textured green foliage and to separate different garden areas, adding elements of surprise and mystery to a tour of the garden. The collection of box now includes many cultivars and is being continually augmented: Ickworth now holds the National Collection for the NCCPG (see Appendix 1). Between two old yew trees, privet and box bushes are typical of planting at Ickworth. In the bed a pendulous privet (*Ligustrum sinense* 'Pendulum') dominates surrounding box bushes, although *Buxus sempervirens* 'Latifolia Maculata', with large leaves splashed with gold, is eye-catching among more sombre greens. *B.s.* 'Handsworthiensis' has green leaves with a pronounced 'blue' tone, and *B. microphylla* 'Curly Locks' is a dwarf spreading bush with small rolled leaves which become distinctly bronze in winter.

In Loudon's 'Gardenesque' style, the Victorian shrubbery, partly evolved as a means of displaying a collection of trees and shrubs. Specimen conifers, newly introduced in the middle of the nineteenth century, and shrubs such as aucuba, arriving from Japan in 1861, augmented the 'evergreen' possibilities, and were planted in contoured island beds where winding paths and boskage disguised the sometimes quite modest proportions of a villa or suburban garden. Today many of these trees and shrubs have grown large, and although the areas are not 'woods', the site offers the conditions that the smaller woodland plants enjoy. One tree in a garden can create woodland conditions for the plants beneath it.

At PECKOVER HOUSE the Victorian shrubbery includes aucuba, hollies with green and variegated leaves, a large

At Dunster most of the views in the outer garden reveal the naturalistic style of the planting, and this is especially true of the riverside effects.

Hydrangea aspera sargentiana, a thriving monkey puzzle (*Araucaria araucana*), the redwood (*Sequoia sempervirens*), planting of the prostrate *Viburnum davidii*, and a massed ground-cover edging of bergenias. At NYMANS the edges of the drive are shaded by tall trees, but the light canopy allows good shrubbery-type planting below. In front of tall holly hedges, plants are tightly packed together to prevent weed germination, and deciduous shrubs such as deutzia, philadelphus and shrub roses spread over good flowering herbaceous perennials which need little attention through the seasons. *Deutzia longifolia* 'Veitchii' has rich lilac clustered flowers in July. Peonies, crambe, catmint, *Trachystemon orientalis* with large coarse leaves, alchemilla and hostas all flower freely in spite of the shade. Through the holly hedge and twining over arches of clipped holly a vigorous small-flowered white rose, probably 'Madame d'Arblay', reaches up to the light.

Four gardens in the South West owned by the National Trust have very favourable microclimatic conditions: high rainfall, mild winter temperatures and prolonged daylight. COLETON FISHACRE, GLENDURGAN, OVERBECKS and TRENGWAINTON provide the conditions most suitable for experimenting with the sort of semi-tropical plants which thrive on Tresco, not far away in the Scillies. At Trengwainton proteas and leucadendrons, plants which need a relatively mild climate, moving air and a soil almost devoid of nutrients, have been planted. Near the walled garden in deep shade a group of olearias succeeds. *Olearia ilicifolia, O. paniculata*, the rarer *O. arborescens* and grey-leaved *O. × mollis* all produce copious white daisy-flowers even in this sunless position. This Australasian genus, the daisy bush or tree daisy, is temperamental, but it is now thought that they prefer a soil low in phosphorus. Many of them are tender and at Trengwainton there is a further selection in the walled 'bays'.

In the Trengwainton woodland, originally of beech, ash and sycamore, further wind shelter has been given by Monterey pines and Monterey cypresses, and a more recently planted stand of Leyland cypress to the south-west in the path of the prevailing wind. In the wood nothofagus species will grow quickly to give overhead canopies. *Eucryphia cordifolia*, its hybrid with *E. lucida*, and *E. moorei*, with evergreen pinnate leaves, are all outstanding. The tender *Lomatia ferruginea* and *Weinmannia trichosperma*, tree ferns (*Dicksonia antarctica*) and the walking fern (*Woodwardia radicans*), which roots at the tips of its fronds, grow in sheltered pockets. Large-leaved rhododendrons such as *RR. grande, falconeri* and *sinogrande* grow with many of the late-flowering smaller species. *R.* 'Rosevallon' (a *neriiflorum* hybrid) has leaves with violet-purple undersides and scarlet flower-trusses. *R. griersonianum* produces its scarlet bell-shaped flowers in June. Under the trees clumps of hydrangeas flower prolifically through autumn until the first frost, and both the blue and white-flowered forms of willow gentian (*Gentiana asclepiadea*) have naturalized all through the woodland. Along the streamside primular, astilbe and rodgersia and many other moisture-loving plants grow in natural drifts.

In the much more open site at GLENDURGAN snowdrops, Lent lilies (*Narcissus pseudonarcissus*) aquilegias and bluebells grow on the steep banks which edge the valley leading down to the harbour. Snowdrops grow in the shade where groves of trees are planted. On other banks St John's wort (*Hypericum calycinum*) makes a weed-suppressing carpet. At TRELISSICK the lavender-

coloured wood anemone (*Anemone nemorosa* 'Allenii') is naturalized in grass.

In the clean atmosphere and humidity of many of the woodland gardens of the South-West, and in the high-rainfall areas
such as Northern Ireland, lichen growth on tree trunks and
branches is a problem; rhododendrons and azaleas are particularly prone. The deciduous azaleas can be sprayed in winter with
tar-oil, and trunks of magnolias and even larger trees also
respond to this treatment. Evergreen forms have to have
branches cut back to make them break below an affected area.
Mr Peter Horder, the Head Gardener at Trengwainton finds
that if plants are cut back early in the season new shoots have
time to harden off before the winter. The rough-barked forms of
rhododendrons are more ready to put out new shoots, but those
which have smooth bark will seldom 'break' again. After trimming back the plants are given a slow-acting fertilizer such as
Enmag, as well as Vitax Q4 as soon as growth begins. Healthy
well-fed plants are much less likely to get disease. At Trengwainton they have stopped using Arbrex on all cut stumps
because it is now believed that nature quickly seals and heals a
'raw' wound. This sort of 'pruning' is also essential in old woodland gardens, and Mr Mike Snowden, the Head Gardener at
ROWALLANE in Northern Ireland, has found that many rhododendrons can be cut back to improve their shapes if half a bush is
done at a time, rather than a drastic overall cut, which puts a lot
of strain on the plant in its efforts to make new growth.

Meadows

Besides encouraging his readers to grow many flowers both
native and foreign 'naturally' in rough grass, which was not
mown until after leaves died down in spring, William Robinson
advocated meadow gardening, where only the true wild flora
would be seen. Today as our native flora is increasingly threat-
ened by farmers' sprays (or the predatory collector) its preservation is as necessary as a new style of more 'natural' gardening is
attractive. Butterflies and other wildlife also benefit, maintenance programmes are less intensive and expensive, and visitors
appreciate the chance to compare the appearance of the wild
member of a genus or a pure species with the highly bred garden

cultivar. In early English gardens up to the end of the seventeenth century, wild flowers were encouraged to grow under orchard trees to make 'flowering meades', but the idea of wild or natural gardening was not accepted again until the time of William Robinson and Gertrude Jekyll. While gardening fashions changed through almost two centuries, wild flowers still continued to flourish, in woods, ditches and hedgerows, and it was only recently that so many became almost extinct. Naturalists say that 95 per cent of the flowery English meadows have disappeared in the last forty years and many that survive are now protected in National Trust open space properties.

In 1881 William Robinson wrote, 'Not to mow is almost a necessity in the wild garden: considering that there is frequently in large gardens much more mown surface than is necessary . . . surely it is enough to have a portion of lawn as smooth as a carpet at all times without shaving off the long and pleasant grass of the other parts of the grounds . . . mowing this grass once a fortnight . . . is a costly mistake . . . we want shaven carpets of grass here and there, but . . . who would nor rather see the waving grass with countless flowers than a close surface without a blossom.'

Partly because of the need for economy, but also to preserve scarce wild and naturalized flowers, the Trust has always taken this advice in appropriate places. In many Trust gardens, as in those privately owned, there are good reasons for establishing or retaining some sort of wild-flower meadow. Today when mowing and edging machines of every type are available for grass cutting, and selective herbicides and fertilizers make lawn management simple (if expensive), gardens can become too manicured. Most gardens do benefit visually from some smooth tightly cut conventional lawn, but even this can look better when a neighbouring area of longer grass presents a pleasant textural contrast. The lawn area can be extended to grass paths which make a firm crisp line beside or around a section where the mowing programme is quite different. From a designer's point of view the rougher section can make as satisfactory a contrast as more colourful flower beds, and the two areas are linked together firmly by the horizontal ground pattern of mown paths. Both Robinson and Jekyll still preserved formality and shaven lawns near the house in the 'inner' garden, but they saw the value of a gradual transition, enhanced by changing height and texture, and hence appearance and colour, from this part to the outer garden edges where orchard trees or even countryside merged with garden plants. If this rougher grass could be encouraged to display a colourful range of flowering plants and grasses, so much the better.

Another reason for gardening in rough grass is to save maintenance costs. Instead of the weekly cut through summer months (usually about 29 times in the whole year, depending on weather conditions), cutting is done much less frequently. It is true that when it is done more work is involved if grass has to be carted off. But it is much less necessary to have a fixed timetable; a few days or even weeks one way or the other allows more relaxed gardening and other essential tasks to be completed. Even gathering and sowing seed to increase a range of plants does not have to be done as an exacting programme. At SIZERGH CASTLE, ROWALLANE and SHEFFIELD PARK, flowers and grasses are only those which arrive 'naturally', their seeds carried by wind or insects (ants are said to transport primrose seed, while many of the daisy-flowered Compositae blow in).

A third and compelling reason for establishing a 'meadow' is in order to preserve the dwindling pasture population of flora and wildlife which modern farm sprays tend to eradicate or destroy. The National Trust, by encouraging this sort of gardening, plays its part in preserving the heritage of native flora, and in general provides an education in ecological gardening, which is much appreciated by the millions of visitors, including parties of school children.

Obviously the wild flowers or exotic bulbs which can also find a place here will vary with the type and pH of the soil. The native flora of chalk soils is different from that of deep clay or strongly acid peaty loam. It is possible to have a 'meadow' in woodland, in shade or sun, on north-facing or south-facing slopes. In moist boggy soil the flowers which thrive are different from those found to do their best in well-drained ground.

In poor soil, especially on chalk or limestone, undisturbed pasture can easily be encouraged to grow native local and other flowers, but establishing attractive 'meadows' where there is nutrient-rich soil is much more difficult. Fortunately where an area has been closely cut as lawn for many years there is usually a low level of fertility and when grass is initially allowed to grow to hay length wild flowers appear without being introduced. Natural colonization will take place over a period of years, but herbs and grasses can be introduced by seed. Small quantities of the seed is mixed with a seed compost and sown in autumn or spring in small pockets. Vetches and clovers are easily established in this way. Seeds can be taken from buttercups (*Ranunculus bulbosus*), ox-eye daisies (*Leucanthemum vulgare*), cowslips (*Primula veris*), fritillaries (*Fritillaria meleagris*) an meadow cranesbill (*Geranium pratense*) growing in some local waste ground, and either sown straight into the meadow or, best of all, raised to be planted out later. If an old pasture is being ploughed up locally it may be possible to obtain a few turves which will contain seed and seedlings of the flora.

If nettles and docks grow luxuriantly in a rough area this is usually an indication of nutrient-rich soils. For a few years the area should be mown tightly and all grass clippings removed. The larger weeds can be sprayed with herbicides. After a time even the most vigorous of the grasses will have been weakened and the 'meadow' programme can begin, and new plants introduced. If feasible the whole area can be ploughed up and reseeded with a fescue/bent mixture to which can be added small amounts of white and red clover seed, and other herbs. Most orchids spread by wind-blown seed, and should never be dug up in the wild.

As well as herbaceous plants, bulbs and tuberous plants will grow strongly in grass which is cut tightly towards the end of the season, or when the leaves have died down. Aconites (*Eranthis hyemalis*) and crocus species, especially *Crocus tommasinianus* and *C. chrysanthus*, flower early and are often grown in lawn which is tightly mown later, as leaves wither quickly, but they will also succeed in the longer meadow grass. The golden aconites prefer light shade from the canopy of a deciduous tree, and like snowdrops multiply most freely in a damp site. *Crocus vernus* grows in many coloured forms at LACOCK ABBEY. Narcissus species and especially the native *Narcissus pseudonarcissus* thrive in acid loam and filter through the woods at STOURHEAD. More showy daffodils can be planted in drifts of different colours. In the orchard at SISSINGHURST CASTLE clumps of daffodils mingle with snake's head fritillaries and other native plants. Moisture is very important for daffodils and they prefer heavy to light soil. At ASCOTT bulbs of anemones, crocuses, fritillaries (*Fritillaria meleagris*), scillas and tulips are planted in the south-sloping banks, while on the level lawn, under and between trees, there are drifts of daffodils alone. At ACORN BANK a steep escarpment falling to the river valley is covered in spring with assorted narcissi, particularly the valuable fragrant late white *Narcissus poeticus recurvus*. Inside the garden among the orchard trees are wild native tulip (*Tulipa sylvestris*) and wood anemone (*Anemone nemorosa* and its double cultivar 'Vestal'). The soil at Acorn Bank is an alkaline clay. On the sloping lawns at ARLING-TON COURT, Japanese primulas thrive naturalized in grass, and the wild primrose, violet and wood anemone continue to spread. In one corner of the lawn at TRELISSICK there is a carpet of pale lavender-blue *Anemone nemorosa* 'Allenii', *Fritillaria meleagris*, and summer snowflake (*Leucojum aestivum*) which spread through Thamesside Oxfordshire meadows, will naturalize in damp sites. In a very dry site, where beech trees take much of the moisture, martagon lilies, daffodils and bluebells grow in rough grass at FARNBOROUGH HALL. At BLICKLING HALL and WALLINGTON the yellow *Lilium pyrenaicum* is naturalized under trees. Dog's tooth violets (*Erythronium dens-canis*) will grow in the thinner turf in partial shade, but are likely to be swamped in more luxuriant grass. Camassia species and white-flowered star of Bethlehem (*Ornithogalum umbellatum*) do not like too strong competitors, but spread where grass is cut soon after they flower. In June the native bluebell (*Hyacinthoides non-scripta*) makes dense carpets of blue in the woods at WINKWORTH ARBORETUM.

Colchicum autumnale and *C. speciosum*, autumn crocus (*Crocus speciosus*) and even the small gold-flowered *Sternbergia lutea* will survive in grass; for the latter, turf is kept as short as possible during the summer, to allow bulbs the maximum sun during the dormant period. Colchicums and autumn crocus usually start to appear for flowering at the end of August and grass-cutting pro-grammes must be adjusted so that no more mowing is done until early November, just before daffodil spikes for the following spring start to shoot. These bulbs can be moved when in leaf early in the summer.

In a relatively large garden, it may be possible to 'stagger' mowing regimes to encourage different types of wild flowers. Snowdrops (*Galanthus nivalis*) and primroses (*Primula vulgaris*) will thrive in grass in which they are planted if it is given a first cut in June. This may coincide with cutting the leaves of natural-ized daffodils, a task which should be left until six weeks after they have flowered, probably sometime in June. At CLANDON

PARK narcissus and cowslips (*Primula veris*) grow happily together, the latter setting and scattering seed at just about the moment when daffodil leaves have faded sufficiently to allow them to be cut down. In another meadow area a mowing regime can be begun in spring, then left for a six-week period in the middle of summer. Grasses and quick-growing 'flowerers' will give a display even in that short period. The third section will not be cut until orchids have seeded in August or September. Whichever system is adopted, all grass-clippings should be removed, for composting if short, or for hay later.

Mr Malcolm Hutcheson, the Head Gardener at SIZERGH CASTLE in Cumbria, is a knowledgeable botanist and has a made a meadow for local flora on a bank east of the castle. He writes:

❧ The meadow garden at Sizergh Castle is a south-facing embankment, which in spring is covered with the local wild daffodil (*Narcissus pseudonarcissus*). The area is then allowed to grow naturally through the summer months and the flowers of the various native plants give a profusion of colour.

After the daffodils sweet violets (*Viola odorata*), wood anemone (*Anemone nemorosa*), cowslips (*Primula veris*), early purple orchids (*Orchis mascula*), a few green-winged orchids (*O. morio*) and double-flowered cardamine (*Cardamine pratensis* 'Flore Pleno') begin to appear. Among a yellow carpet of dandelions the tiny adder's tongue fern (*Ophioglossum vulgatum*) can be seen. As these plants fade they are replaced by the meadow and wood cranesbill (*Geranium pratense* and *G. sylvaticum*), moon or ox-eye daisies (*Leucanthemum vulgare*), bugle (*Ajuga reptans*), bird's-foot trefoil (*Lotus corniculatus*), fox and cubs (*Hieracium aurantiacum*), a few twayblade (*Listera ovata*) and numerous greater butterfly orchids (*Platanthera chlorantha*).

The soil of the bank is shallow as it overlays local limestone. It does not contain much humus and is starved, thus discouraging the taller 'rank' grasses. As a consequence, a range of the finer grasses prevails in the summer months, their nodding flower-heads and arching leaves adding much to the attraction of the meadow. Timothy (*Phleum pratense*), quaking and sweet vernal grasses (*Briza media* and *Anthoxanthum odoratum*), Yorkshire fog (*Holcus lanatus*) and wild oats (*Avena fatua*) are in evidence.

Grass cut at different levels, with tightly mown lawn in the foreground, creates contrasting effects. At Sizergh Castle daisies give a natural, unmanicured appearance.

Among the final show are hardheads (*Centaurea nigra*), betony (*Stachys officinalis*) and the green and red fruits of lords and ladies (*Arum maculatum*) growing under the canopies of trees.

Maintenance of the area is relatively simple, as the first cut is not done until late August or early September, according to the season. By delaying cutting until this time of year most of the plants have seeded naturally, which is particularly important for the daffodils and various orchids. A wet season may give a longer show of colour, even if some of the grasses are flattened by the rain.

Cutting is done by rotary mower and all the cut 'hay' is removed and used for making compost. The whole area is then cut once or twice during the remainder of the growing season to produce a short turf to withstand the winter and to allow the bulbs to give a good show the following spring and summer.

The 'starved' soil, which is neither strongly acid nor alkaline, accounts for such a wide range of plants appearing on the site. No seed from a commercial or other source has been introduced. It is particularly pleasing to note that after some fifteen years of the same treatment some of the orchids, including the Fly Orchid (*Ophrys insectifera*) which is at the northernmost limit of its habitat here, and rarer flora are increasing. ❧

At SHEFFIELD PARK to the east of the third lake on the site of an old cricket pitch (where Australian teams played in the 1800s), a meadow of wild flowers, of interest to botanists and the conservationists, has been encouraged to develop. Each year the Head Gardener ensures that all the wild flowers are allowed to seed and disperse before the grass is cut. Orchids include *Dactylorhiza fuchsii*, its stout stem rising from spotted leaves to bear lilac or whitish flower-heads. Butterflies also have greatly benefited from this meadow area.

At ROWALLANE in Northern Ireland a paddock is being treated as a meadow for wild flowers. Mown paths round the edge and a swathe through the centre define the shapes of the meadow area where cuts of the long grass are timed to allow seeding. Here the soil is also lime-free. Plants such as lady's bedstraw (*Galium verum*) and marsh bedstraw (*G. palustre*) mingle with knapweed or hardheads (*Centaurea nigra*), moon-pennies or ox-eye daisies (*Leucanthemum vulgare*). Vetches which do not need calcareous soil are also found here.

Orchis mascula flowers in late spring, and the cowslip and oxlip hybrid (*Primula veris* × *elatior*) has made a colony. The grass is cut in August when seeding is complete and then cut regularly until winter.

——————BULBS AT WIMPOLE——————

As in many large estate gardens, extensive plantings of daffodils can be found in the pleasure grounds at WIMPOLE HALL. Here nearly all the bulbs were first forced for house decoration, but were then planted out each year. Describing the culture as 'nothing out of the ordinary', Mr Philip Whaites, the Head Gardener, attests that the display gets better every year:

❧ From November onwards, grass cutting ceases. The bulbs continue to grow throughout the winter, flower in spring, and are then allowed to dry off completely until the end of July. At that point the area is finally cut as hay, dried to allow the wild flower seeds to fall to the ground and is then carted off and baled. The bulb area is then cut every 14 days or so with a ride-on rotary mower, and cuttings are left on the surface.

By this particular method of culture we not only get a spectacular show of daffs, but also a marvellous collection of wild flowers, including cowslips, celandines, primroses, bluebells, blue and white violets, snowdrops, twayblades, forget-me-nots and lesser purple, early purple and bee orchids. ❧

Narcissi at Wimpole

'Actaea'	'Geranium'	'Mrs Barclay'
'Bath's Flame'	'Golden Harvest'	'Mrs Ernst H. Krelage'
'Beersheba'	'John Evelyn'	'Mrs R. O. Backhouse'
'Carlton'	'King Alfred'	'Red Rascal'
'Cheerfulness'	'Mary Copeland'	'Rembrandt'
'Cragford'	'Mount Hood'	'Sempre Avanti'
'Fortune'		

Natural planting and low maintenance

William Robinson's theories on wild or 'natural' planting discussed under woodland gardens always sound invitingly labour-saving and practical. In fact this not always so. Plants grown together in the ways he recommends seldom develop at the same rate, and the most vigorous tend to dominate the planting scheme after a few years. The skill in this sort of gardening lies not only in being able to visualize the ultimate 'picture' in an artistic sense, in some cases not to be realized for many years, but also in placing plants together which will grow in the same conditions *and* will enhance each other, and most importantly not need constant re-shuffling and careful hand-weeding where soil is bare between plants or groups of plants. Many gardens besides those belonging to the Trust show his influence but there are degrees of so-called 'natural' planting between the careful placing of suitable hardy plants in beds in light woodland and on the outer fringe of the garden, true meadow gardening and gardening at a low level of maintenance, where random seeding of desirable plants is encouraged, and grass is not kept as smooth and weed-free as a bowling alley.

To many gardeners the sight of dandelions growing in

pavement or colonizing a meadow brings to mind the dread of wind-blown seed. In some seasons if conditions of sun and rain have been just right the summer before and, if the previous autumn was warm and sunny, there is suddenly an explosion of germinating seedlings: alchemilla, brunnera, campanula, violas and biennial foxgloves and evening primrose to name but a few. Brambles, elders and milk-thistle benefit from the same conditions and become a pest, needing careful removal by hand, or judicious use of sprays (or a glove specially impregnated with a contact herbicide).

Many old gardens, in fact, become overrun not with traditional weeds but with plants which, originally planted as part of the design, have become weeds, as they are unwanted in particular places. The Welsh poppy (*Meconopsis cambrica*), the Byzantine gladiolus (*Gladiolus communis byzantinus*), *Allium siculum* (now more correctly *Nectaroscordum siculum*), tall verbascum, biennial evening primrose (*Oenothera biennis*) and *Alchemilla mollis* are all good garden plants but if allowed to seed freely will, in time, spoil planting schemes. This is particularly so if colour planning is strict in a garden.

At the same time the gardener in the very dry garden like the American Garden at FELBRIGG HALL, where old trees take much of the moisture, will envy the natural effects gained in a favoured garden with damp acid soil, such as TRENGWAINTON, where the willow-gentian, both blue *Gentiana asclepiadea* and its white form *G.a. alba*, make groups between exotic rhododendron or olearia bushes, and the walking fern (*Woodwardia radicans*) is vigorous in between specimen tree ferns (*Dicksonia antarctica*). At Trengwainton primulas seed along the stream but if the giant cow parsley (*Heracleum mantegazzianum*) was allowed to seed here it would quickly overrun and destroy other smaller plants. Yet it is statuesque and beautiful along the lake at BLICKLING HALL, at BUSCOT PARK and on the orchard edge at HARDWICK HALL.

Low-upkeep gardening becomes a delicate balance between nature literally taking over the garden and a degree of disorder which is acceptable but will not become a danger to existing and desirable design effects, or to good ornamental plants. At GLEN-DURGAN snowdrops, Lent lilies (*Narcissus pseudonarcissus*) aquilegias and bluebells grow on the steep banks which edge the valley leading down to the harbour. On other banks in the garden St

At Anthony House in Cornwall there is a
natural meadow of campions and buttercups.

John's wort (*Hypericum calycinum*) makes a weed-suppressing carpet. Bluebells can quickly spread, their seed carried by birds, to neighbouring flower beds where they multiply and can become a problem if left unchecked.

In the last forty or fifty years the use of ground-covering plants has been recommended for reducing the high cost and burden of routine garden maintenance. There is still, however, considerable confusion in the mind of the amateur about how to use them, as well as about the necessary time-scale which enables these plants to grow together and become effective weed-smotherers. By visiting National Trust gardens and by hearing the behind-the-scenes story from the gardeners themselves, it is possible to assess how this sort of planting works.

The flower beds at HIDCOTE already planted in the first thirty years of this century made use of the same principles. Hardy perennials were densely packed together so that there was no space for weeds to develop. Today we usually consider ground-cover plants as those with strong foliage, in different textures and shades of green (and other colours); these plants are chosen for their density of habit rather than for their flower colour or seasonable performance. Ground-cover plants are those which over a period will grow together shading the soil beneath to discourage the germination of unwanted plant seedlings. The best-ground-cover plants are those which have attractive foliage which is itself an asset. (Grass, of course, cut at different levels is a ground-cover, and its maintenance is far from being labour-free.) Other plants which quickly grow together such as St John's wort, most comfreys (symphytum), lamiums, brunnera, forget-me-not and forms of knotweed (fallopia) can be as invasive as ground-elder or creeping buttercup.

Ivy will flourish in deep shade, and other 'natural' climbers such as *Hydrangea anomala petiolaris* and forms of parthenocissus will quickly spread on the horizontal. Ground-cover works in layers. Shrubs act as weed-suppressants under the canopies of trees; low-growing woody or creeping herbaceous plants and bulbs cover the soil at ground level. Gardening economically means a constant balance between using plants which grow together and keep at bay the unwanted intruder and the problems these plants then create by themselves being so vigorous.

At KNIGHTSHAYES COURT, in the woodland garden made since 1945, foxgloves of the *Digitalis* Excelsior strain give interest after the predominantly spring-flowering plants are finished. The Head Gardener, Mr Michael Hickson, always 'rogues' out those with flowers of pink or mauve at first flower, while encouraging the white forms to multiply. In many Trust gardens like KILLERTON, cyclamen, both autumn-flowering *Cyclamen hederifolium* and spring-flowering *C. coum* and *C. repandum*, appear in drifts under trees and shrubs, their marbled leaves contributing colour at different seasons.

At TINTINHULL blue scillas, *Anemone blanda* from south-east Europe and the Apennine anemone (*A. apennina*) spread in well-mulched soil; flowering to make a carpet of blue in early spring, they convey a feeling of maturity to the garden. These are all plants which can reasonably be controlled. More dangerously the Welsh poppy (*Meconopsis cambrica*) has been encouraged to seed in selected beds; elsewhere the biennial evening primrose

(*Oenothera biennis*) flowers at evening and dusk through the last three months of summer, and the little yellow fumitory (*Corydalis lutea*) lurks in corners of steps. All these plants which cover the ground and control germination of 'true' weed seeds can become a nuisance.

At KNIGHTSHAYES forms of erythronium, omphalodes, Californian Hybrid iris and *Maianthemum bifolium* make an effective under-carpet to the taller shrubs. The latter and erythroniums from different parts of the world are also a feature at STAGSHAW, the woodland garden at Ambleside overlooking Windermere, where beds are less formally arranged and these plants seem to spread at will. Plants grown in this way need less attention than when grown in more formal borders. As William Robinson says in his book *The Wild Garden*, 'No disagreeable effects result from decay. The raggedness of the old mixed border after the first flush of spring was intolerable . . . when lilies are sparsely dotted through masses of shrubs, their flowers are admired more than if they were in isolated showy masses; when they pass out of bloom they are unnoticed amidst the vegetation, and not eyesores, as when in rigid unrelieved tufts in borders.' In fact many of these plants help each other: their foliage not only acts in time as a self-perpetuating natural mulch, but often protects the emergent shoots of some later-flowering plant. The almost evergreen and decorative leaves of spring-flowering hellebores provide the perfect cool yet frost-free cover for young lily shoots which flower in mid- or late summer.

Many plants such as the statuesque giant cow parsley (*Heracleum mantegazzianum*) would be too coarse for a flower bed, but find a place in a rough orchard or on the edge of woodland where they will seed freely in rough grass, as at ROWALLANE. Some foreign introductions such as winter heliotrope (*Petasites fragrans*) spreads and overwhelms choicer border plants, but a colony along a stream bank controls grass and needs little attention.

This sort of gardening calls for an understanding and awareness of the needs of both native and foreign plants, which, in turn, dictates their appropriate use in the informal garden. In planning ahead more consideration is given to plant associations which could occur naturally than to prescribed colour theme or definite seasonal effect. On a sunny bank brooms, cistus and ceanothus will make satisfactory companion plants; in woodland American and Asiatic shrubs thrive together in deep loamy soil;

by streams or pond-side moisture-loving plants from all over the northern and temperate zones of the world, often with strong architectural foliage, look good together. Primulas such as *Primula pulverulenta*, *P. japonica* and *P. florindae* (the latter thriving even in alkaline soils) flower and seed to become naturalized in the right conditions. At TRENGWAINTON they colonize as space permits, almost becoming garden weeds, but useful when transplanted in establishing new garden extensions.

At MONTACUTE HOUSE groups of decoratively foliaged hostas (*Hosta fortunei hyacinthina*) are used under shrub roses. Planted about 30 cm (12 in) apart hostas grow together within a few years, and the more vigorous large-leaved forms such as *Hosta sieboldiana* become impenetrable to weeds. On the west front at Montacute the very vigorous bramble *Rubus tricolor* spreads under the canopy of tall shrubs. Its attractive burnished leaves have silvery undersides, and it can be invasive if put in the wrong place. In a shady very dry corner at TINTINHULL under a pair of *Quercus ilex* a mass of the less common periwinkle, *Vinca difformis*, grows thickly, allowing hellebores, martagon lilies and even spring-flowering *Cyclamen repandum* to push through its foliage. It has very pale blue flowers which it bears in the winter, above pointed green leaves, on arching stems which root as they grow. Up the woodland drive at NYMANS strong-growing perennials such as alchemilla and herbaceous geraniums are massed to save hand-weeding. At BATEMAN'S the creeping *Waldsteinia ternata* grows tightly under a yew hedge and controls the emergence of weeds, although it itself needs sun to flower. At HIDCOTE stream banks are covered with *Symphytum* 'Hidcote Blue'. At GREYS COURT the bright blue-flowering *Lithospermum purpureocaeruleum* (now more correctly called *Buglossoides purpurocaerulea*) grows under a complete canopy of wisteria. This plant certainly suppresses weeds, but can itself become an invasive problem and needs cutting back. At CHARLECOTE PARK the little wild garden in light woodland is carpeted with lamiums, lungworts, herbaceous geraniums and other dwarf plants and bulbs to give a pleasantly informal air, and is very labour-saving. At DUNSTER CASTLE evergreen shrubs cover the ground under tall trees. Banks of *Hypericum calycinum* and *Brachyglottis* 'Sunshine'

At Glendurgan the steep banks above the mouth of the Helford river provide a natural setting for bluebells under the more exotic shrubs.

make weed-free cover on steep slopes where weeding is difficult. In another area the vigorous *Rubus tricolor* spreads under new planting of arbutus groves.

Today it is possible to say that gardening in formal patterns is no more labour-intensive than the constant shuffling and rearrangements of plants in so-called Robinsonian or 'naturalistic' garden areas. By the judicious use of chemicals and plastic sheeting, a knot or maze of a hedging plant set among gravel, or even gravels in different colours, as at LITTLE MORETON HALL or MOSELEY OLD HALL, needs little attention except for an annual clipping and weedkilling using an appropriate contact weedkiller. Even summer bedding needs little attention except for dead-heading, once the tightly packed flowers have grown together. Much of the work involved is in their production towards the end of the winter, and the adequate preparation of the beds and planting, a task usually completed at the time of the autumn planting of winter- and spring-flowering plants.

Gertrude Jekyll followed Robinson in encouraging another sort of labour-saving gardening. She loved to grow what she called 'free-growing' roses, letting them find their way up into old orchard trees or a shabby holly. With small-flowered species clematis and honeysuckle to extend the flowering season, pruning and tying in once a year is all the attention necessary. She planted her favourite white roses, 'The Garland' and 'Aimée Vibert', to grow as cascading fountains where the bloom would hang downwards for all to see, rather than flower-heads opening at the top of a pergola. Today at KNIGHTSHAYES, LYTES CARY, NYMANS, SIZERGH CASTLE and TRERICE, roses such as *R. filipes* and its giant cultivar 'Kiftsgate', 'Bobbie James', 'Francis E. Lester', 'Rambling Rector' and many others give these natural effects, and are as beautiful as any fruit blossom early in the season. These bushes should be planted a few feet from the base of their 'host' and mulched thickly in the spring. At first young shoots are guided upwards into the branches of the tree, but after a season new shoots push up farther to the light and trail downwards to flower with little further help. Pruning consists of removing old wood. Some of these roses can be used as ground cover, growing horizontally, or even pegged down to make a weed-smothering mass of foliage. Some roses such as *Rosa* 'Paulii' and its pink-flowered hybrid *R.* 'Paulii Rosea' actually grow naturally in this way.

—— V ——

PRACTICAL

MAINTENANCE

——

Practically all gardeners welcome the idea of reducing the many hours spent doing repetitive tasks such as mowing grass and edging lawns, cutting hedges, brushing stonework, raking up leaves in autumn and composting garden materials for feeding and mulching flower beds. The National Trust have exactly the same problems of upkeep as the private owner, but because the Trust is a large organization each Head Gardener, Gardener-in-Charge or Gardening Tenant receives advice and guidance not only on policy and planting but also on the technical aspects of gardening. The right choice of a machine to do a specific job entails a decision about the level of maintenance desired. The right choice of ornamental plants will also determine how much time is spent dealing with weeds, the unwanted invaders which spoil a garden scheme.

Labour-saving gardening and the understanding of the use of good ground-cover planting, which with mulches will suppress annual weed germination, is synonymous today with good gardening techniques. Borders beside lawns are edged with brick or stone, tanalized wood or steel strip is used to make neat grass edges, soil is sterilized to control perennial weeds and prevent replant disease, and good organic practice helps combat weed infestations.

LAWN AND TURF CARE

The smooth or textured appearance of grass areas is an intrinsic part of a garden's design. In gardens where a manicured look is an essential part of formality, cylinder machines do weekly (or more frequent) cuts, and grass mowings are picked up. Immaculate edges are necessary to tightly mown lawns, and attending to these is time-consuming. In many Trust gardens beds and borders are firmly outlined with stone or brick set just below the level of the surrounding lawn, allowing plants to spill over the edges without making mowing difficult, and eliminating the need for maintaining firm verged grass edges.

In less formal areas of the garden, however, grass laid at different levels is very visually satisfying, contrasts of colour and

At West Green House an octagonal fruit cage, shown here before restoration, is decorative as well as functional.

texture making a firm pattern. Varying heights can be used to define different areas: in the wilder woodland-type garden, where grass can be kept longer, more closely mown strips will define a pathway and direct the feet. Longer grass can be cut perhaps only 13 or 14 times during a growing season if a length of about 10 cm (4 in) is satisfactory; the average is about 29 times for a smooth lawn.

At ROWALLANE lawn areas, except for those directly round the house, are not kept tightly mown. Instead, paths which wind through woodland and more open glades are cut weekly; under the specimen trees the grass is allowed to grow longer and give an informal atmosphere. At ANGLESEY ABBEY the formal avenues are further emphasized by grass at varying levels. At ARLINGTON COURT spring bulbs and small plants such as primroses, claytonias and violets grow naturalized in the grass, and mowing is delayed until these have set seed.

The care of the well-kept lawn which is an essential feature of a typical English garden is one of the most time-consuming tasks of garden maintenance, and mowing alone can be responsible for about 60 per cent of the cost of lawn upkeep. **Mr James Marshall**, one of the National Trust's Gardens Advisers, analyses the interrelationship of mowing frequency, height of cut, grass varieties and overall appearance, and summarizes other factors in the maintenance of a good-looking and healthy lawn:

MOWING HEIGHTS AND FREQUENCIES

❧ A long-term trial on intensive turf culture by Reading University has come up with some interesting conclusions – confirming, for instance, that regular mowing is better than irregular mowing for intensively managed turf. Very close mowing, 10 mm (½ in) and less, can be damaging to the grass root systems and has to be counterbalanced with irrigation and generous amounts of nutrients. Higher cutting i.e. 15 mm (¾ in), creates a sward that is both more resistant to drought and better looking in the winter months. The longer grass needs less frequent cutting, and the sward proves to be perfectly acceptable when compared with close mowing done at monthly intervals. A major cost reduction is possible by opting for the slightly longer grass.

For all lawns except bowling and golf greens, clippings need be removed only during periods of excessive growth – spring and early summer – so as to help recycle nutrients, provided that mowing is done frequently and kept at 15 mm (¾ in).

Frequency of cut is now being considered an important characteristic when breeding new turf cultivars. A choice of grass mixtures including small bent grasses (agrostis), creeping red fescues, shade-tolerant mixtures and smooth-stalked meadow grass can reduce the frequency of mowing. However, where the sward has to withstand appreciable wear, new sports turf cultivars of perennial rye grass need to be considered.

It is also a question of style. Zones of different lengths of grass can help to differentiate between formal areas, pleasure grounds and wild gardens. The close-mown turf of the manicured lawn, 10–15 mm (½–¾ in), is obviously the most expensive and labour-intensive, requiring regular cuts with a cylinder mower with the clippings boxed at the appropriate time.

Medium-mown turf, 35–100 mm (1¼–4 in) high, in shrubberies, pleasure grounds and wild gardens, needs regular cuts with cylinder or rotary mowers, perhaps using a flail mower for the higher cut. It is possible to economize with 'medium' turf, but a balance has to be achieved between using the manoeuvrable triple-cylinder mowers at frequent intervals and rotary/flail mowers less frequently, but leaving more grass clippings lying on the surface.

Long grass meadows are more than simply the result of allowing grass to grow long. It is important to stress the time necessary to establish a meadow field from a relatively high-nutrient turf sward. To encourage a varied flora but not the competitive and vigorous grass species, the soil needs a low nutirent level and high pH. Other critical factors are the timing and method of cutting. If hay is required, reciprocating cutter-bar machines can be considered, but if hay is not a problem, flail mowing is the best alternative; even a forage harvester might be chosen for larger gardens.

FERTILIZERS AND TOP DRESSINGS

Grass, like all living plants, needs basic nutrients – especially when the foliage is regularly cut off and collected rather than recycled. Fertilizers, however, are expensive, and it is pointless to apply nutrients that will only increase the frequency of mowing. Apart from fine sports areas, lawns need to be fed only in the following situations: in important and formal areas where

the clippings are collected; where an area of wear-and-tear needs to be invigorated; after a period of drought; where a lawn is on very thin, hungry soils. Good results can be obtained from relatively small applications of slow-release compound fertilizers: 35–50 g per square metre (1–1½ oz per square yard). A suitable analysis is 11 per cent nitrogen, 9 per cent potash, 6 per cent phosphate, with the possible addition of 1 per cent magnesium or iron to improve colour and disease-resistance.

Top dressing is a very good way of improving the structure of the soil, and is beneficial after scarification and aeration of a lawn. Most top dressings are a mixture of loam and sand, and a fertilizer can be added to promote growth. Apply at no more than 1 kg per square metre (2.2 lb per square yard).

Scarification (see also under 'Machinery and equipment') is best done in autumn, early winter or early spring. It is used in prestige lawns where 'thatch' has built up and in compacted areas in conjunction with slitting and hollow tining. In small areas, hand raking with a wire rake can help to lift procumbent grasses to meet the mower blades and thereby achieve a finer appearance.

WEED AND PEST CONTROL

Regular herbicide treatment is necessary only in formal areas and prestige lawns. Combining a herbicide with a granular fertilizer is a simple, although expensive, method of application.

Moss infestations are often attributed to poor drainage, but may also be caused by low nutrient, lack of adequate aeration, and too low a setting of mower blades. Chemical control is only a temporary solution: it is far better to improve cultivation techniques, including the avoidance of compaction, improving drainage, correcting over-acidity and avoiding close mowing.

Lawns with a high level of nutrient can be prone to diseases, but red thread disease (*Corticium fuciforme*) can be a problem in all areas of turf. Brownish, bleached patches appear typically in conditions of damp, mild, humid weather. In most cases it is not necessary to apply fungicides, as the disease goes away after a change in the weather.

Moles are an increasing problem in fine-textured lawns: the most successful means of control is trapping. Leatherjackets,

(Previous pages) At Standen the lawn is cut in traditional cross stripes. This sort of effect can only be achieved with a cylindrical mower.

the larvae of the crane-fly, can cause dead brown patches on lawn surfaces. Damage in spring is usually most severe following a wet autumn and mild spring. Earthworms, on the other hand, need to be encouraged, certainly not controlled, as they are excellent aerators of the soil. ❧

Mr Marshall gives a more detailed survey of the range of machinery for mowing and other aspects of lawn maintenance in the section on 'Machinery and equipment', overleaf.

Mr Ted Bullock, the Head Gardener at FELBRIGG HALL, has found that wooden edging on all the lawns make maintenance much easier. It prevents the crumbling edges and 'side-wall' growth of grass and weed, which is so difficult to extract when edging in a conventional way. The wooden planks, correctly put in place, give years of effortless lawn-edging, although the initial cost is high. Mr Bullock describes the method used at Felbrigg to fix the planks in position:

❧ The timber, pressure-tanalized deal, is cut in 3.7 m (12 ft) lengths, 10 cm (4 in) wide by 2 cm (¾ in) thick. At Felbrigg the method employed to fix the planks is the following: the turf edge is cut and rolled back about 30–35 cm (12–14 in). A garden line is then stretched along the face of the soil, usually just inside the line of the turf edge, and a channel about 15 cm (6 in) deep is taken out. The board is inserted and three pegs are driven in on the *inside* (the lawn side, not the path side), to just below the top of the board. The pegs used at Felbrigg are also of tanalized timber, 5 × 5 × 30 cm (2 × 2 × 12 in) long, and sharply pointed. The board is drilled and then screwed into position.

The turf, when replaced, should ideally be just above the top of the board. We have experienced little sinkage of the turf by using the above method.

Some lawn edges are undulating and in order to obtain a good level finish against the boards, it is necessary to add a little soil to raise the level of the turf (if it is lower than the edge of the board), or, of course, to scrape away some earth if the turf level is too high.

On lawns with curves it is possible to achieve reasonable bending of the timber edging by soaking it thoroughly before use. If the curve is a very tight one this may be difficult, and it

FIGURE 2 WOOD EDGING

may be necessary to make some shallow saw cuts. Strong metal stakes are used to hold curved lengths in position temporarily, until the planks can be screwed securely against their pegs, and on curved lengths extra pegs are advisable to hold the edging more firmly. ❧

MACHINERY AND EQUIPMENT

The reasons for using machinery in a garden are to maintain the garden as efficiently as possible, and to do menial work such as grass cutting, leaf sweeping and hedge cutting as speedily as possible. Many National Trust gardens could not be maintained to the required standard without either more staff or the use of appropriate machinery, and here **Mr James Marshall** appraises the range of types available for different functions.

Just how much to mechanize depends on the size and, perhaps more importantly, on the style of garden. A balance has to be achieved between under-equipping and using small machines which are under-powered on the one hand and over-equippping with lots of machines which are hardly used on the other. Hiring or even sharing specialist equipment such as turf scarifiers and slitters can avoid the latter danger, but poor maintenance is an obvious ill consequence of sharing.

—— *TYPES OF MOWING MACHINERY* ——
CYLINDER MOWERS

❧ The cutting action consists of revolving blades on a cylinder which bear on a fixed plate; a clean scissor-like cut therefore occurs. The number of blades on the cylinder determines the quality of cut.

ROTARY MOWERS

The principle relies on a rotary disc on which are mounted several flexible blades, the grass being cut by macerating action. Such mowers have become very popular because they are more versatile and need less maintenance and fewer blade adjustments. The hover types are especially useful for cutting banks and slopes. However, they do not make a fine cut and they tend to need more fuel to power the high-speed blades. Collecting grass is more difficult than with cylinder mowers, and swards cut continually by rotary mowers tend to develop more weeds and moss.

RECIPROCATING KNIFE MOWERS

In this case a reciprocating knife is mounted on the front of a wheeled unit. Limited use, mainly for cutting long grass.

FLAIL MOWERS

Here a series of free-moving flail-type blades are mounted on a rotary cylinder. These are generally too big for small gardens and in the main used only on long grass areas. Some models have spring-loaded, quick-change knives, which depending on the type of knife fitted can be used to cut grass, scarify turf, or pick up leaves.

BRUSH CUTTERS

These have a high-speed rotating disc to which are attached nylon cord flails, solid blades or even a circular saw. The nylon flails are perhaps the most useful for cutting grass fringes under trees, shrubs and fence lines, but care should be taken not to damage the tree bark. Their cutting rate is about four to five times as fast as hand scything. The electrical powered ones are not very robust, whereas the more useful two-stroke petrol-engined models are noisy and can be very fatiguing. There is now a front-mounted wheeled model which is far less tiring and much quieter.

POWER FOR MOWER UNITS

ELECTRICITY

Minimum maintenance required; free from starting troubles, but not as powerful as petrol engines. Maximum width of cutting unit being 35 cm (14 in). Only applicable to small gardens. Power breakers should always be used.

PETROL

Very reliable, long-lasting engines, but require routine maintenance. Over 12HP, engines are less economical than the equivalent diesel engine.

DIESEL

Less maintenance than petrol engines but more expensive in initial cost; water-cooled engines are far less noisy and smelly than air-cooled engines. An equivalent water-cooled diesel engine uses about 40 per cent less fuel than a petrol engine.

Adequate manoeuvrability is essential in deciding the width of cut. For a series of small lawns and flower beds, 30–35 cm (12–14 in) should be used. For larger areas 45 cm (18 in), and for extensive areas of grass, triple-type cylinder mowers with widths up to 2.3 m (86 in) can be used. At Anglesey Abbey the width of cut is 3.4 m (11 ft).

There has been an upsurge of interest in combining the haulage capacity of a mini-tractor with a mid-mounted rotary mower. The advantages are obvious, but the main danger is to overuse an under-powered engine, and such a combination is less manoeuvrable and efficient for mowing than a front-mounted rotary mower.

—TURF MAINTENANCE EQUIPMENT—

POWERED SCARIFIERS

The continual use of mowers and the passage of feet can compress the turf, thus reducing the penetration of water, nutrients and air, causing dead 'thatch' to build up round the grass roots. This dead organic material needs to be pulled out of the lawn and there is a range of powered scarifiers both for the large and small garden. The frequency of the operation depends on the type and size of the lawn and the priority of a fine surface.

EDGE TRIMMERS

The rechargeable battery-powered trimmers are very economical and can edge a length of lawn five times as quickly as hand edging shears, but all powered trimmers need a firm edge to cut to. Petrol edgers are also available.

OTHER EQUIPMENT

MECHANICAL HEDGE CUTTERS

Both electrical and petrol-operated hedge cutters work on the principle of a reciprocating cutter bar. Twin-edged blades have become popular and are very useful for left-handed people. Depending on the size of the cutter bar, such machines can cut hedges at five or eight times the rate of hand shears.

Electrical cutters, operated from the mains and battery- or generator-powered, are relatively quiet, light and efficient. If a large number of hedges are to be cut, a portable generator would be a good investment. Most recorded accidents occur with hedge cutters and great care should be taken.

CHAIN SAWS

Powered chain saws are now generally used and have done much to increase efficiency. When selecting a chain saw, due note must be taken of weight, engine performance, vibration and safety factors. All saws are potentially dangerous and a very useful Code of Practice is published as a safety guide by the Forestry Safety Council, entitled 'The Chain Saw'. No chain saw should be used without suitable safety clothing.

LEAF SWEEPERS

The collection of fallen leaves in the autumn can be a major problem, and although there are a number of types of leaf sweepers on the market none is completely efficient. The main problem is that leaves can be very wet in the autumn.

The blower type works on the principle of a powerful directional fan which blows the leaves into heaps which can then be conveniently picked up.

The 'Hoover' type works on the principle of a great vacuum cleaner. These are available in a range of widths, engine units and bag sizes. Most are excellent when picking up leaves from hard paths and gravel drives, but are more limited on wet grass.

Trailed leaf sweepers consist of rotating nylon brushes which flick the leaves into a collecting bag. Over a large area the use of an independent engine to power the brushes is very worth while.

The flail type is very useful for large areas, and with the addition of a mulching screen the leaves are ground up and can be used as a shrub mulch.

It has been estimated that in ideal conditions either a 'Hoover' type or a trailed sweeper can do the work of ten people with brooms.

Fertilizer distributors

Even spreading of fertilizers over large areas of grass is really only possible by some mechanical distributor. There are two main types available, and both are either hand-propelled or drawn behind a tractor.

The spinner type is the best. If possible always use a stainless steel hopper with a plastic spinner. The other type works on the principle of a revolving rubber belt, but however clean it is kept it tends to get clogged up, even when applying granular fertilizers.

Sprayers

Hand-pumped knapsack sprayers are a very simple and efficient means of applying chemicals; the main drawback is the quantity of water that needs to be carried.

The Controlled Droplet Applicator is a development by which the minimum active ingredient is applied, thus reducing the risk of drift and run-off. An added advantage is that the operator does not come into contact with the chemical and therefore less safety clothing is required. ❧

Winter protection

Mr Ted Bullock describes some of the tactics used at FELBRIGG HALL to protect plants against damage in winter:

CUTTINGS OF TENDER PLANTS

❧ Cuttings of tender plants are taken in August and September. Any plants which are prone to possible damage in a severe winter are included. In the relatively severe climate of Norfolk, these include bays, *Carpenteria californica*, cistus, ceanothus, hebe, myrtles, rosemary, thymes, lemon-scented verbena, pineapple sage (*Salvia elegans* 'Scarlet Pineapple') and others. These are rooted in the greenhouse or frame over winter as a precaution that is taken every year to guard against losses which may be difficult to replace next season.

PROTECTION OF SHRUBS
IN WINTER

Protection of some of the tender shrubs and plants is done before Christmas, using hessian and straw mats. This particularly applies to ceanothus, myrtles, bays and *Carpenteria californica*. We find that the old mats, made up of old wire netting (rabbit or chicken wire) joined together, with a good thick layer of straw or bracken in the middle – like a sandwich – are particularly effective against the freezing winds. ❧

At KNIGHTSHAYES COURT Mr Michael Hickson uses a similar standard protection for young plants. Knightshayes has a much milder climate than Felbrigg, and a higher rainfall. In winter lowest ground-temperatures experienced are −10°C (14°F) but the important chill factor can reach as low as −21°C (−1°F), easily freezing the sap in young rhododendrons or tender woody plants. Wire rabbit netting is laid on the ground; a half-section is filled with straw laid out in vertical strips as in thatching, to ensure that rain will run downwards once it is fixed in an upright position, then it is doubled over like a sandwich. Wire or tarred string is threaded through the mesh to bind it. Stiff strands of wire are used to stiffen the completed 'mat' and it is fitted round a plant, fixed to the inside of a tripod of stakes, and then tied securely to the stakes, leaving some movement for air between the plant and the mat. At the top a further wigwam can be erected, Indian-style, and bound together, using fronds of Christmas trees or other conifers. For smaller plants Michael Hickson makes a wigwam in the same fashion, but at ground level.

COMPOST

M r **Graham Kendall**, the Head Gardener at MONTACUTE HOUSE, describes his method of making compost:

❧ Most National Trust gardens have been cultivated for a very long time, and Montacute has been a garden for three and a half centuries. As soils inevitably become leached and tired, nutrients have to be added either by using proprietary fertilizers or by the application of manures and composts, which have the additional benefit of improving the soil structure.

We do use proprietary fertilizers because they are quick and easy to apply, but we also prepare our own compost, which we use mainly as a mulch. Time, however, prohibits too scientific an approach to the preparation of our heap, and lack of availability of plant material limits its quality. The bulk of our material consists of grass cuttings through the growing season and fallen leaves gathered in the autumn. We acquire these in large enough quantities to swamp other ingredients, which include fibrous rooted weeds – hopefully with some soil still attached – and bonfire ash. The latter, while containing potash, is of more dubious benefit and is composted as a convenient method of disposal. A limited range of ingredients can still produce a very useful compost. Grass cuttings are rich in nitrogen, phosphate and potassium as well as other nutrients. Leaf litter, especially beech leaves, which are plentiful here, has virtually no nutrient value, except for calcium which is retained in the leaf skeleton. This skeleton, together with clippings from our hedges, adds fibre to the heap, which forms humus. Humus is a black colloidal material which coats individual soil particles. On light soils it will hold the particles together and retain water. On heavy soils it reduces stickiness and makes soil more friable.

Our heap is started in early spring, on forked-over earth. It is contained in a bay constructed of corrugated iron sheets. We use compost left over from the previous year as an activator to add the active bacteria and micro-organisms. As we are constantly adding to it, we do not cover the heap, although it would be beneficial to do so through the winter to keep heat in and prevent the leaching of nutrients.

The more often a heap can be turned the better, especially when using a large amounts of grass clippings which tend to stick in one soggy mass. A more open structure allows air into the heap, encouraging the right organisms for decomposition. Moisture is also necessary and, because of the amount of grass used, our heap seldom dries out. We make our heap wide and low and this increases the surface area for absorbing rainfall. The compost from the first year is ready to use in the spring of the second, and is put on as soon as the soil is warm enough to accept the mulch. ✻

APPENDICES

APPENDIX 1:
NATIONAL COLLECTIONS IN
NATIONAL TRUST
GARDENS

Over a thousand different kinds of cultivated plant are lost each year from Britain's gardens: plants may be destroyed by disease or simply go out of fashion and disappear, and those that are slow or difficult to propagate are often dropped by the nursery trade. The National Council for the Conservation of Plants and Gardens was formed from the Royal Horticultural Society in 1978, and since then has built up over 550 National Collections of cultivated plants that would otherwise be in danger of disappearing from gardens. **Mr Anthony Lord**, one of the National Trust's former Gardens Advisers, writes of the role of the Trust in maintaining National Collections for the NCCPG:

❧ Gardens of the National Trust come to hold National Collections not by chance, nor by the whim of their latter-day staff, but through the recognition of groups of plants, usually already in the gardens, which are particularly suited to their traditions and character.

The character of historic gardens derives largely from the plants they contain. To conserve gardens it is therefore necessary to conserve the character of the planting. This may have evolved over many centuries, by association with one or a number of families who added the plants they liked over successive generations. The Trust's gardens now comprise a plant collection of extraordinary richness and scope which must surely constitute the largest such collection in single ownership.

The style of planting was often determined by either fashion or function: the border planting at Packwood in Warwickshire is of hardy herbaceous, mixed perennials planted in a style that was fashionable from Victorian times until the last war, but which have since markedly lost their popularity; flowers for cutting were required in most houses and the choice of plants for the border and cut-flower garden was clearly influenced by the plants' suitability for this function; fruit and vegetables had to provide crops under local conditions to suit local tastes and the choice of varieties differed widely around the country accordingly. Even now, when fashions have changed and the functions required of the plants are different, the Trust must continue such traditions of planting, irrespective of modern taste as, for example, at Calke Abbey.

Accordingly, the fruit trees planted at Nunnington in Yorkshire are of varieties long popular in the area but seldom available from nurseries. In Cornwall, quite different varieties of orchard fruit were preferred and the Trust continues to use these for its Cornish gardens, although most are not grown by nurseries and have to be propagated specially.

The particular enthusiasms of individuals, whether for a range of plants or for a particular genus, are still apparent in many gardens. At Antony House in Cornwall, the nearly 500 day-lilies collected by the late Lady Cynthia Carew Pole remain an integral part of a genus which continues to be much changed by the plant breeder. (This is now a part of the National Collection of *Hemerocallis*). Other enthusiasts subscribed to plant-hunting expeditions and the introductions of, for instance, Harold Comber from Chile or Frank Kingdon-Ward from the eastern Himalayas, still contribute significantly to the character of planting at Nymans and Trengwainton respectively. This tradition continues and plants raised from seed collected in the wild by plant hunters such as Roy Lancaster give interest to Nymans and numerous other Trust gardens.

Specialized gardens such as the pinetum, fernery or rock garden, each housed their own particular range of plants, each of which contained many representatives, almost collections, of certain genera.

Thus the gardens of the National Trust have come to hold a great wealth and diversity of plants chosen over the centuries to suit all tastes and conditions. A study of the contents of each garden will reveal trends in the planting: occasionally we find that a garden might contain large numbers of a particular sort, family or genus of plants which may be regarded as a collection. Enriching the content of such groups to make more comprehensive collections is one means of sharpening the individuality of our gardens. These groups are not necessarily botanical: for instance, there are collections of autumn colour plants at Sheffield Park, plants raised by the Veitch nursery at Killerton, dwarf conifers at Sizergh and Shakespearean period plants at Charlecote. When a garden has sufficient area, resources and staff to house and maintain a collection of most of the representatives of a certain botanical group of plants, and when this group is appropriate historically and aesthetically to the garden, the Trust can consider proposing it as a National Collection.

The Trust houses just over thirty collections at present, but each year more are designated as such by the NCCPG. It is important that the Trust should only undertake such collections where they can be adequately housed without altering the character of the garden. Not even the largest of our gardens could accommodate the 4,000 fuchsias believed to exist in Britain without their significantly changing the character of the garden. The estimated 30,000 extant cultivars of *Hemerocallis* would be even more overwhelming. The Trust's paramount objective must remain the conservation of its properties, including gardens. Rare garden plant conservation is a worthwhile secondary objective and is supported wherever it helps fulfil this primary role.

Collecting tree genera is often difficult; many sorts of, for instance, oak or lime are available and a large number would dominate the character of even our largest garden. Whitebeams (*Sorbus* section *Aria*) are smaller and more manageable. These were favourites of Dr Wilfrid Fox, the founder of Winkworth Aboretum, where they are held with the smaller *Sorbus* section *Micromeles* as a National Collection. Dr Fox is commemorated by the fine whitebeam bearing his name which grows at Winkworth.

At Mottisfont, a vast London plane, in fact two trees fused together, is the largest tree and therefore the biggest living object in the country. What better place to house a National Collection of planes (*Platanus*), which appreciate being near to the water of the 'font' or fountain which gives the place its name? Also at Mottisfont is one of the largest and most impressive of the Trust's National Collections, that of old roses dating from before 1900. These were assembled by the Trust's former Gardens Adviser, Mr Graham Stuart Thomas, and are mainly French in origin. They provide a spectacular and sweetly scented display in the walled garden through late June and early July.

Another tree genus, of which the Indian bean tree (*Catalpa bignonioides*) is the best known, is collected at Cliveden, and at

Kingston Lacy there is the National Collection of lily-of-the-valley, with unassuming and pretty flowers, exquisitely perfumed, pink or white, single or double, and leaves of plain green or striped with gold. Wood anemones are another charming group collected here, useful in the woodland garden or among herbaceous planting where they can provide a useful spring display before other plants have leafed. They, too, can have single or double flowers, in many shades of pink, mauve, blue, white, yellow or green.

Bodnant boasts four National Collections, all of them of genera particularly suited to the character of the garden. Of the tree genera, magnolias start the season with their mostly spring blooms of white or pink. These are followed by forms of *Embothrium*, the dazzling scarlet Chilean Fire Bush, in May and June, the season continuing through to autumn with eucryphias. The fourth Bodnant collection is of the scarlet-flowered *Rhododendron forrestii* and its close allies, excellent low-growing plants flowering mostly in April and May.

Also strictly rhododendrons, the collection of Ghent azaleas at Sheffield Park provides scent and colour in May and June and includes a number of historic nineteenth-century varieties.

Box has always grown in the garden at Ickworth. Although always neat and attractive, both for hedging and for understorey planting in shrubberies and woodlands, the usefulness of this worthy shrub is often overlooked. Ickworth's National Collection contains most of the cultivars and species in cultivation in this country.

Elder, like box, is remarkable for its tolerance of dry shade and the collection of *Sambucus* at Wallington contains forms of the common elder (*S. nigra*) of much more garden interest than the plain green form, with leaves variegated, gold, purple or finely divided, as well as numerous other species.

When the garden at Erddig was restored, its many shady brick walls needed some planting to soften their hard appearance. A National Collection of ivies filled this role admirably; the plants are allowed to grow both up the wall and over the adjoining ground to prove their merit as ground cover.

At Hidcote the collection of peony species and primary hybrids (first generation offspring of a cross between two species) bridges the gap between shrubs and herbaceous plants. Since the days of its creator, Lawrence Johnston, the garden has contained many of these, both tree peonies and herbaceous ones, and the Trust hopes to plant yet more. Although the species are mainly single and fleeting in flower, they have a charm and beauty which the larger, double hybrids lack.

The planting of the terrace borders at Upton derives largely from the first half of this century. Throughout this time, aster borders were a feature of many gardens and were championed by many leading gardeners including Gertrude Jekyll. The Michaelmas daisies (*Aster novi-belgii* and *A. novae-angliae* forms) which made up the bulk of the planting in these, have become prone to mildew in recent decades and most are no longer good garden plants; most need staking, a job for which few gardeners can find time today. Small-flowered asters such as *A. cordifolius* and *A. ericoides* cultivars and hybrids and also the cultivars and hybrids of *AA. amellus* and *thomsonii* do not suffer from these disadvantages and have been unjustly neglected recently. The Aster Border at Upton houses the National Collection of these and includes a number of excellent varieties, many of which had been lost from British gardens and had to be re-introduced from Europe.

Scabiosa caucasica is another plant which has lost popularity recently and many varieties have disappeared. The remainder have found a home as a National Collection in the cut-flower border at Hardwick Hall, where they are perfectly suited to both the alkaline soil and the traditions of the house.

Not all herbaceous plants are fully hardy and it is such rather tender plants that can most easily be lost from cultivation. Many of the more tender *Crocosmia* hybrids (montbretias) bred in France and Britain late in the last century and early in this century, are extinct but the survivors, along with the species and more recent hybrids, are grown as a National Collection at Lanhydrock in Cornwall.

The disappearance of many penstemons may be attributed to their inability to survive cold winters and seventeen years ago it seemed that only a handful of large-flowered hybrids remained. The assembling of some four dozen *P. gloxinioides* and *P. campanulatus* hybrids to form a National Collection at Rowallane demonstrates that an excellent range of these still exists; the plants themselves bear witness to their continuing value for dazzling late summer display.

Felbrigg Hall is renowned for its plantings of *Colchicum*

tenorei and the success of this and other meadow saffrons in the garden have led to the establishment of a National Collection there.

At Sizergh Castle, the impressive rock garden, which dates from 1926, is particularly suited to the growing of ferns and contains good collections of a number of genera. Of these, four are particularly suited to conditions in the garden and have been designated National Collections. Osmundas, including the native royal fern, enjoy the damp conditions alongside the stream which runs through the garden, while *Cystopteris* thrive in damp crevices, particulary beside waterfalls. Aspleniums, including forms of the native hart's tongue, appreciate the alkaline soil of the garden, while *Dryopteris* species and forms thrive where conditions are akin to their native woodland. More recently, Powis Castle in North Wales, built by the Princes of Powis, was accepted as NCCPG collection holder for *Aralia* and *Laburnum*. The *Aralia* is probably one of the finest of all ornamental hardy shrubs and is often referred to as the Japanese Angelica Tree. The *Laburnum* signifies the onset of summer when it produces glorious racemes of golden yellow pea-like flowers in late May and June.

Of cultivated plants in Britain, the species are generally well conserved by botanic gardens, and most are secure in their natural habitats around the world, but gardeners must conserve garden varieties if they are to survive. By doing this and by supporting the National Collections' scheme of the NCCPG, the National Trust helps to preserve the richness of our garden flora and to make our gardens more interesting and attractive for us all. ❧

APPENDIX 2:
FEATURES IN NATIONAL TRUST GARDENS

NOTE The chart indicates National Trust gardens where subjects discussed in the book may be seen: it is not a comprehensive listing of every type of features in these gardens.

	Landscape	Hedging	Avenue	Pleaching/Pergolas etc	Topiary	Knot Garden	Maze	Formal Parterre	Ornaments	Container Planting	Borders	Rose Garden
Acorn Bank *Cumbria*		■	■						■		■	
Anglesey Abbey *Cambridgeshire*		■	■	■					■			
Antony *Cornwall*	■	■	■	■	■	■			■		■	
Ardress *Co Armagh*										■		■
Arlington Court *Devon*				■					■	■	■	
Ascott *Buckinghamshire*		■	■		■			■	■		■	
Ashdown *Oxfordshire*			■					■				
Barrington Court *Somerset*		■	■	■					■		■	
Basildon Park *Berkshire*	■								■			
Bateman's *East Sussex*		■		■							■	■
Belton House *Lincolnshire*	■	■	■		■				■	■	■	
Beningbrough *North Yorkshire*		■	■						■	■	■	
Benthall Hall *Shropshire*		■		■	■				■	■	■	
Blickling Hall *Norfolk*		■	■	■	■			■	■	■	■	
Bodnant *Gwynedd*	■	■		■					■		■	■
Buscot Park *Oxfordshire*		■	■	■				■	■		■	
Canons Ashby *Northamptonshire*		■	■		■						■	
Castle Drogo *Devon*		■		■							■	■
Castle Ward *Co Down*	■		■	■						■	■	
Charlecote Park *Warwickshire*	■	■	■		■				■	■	■	
Chartwell *Kent*		■		■					■	■	■	■
Chirk Castle *Clwyd*	■	■	■		■				■		■	■
Clandon Park *Surrey*		■		■			■	■	■	■		
Claremont *Surrey*	■	■							■			
Clevedon Court *Avon*		■		■							■	
Cliveden *Buckinghamshire*		■	■		■			■	■	■	■	■
Coleton Fishacre *Devon*		■							■	■		
Cotehele *Cornwall*		■			■						■	
Cragside *Northumberland*										■	■	
Dudmaston *Shropshire*	■								■	■	■	
Dunham Massey *Gtr. Manchester*	■						■	■		■		
Dunster Castle *Somerset*										■		
Dyrham Park *Avon*	■								■			
Emmetts *Kent*												■

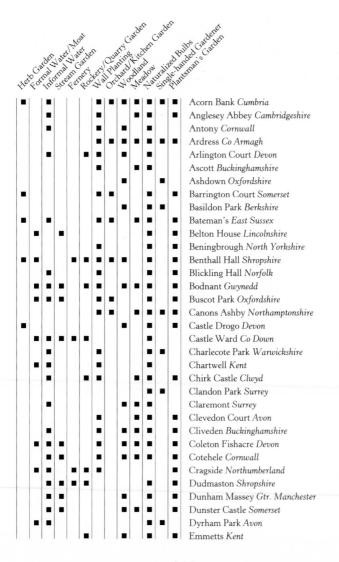

	Herb Garden	Formal Water/Moat	Informal Water	Stream Garden	Fernery	Rockery/Quarry Garden	Wall Planting	Orchard/Kitchen Garden	Woodland	Meadow	Naturalized Bulbs	Single-handed Gardener	Plantsman's Garden
Acorn Bank *Cumbria*	■		■				■	■	■		■	■	■
Anglesey Abbey *Cambridgeshire*			■				■		■	■			■
Antony *Cornwall*			■				■	■	■				
Ardress *Co Armagh*			■			■	■	■	■	■	■	■	■
Arlington Court *Devon*			■		■	■		■		■			
Ascott *Buckinghamshire*			■				■		■	■			
Ashdown *Oxfordshire*							■			■			
Barrington Court *Somerset*	■						■	■		■			■
Basildon Park *Berkshire*							■		■	■	■		
Bateman's *East Sussex*	■		■				■	■		■			■
Belton House *Lincolnshire*		■		■					■				■
Beningbrough *North Yorkshire*							■		■				■
Benthall Hall *Shropshire*	■	■			■	■	■	■	■				■
Blickling Hall *Norfolk*		■					■		■				■
Bodnant *Gwynedd*	■	■	■		■	■		■	■	■			■
Buscot Park *Oxfordshire*	■	■	■			■	■		■				■
Canons Ashby *Northamptonshire*						■	■		■	■	■	■	■
Castle Drogo *Devon*	■						■		■				■
Castle Ward *Co Down*	■	■	■	■	■	■			■				
Charlecote Park *Warwickshire*		■					■		■	■			
Chartwell *Kent*	■	■					■		■				
Chirk Castle *Clwyd*		■			■	■			■	■			■
Clandon Park *Surrey*									■	■	■		
Claremont *Surrey*		■					■	■	■				
Clevedon Court *Avon*			■					■	■				■
Cliveden *Buckinghamshire*		■				■	■	■	■				■
Coleton Fishacre *Devon*	■	■	■			■		■	■	■			■
Cotehele *Cornwall*		■	■			■		■	■	■			■
Cragside *Northumberland*	■	■		■	■	■							■
Dudmaston *Shropshire*		■	■	■	■	■			■				■
Dunham Massey *Gtr. Manchester*							■		■				■
Dunster Castle *Somerset*		■	■				■	■	■				■
Dyrham Park *Avon*		■	■	■					■	■			
Emmetts *Kent*					■			■		■			■

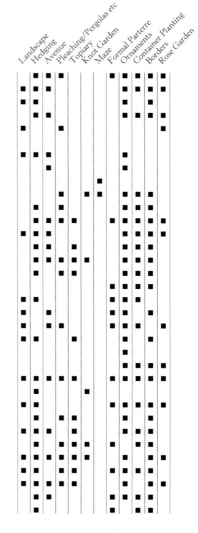

	Landscape	Hedging	Avenue	Pleaching/Pergolas etc	Topiary	Knot Garden	Maze	Formal Parterre	Ornaments	Container Planting	Borders	Rose Garden
Erddig *Clwyd*		■	■	■				■	■	■	■	■
Farnborough Hall *Warwickshire*	■	■	■						■	■	■	■
Felbrigg Hall *Norfolk*	■	■							■		■	
Fenton House *London*		■	■						■	■	■	■
Florence Court *Co Fermanagh*	■			■								■
Fountains Abbey & Studley Royal *North Yorkshire*	■	■	■						■			
Gawthorpe Hall *Lancashire*			■						■			
Glendurgan *Cornwall*							■					
Greys Court *Oxfordshire*				■		■	■		■	■	■	
Gunby Hall *Lincolnshire*		■		■					■	■	■	
Ham House *Surrey*		■	■	■	■			■	■	■	■	■
Hanbury Hall *Hereford & Worcester*	■	■	■						■	■	■	■
Hardwick Hall *Derbyshire*		■	■		■				■	■	■	
Hidcote Manor *Gloucestershire*		■	■	■	■	■			■	■	■	
Holt: The Courts *Wiltshire*		■		■	■				■	■	■	
Hughenden Manor *Buckinghamshire*								■	■	■		
Ickworth *Suffolk*	■	■							■	■	■	
Killerton *Devon*	■		■						■	■		■
Kingston Lacy *Dorset*	■		■	■					■	■	■	■
Knightshayes Gardens *Devon*	■	■			■				■		■	
Lacock Abbey *Wiltshire*									■			
Lamb House *East Sussex*									■	■	■	■
Lanhydrock *Cornwall*	■	■	■	■	■			■	■	■	■	■
Little Moreton Hall *Cheshire*		■				■						
Lyme Park *Cheshire*	■	■						■	■	■	■	■
Lytes Cary *Somerset*		■		■	■				■		■	
Montacute *Somerset*	■	■	■		■				■	■	■	
Moseley Old Hall *Staffordshire*				■	■	■		■		■	■	
Mottisfont Abbey *Hampshire*	■	■	■	■	■	■			■		■	■
Mount Stewart *Co Down*	■	■		■	■			■	■	■	■	
Nymans *West Sussex*	■	■	■	■	■				■		■	■
Overbecks *Devon*		■	■					■	■	■	■	
Oxburgh Hall *Norfolk*		■						■		■	■	

Herb Garden	Formal Water/Moat	Informal Water	Stream Garden	Fernery	Rockery/Quarry Garden	Wall Planting	Orchard/Kitchen Garden	Woodland	Meadow	Naturalized Bulbs	Single-handed Gardener	Plantsman's Garden	
■	■				■	■		■					Erddig *Clwyd*
		■						■	■	■			Farnborough Hall *Warwickshire*
■					■	■		■	■			■	Felbrigg Hall *Norfolk*
					■	■		■	■	■		■	Fenton House *London*
		■	■				■	■	■	■		■	Florence Court *Co Fermanagh*
	■	■						■					Fountains Abbey & Studley Royal *North Yorkshire*
	■						■						Gawthorpe Hall *Lancashire*
	■	■			■			■	■	■		■	Glendurgan *Cornwall*
			■		■	■		■	■	■	■	■	Greys Court *Oxfordshire*
■	M					■		■	■			■	Gunby Hall *Lincolnshire*
					■	■		■	■				Ham House *Surrey*
	■				■	■		■	■	■	■	■	Hanbury Hall *Hereford & Worcester*
■					■	■		■	■			■	Hardwick Hall *Derbyshire*
		■		■	■	■	■		■			■	Hidcote Manor *Gloucestershire*
■	■	■	■		■	■		■	■			■	Holt: The Courts *Wiltshire*
					■	■		■	■	■	■	■	Hughenden Manor *Buckinghamshire*
	■			■			■	■	■			■	Ickworth *Suffolk*
		■		■	■		■	■	■			■	Killerton *Devon*
			■		■			■	■			■	Kingston Lacy *Dorset*
	■							■	■			■	Knightshayes Gardens *Devon*
	■	■							■	■			Lacock Abbey *Wiltshire*
■					■	■						■	Lamb House *East Sussex*
		■	■		■			■		■		■	Lanhydrock *Cornwall*
■	M						■			■			Little Moreton Hall *Cheshire*
		■	■		■			■		■			Lyme Park *Cheshire*
					■	■		■		■	■	■	Lytes Cary *Somerset*
					■			■					Montacute *Somerset*
■					■	■		■					Moseley Old Hall *Staffordshire*
		■	■		■			■				■	Mottisfont Abbey *Hampshire*
		■	■	■	■			■				■	Mount Stewart *Co Down*
					■		■	■	■			■	Nymans *West Sussex*
					■			■				■	Overbecks *Devon*
	M				■		■		■				Oxburgh Hall *Norfolk*

	Landscape	Hedging	Avenue	Pleaching/Pergolas etc	Topiary	Knot Garden	Maze	Formal Parterre	Ornaments	Container Planting	Borders	Rose Garden
Packwood *Warwickshire*		■	■		■						■	
Peckover House *Cambridgeshire*				■	■				■	■	■	■
Penrhyn Castle *Gwynedd*				■								
Petworth *West Sussex*	■								■		■	
Plas Newydd *Gwynedd*	■	■			■				■	■	■	
Polesden Lacey *Surrey*	■	■	■	■	■				■		■	■
Powis Castle *Powys*	■	■			■				■	■		
Rowallane *Co Down*	■								■		■	
Rufford Old Hall *Lancashire*					■						■	
Saltram *Devon*	■		■						■	■	■	
Scotney Castle *Kent*	■								■	■		
Sheffield Park *East Sussex*	■		■									
Shugborough *Staffordshire*	■				■				■	■	■	■
Sissinghurst Castle *Kent*		■	■	■					■	■	■	■
Sizergh Castle *Cumbria*	■		■								■	
Snowshill Manor *Gloucestershire*		■	■								■	
Springhill *Co Londonderry*												
Stagshaw *Cumbria*												
Standen *West Sussex*		■									■	■
Stourhead *Wiltshire*	■								■		■	
Tatton Park *Cheshire*	■	■	■	■	■	■	■	■	■	■	■	■
Tintinhull *Somerset*		■			■				■	■	■	
Trelissick *Cornwall*	■										■	
Trengwainton *Cornwall*				■						■	■	
Trerice *Cornwall*		■									■	
Upton *Warwickshire*		■							■	■	■	■
The Vyne *Hampshire*		■	■								■	
Waddesdon Manor *Buckinghamshire*	■	■		■	■			■	■			
Wakehurst Place *West Sussex*	■	■							■	■	■	
Wallington *Northumberland*	■	■	■						■	■	■	
Westbury Court *Gloucestershire*		■		■	■			■	■	■	■	
West Green House *Hampshire*		■	■	■	■				■			
Wightwick Manor *Staffordshire*		■		■	■				■	■	■	■
Winkworth Arboretum *Surrey*	■											

Herb Garden	Formal Water/Moat	Informal Water	Stream Garden	Fernery	Rockery/Quarry Garden	Wall Planting	Orchard/Kitchen Garden	Woodland	Meadow	Naturalized Bulbs	Single-handed Gardener	Plantsman's Garden	
	■					■			■				Packwood *Warwickshire*
				■	■	■						■	Peckover House *Cambridgeshire*
		■				■			■			■	Penrhyn Castle *Gwynedd*
		■				■	■	■	■				Petworth *West Sussex*
		■				■	■	■	■			■	Plas Newydd *Gwynedd*
				■	■			■	■				Polesden Lacey *Surrey*
		■		■	■	■	■	■	■			■	Powis Castle *Powys*
	■	■			■	■		■	■	■		■	Rowallane *Co Down*
						■			■		■		Rufford Old Hall *Lancashire*
		■				■			■	■		■	Saltram *Devon*
■	M	■				■			■	■		■	Scotney Castle *Kent*
	■	■	■				■	■	■			■	Sheffield Park *East Sussex*
						■			■	■		■	Shugborough *Staffordshire*
■		■				■			■	■		■	Sissinghurst Castle *Kent*
	■	■	■	■	■	■			■	■		■	Sizergh Castle *Cumbria*
	■						■			■	■		Snowshill Manor *Gloucestershire*
■			■			■			■	■		■	Springhill *Co Londonderry*
		■					■		■	■	■	■	Stagshaw *Cumbria*
		■	■	■	■	■		■	■	■	■	■	Standen *West Sussex*
		■	■	■		■		■	■	■			Stourhead *Wiltshire*
		■		■		■		■		■		■	Tatton Park *Cheshire*
						■	■			■	■	■	Tintinhull *Somerset*
			■			■		■		■		■	Trelissick *Cornwall*
		■	■	■	■	■		■	■	■		■	Trengwainton *Cornwall*
						■	■			■	■	■	Trerice *Cornwall*
	■		■		■	■	■			■		■	Upton *Warwickshire*
		■							■	■	■		The Vyne *Hampshire*
					■				■	■			Waddesdon Manor *Buckinghamshire*
		■	■			■		■	■	■		■	Wakehurst Place *West Sussex*
		■	■			■	■	■	■	■		■	Wallington *Northumberland*
	■	■				■	■				■	■	Westbury Court *Gloucestershire*
■		■	■			■	■	■		■		■	West Green House *Hampshire*
		■				■	■	■		■			Wightwick Manor *Staffordshire*
		■						■	■	■		■	Winkworth Arboretum *Surrey*

Appendix 3:
National Trust Gardens

Skegness
GUNBY HALL
Lincoln
HARDWICK HALL
Worksop
M1
Hull
M18
BENINGBROUGH
York
Wakefield
Leeds
LITTLE MORETON HALL
FOUNTAINS ABBEY AND STUDLEY ROYAL
Bradford
M62
Middlesbrough
A1
Blackburn
Manchester
Stockport
LYME PARK
Durham
GAWTHORPE HALL
Preston
M61
TATTON PARK
M6
Newcastle-upon-Tyne
Morpeth
Alnwick
CRAGSIDE
WALLINGTON
ACORN BANK
SIZERGH CASTLE
Lancaster
Liverpool
QUARRY BANK
M56
Penrith
M6
STAGSHAW
Kendal
RUFFORD OLD HALL
Carlisle
PENRHYN
Bangor
Plas Newydd
Plas-yn-Rhiw
BODNANT

NORTHERN IRELAND

MOUNT STEWART
Belfast
Castle Coole
Coleraine
A2
A6
ROWALLANE
CASTLE WARD
A1
Londonderry
SPRINGHILL
Dungannon
ARDRESS HOUSE
Newry
A4
FLORENCE COURT
Enniskillen

Tower
BUCKLING HALL
FELBRIGG HALL
Norwich
King's Lynn
Stowlham
OXBURGH
Bury St Edmunds
ICKWORTH
OBELTON HOUSE
Wisbech
PECKOVER
Peterborough
ANGLESEY ABBEY
Cambridge
Canterbury
Dover
Folkestone
SISSINGHURST CASTLE
LAMB HOUSE
Rye
Hastings
Maidstone
Croydon
Tunbridge Wells
Brighton
Guildford
Crawley
FOR INSET SEE OVERLEAF
Chichester
Portsmouth
Aylesbury
High Wycombe
BASILDON PARK
Reading
Basingstoke
Nottingham
Northampton
Banbury
CLANDON PARK
HARTLEBURY CASTLE
FARNBOROUGH HALL
Oxford
Faringdon
THE VYNE
BUSCOT PARK
Swindon
MOTTISFONT ABBEY
Southampton
Salisbury
Romsey
WINKWORTH ARBORETUM
Stoke on Trent
Derby
SHUGBOROUGH
Stafford
MOSELEY OLD HALL
Wolverhampton
Birmingham
PACKWOOD HOUSE
Stratford-upon-Avon
HANBURY HALL
UPTON HOUSE
HIDCOTE MANOR
SNOWSHILL MANOR
WIGHTWICK MANOR
DUDMASTON
Worcester
Cheltenham
Gloucester
DYRHAM PARK
LACOCK ABBEY
WESTBURY COURT
Bristol
Bath
THE COURTS
Trowbridge
STOURHEAD
LYTES CARY
TINTINHULL
MONTACUTE
Wrexham
ERDDIG
Llangollen
CHIRK CASTLE
Shrewsbury
Telford
BENTHALL HALL
Bridgnorth
Welshpool
POWIS CASTLE
Ramsbury
CLEVEDON COURT
Cardiff
ARLINGTON COURT
DUNSTER CASTLE
BARRINGTON COURT
Ilminster
KINGSTON LACY
Wimborne Minster
KNIGHTSHAYES
Okehampton
Tiverton
Exeter
CASTLE DROGO
COTEHELE
Bodmin
LANHYDROCK
ANTONY HOUSE
Plymouth
SALTRAM
OVERBECKS
Salcombe
Truro
Dartmouth
COLETON FISHACRE
TRELISSICK
TRERICE
Penzance
TRENGWAINTON
GLENDURGAN

Miles 0   25   50   75
Km   0   50   100

Leighton Buzzard ●
ASCOTT ○
WADDESDON MANOR ○
● *Aylesbury*

M1   A1   A10
A11   M11

M40
HUGHENDEN MANOR ○
● *High Wycombe*
M25
GREYS COURT ○
CLIVEDEN ●
A40
FENTON HOUSE ○

M4   ● *Reading*
WEST GREEN HOUSE ○
HAM HOUSE ○
A23   A20
Esher ○
CLAREMONT ○
● *Croydon*
M20   A2

A3
POLESDEN LACEY ○
M25
Westerham ●   EMMETTS ○
A20

Guildford ●
○ CLANDON PARK
CHARTWELL ○

A3
● *Godalming*
○ WINKWORTH ARBORETUM
M23
A21

● *East Grinstead*
○ STANDEN
SCOTNEY CASTLE ○

○ WAKEHURST PLACE

A3
○ NYMANS
Cuckfield ●

Midhurst ●   ○ PETWORTH HOUSE
○ SHEFFIELD PARK
○ BATEMAN'S

A23
Miles 0   5   10   15
Km 0   10   20

GARDENS IN AND AROUND LONDON

INDEX